STORIES FROM THE STALAGS

STORIES FROM THE STALAGS

ALLIED AIRMEN BEHIND THE WIRE IN WW2

MARTIN W. BOWMAN

AIR WORLD

STORIES FROM THE STALAGS
Allied Airmen Behind the Wire in WW2

First published in Great Britain in 2024 by
Airworld
An imprint of
Pen & Sword Books Ltd
Yorkshire – Philadelphia

Copyright © Martin W. Bowman, 2024

ISBN 978 1 39907 330 1

The right of Martin W. Bowman to be identified as Author of this work has been asserted by him in accordance with the Copyright, Designs and Patents Act 1988.

A CIP catalogue entry for this book is available from the British Library.

All rights reserved. No part of this book may be reproduced or transmitted in any form or by any means, electronic or mechanical including photocopying, recording or by any information storage and retrieval system, without permission from the Publisher in writing.

Typeset by SJmagic DESIGN SERVICES, India.

Printed and bound in the UK by CPI Group (UK) Ltd.

Pen & Sword Books Ltd includes the Imprints of Atlas, Archaeology, Aviation, Discovery, Family History, Fiction, History, Maritime, Military, Military Classics, Politics, Select, Airworld, Frontline Publishing, Leo Cooper, Remember When, Seaforth Publishing, The Praetorian Press, Wharncliffe Local History, Wharncliffe Transport, Wharncliffe True Crime and White Owl.

For a complete list of Pen & Sword titles please contact

PEN & SWORD BOOKS LTD
George House, Units 12 & 13, Beevor Street, Off Pontefract Road,
Barnsley, South Yorkshire, S71 1HN, England
E-mail: enquiries@pen-and-sword.co.uk
Website: www.pen-and-sword.co.uk

or

PEN AND SWORD BOOKS
1950 Lawrence Rd, Havertown, PA 19083, USA
E-mail: uspen-and-sword@casematepublishers.com
Website: www.penandswordbooks.com

Contents

Chapter 1	Shot Down in a Fjord – Allan Hurrell	1
Chapter 2	Young Winston – Sergeant Winston Churchill Parker	14
Chapter 3	No Particular Courage – Sergeant Harold 'Harry' Church	22
Chapter 4	Lamsdorf and Beyond – Sergeant Edward Humes	46
Chapter 5	Behind the Wire – Major Ronald V. Kramer	65
Chapter 6	Gefangenennummer 331 – Sergeant Jack Warrington	92
Chapter 7	Wheeler's War – Flying Officer John P. Wheeler	101
Chapter 8	Life as a PoW – Flight Sergeant Denis Innell Humphrey	110
Chapter 9	Raid on Nuremburg – Doug Cady	122
Chapter 10	Barth – The Final Days	145
Chapter 11	'We'll be home for Christmas, if only in a dream' – Len R. Clarke	165
Index		171

Chapter 1

Shot Down in a Fjord

Coastal Command flew 517 sorties, of which 37 were on convoy escort. Shipping protection patrols by Fighter Command involved 791 sorties. A total of 133 aircraft of Bomber Command and six aircraft of Coastal Command laid 306 sea mines. Eleven aircraft are missing. Two forces were despatched to attack the Prinz Eugen, *which had been sighted steaming to the southward off the Norwegian coast.*

The first force was unable to locate the cruiser, but part of the second force, which consisted of 52 aircraft, including 27 torpedo-carrying Beauforts, carried out an attack. Two possible hits with torpedoes are claimed. Considerable enemy fighter opposition was encountered and nine of our aircraft failed to return. Five enemy fighters were destroyed. The Prinz Eugen *has since been identified by photographic reconnaissance as having arrived at Kiel.*

A successful attack was carried out by Hudsons on two convoys off Texel and Terschelling respectively. Three ships (one of 4,500 and two of 2,500 tons) were hit and left burning and seven others of between 2,000 and 6,000 tons were hit. Of the 18 Hudsons despatched, five are missing.

Another Hudson made five hits on a 350ft camouflaged vessel near Molde. A large cloud of smoke was seen issuing from the bows.

Spitfires and Hurricane bombers made a number of attacks on small craft, as a result of which a minesweeper, a barge and a launch were sunk and other vessels damaged. Enemy air activity off our coasts was again on a small scale, consisting mainly of shipping and weather reconnaissances. No attacks on our coastal shipping have

STORIES FROM THE STALAGS

been reported. Three aircraft were destroyed by our fighters and a further five were damaged.

From the Air Situation Report for the week as reported to the British War Cabinet. On 16 May 1942, *Prinz Eugen* made the return voyage to Germany under her own power. While en route to Kiel, the ship was attacked by a British force of 19 Bristol Blenheim bombers and 27 Bristol Beaufort torpedo bombers commanded by Wing Commander Mervyn Williams, though the aircraft failed to hit the ship. During the attack, for which he was awarded the DSO, Williams' aircraft was shot down. He was subsequently recovered from the sea by the Germans; the only survivor from his four-man crew. He became a prisoner of war, held at Stalag Luft III where he became camp intelligence officer and was involved in planning the 'Great Escape'.

'There were four Beaufort squadrons stationed at various aerodromes down the Scottish east coast,' wrote Allan Hurrell, a Rhodesian Beaufort pilot on 86 Squadron. 'They were 22 Squadron, 317, 42 and 86. My squadron [86] was based at Wick in Scotland, where our objective was to strike any enemy ships moving along the Norwegian coast. It was on 17 May 1942 that reports were coming in that the German battle cruiser the *Prinz Eugen* had been sighted making its way down the coast of Norway. Our squadron at Wick was immediately ordered to attempt to intercept the battle cruiser, which was expected to be somewhere south of Stavanger, probably making its way into the Baltic. Eighteen Beauforts took off loaded with torpedoes, flying at sea level to avoid being picked up by enemy detection apparatus (radar as such was not, I understand, available to German coastal defences at that time). Number 86 was later taken over by a Boeing Fortress squadron after I had been shot down and the Beauforts were posted to Malta. My friend Johnnie Atkinson crashed on take-off in England; he and his crew didn't survive. Cliff Thomson did a number of sorties from Malta and was eventually shot down, captured and taken to Italy as a PoW. I also learned that Roy Pitkin had been shot down in his Hudson and killed.

'We were escorted by four Beaufighters to provide air cover and to strafe the battleship whilst the Beauforts got into position to drop their torpedoes. To be effective, a torpedo had to be dropped at 90ft above sea level, aircraft speed reduced to 180 knots and the aircraft also had to be so positioned that the running torpedo would intercept the ship. Warships had tremendous fire power against attacking aircraft and, of course, made zigzag turns, making it very difficult to get into position. The idea was that as many torpedo aircraft as possible would attack from different angles, hopefully drawing away some of the flak and perhaps one torpedo would find its target. As it happened, the *Prinz Eugen* was not found sailing south of Stavanger. The wing commander, after a search along the coast, decided to fly north to Stavanger, as it was thought the *Prinz Eugen* may have found shelter in the harbour. As we swept the dock area, there was no sign of it or any other shipping.

'As we all turned away to fly back down the coast, German fighter aircraft could be seen taking off from an airfield. The squadron was still in formation and as we turned about, I was on the inside of the turn and consequently had to reduce speed a little to keep station. Shore anti-aircraft batteries opened up. I could see the plumes of water following me as they got the range. Suddenly they ceased and the rear gunner warned me that a fighter, a Me 109, was coming up fast. Almost immediately, machine gun and cannon tracer appeared just under us. I tried to jerk the aircraft out of the line of fire but a quick burst of bullets and cannon struck the fuselage and wing tanks.

'A piece of shrapnel must have entered my lower jaw and knocked me unconscious for what must have been a very short time. I recovered consciousness to find "Stuffy" Collins the navigator looking into my face. His face, I remember, was spotted in blood; on reflection the blood must have been from me as I breathed. I immediately took over the controls to find that we were flying almost at right angles to the sea. Once righted, the cabin began to fill with smoke and flames were engulfing the starboard wing. Both engines were still functioning. The heat became intense. We were too low to bail out, so it was imperative to force land onto the sea. At the same time, I opened the entrance hatch above my head to try to let in some fresh air. I managed to manoeuvre the Beaufort into a landing position. Just before we hit the water, I released the parachute safety harness [in the Beaufort, the pilot sat on his packed parachute]. This action I am sure was instrumental in saving my life. As we hit the water, my last thought was "this is it" and I would now be meeting Jesus.

STORIES FROM THE STALAGS

'As the flaming Beaufort hit the waves, I completely blacked out. I came to in a sea of flame[s] all around me, except for a narrow channel through which I managed to swim clear of the petrol flames. Once I had swum clear, I tried to inflate my Mae West through the tube designed for this purpose, only to discover that I couldn't inflate anything as part of my bottom lip and eight incisor teeth, four on top and four below, had been shot away. Before the operation I discovered that someone had taken my Mae West from my locker. The only one left was very soiled and had been thrown in a corner. I looked around and could see no sign of any of my crew or the aircraft. However, from somewhere, a wing petrol tank floated past. I attempted to climb onto it and as I did so, the lever which activated the air bottle on the Mae West (which I hadn't tried as I was convinced there wasn't one) caught on the side of the petrol tank. Lo and behold, the Mae West inflated beautifully with no leaks. I hung onto the petrol tank for a minute or two but the sea seemed too rough, so I dropped back into the water, which surprisingly seemed quite warm, which I learned was due to the warm Gulf Stream that flowed down the coast of Norway to the North Sea.

'As the 109 flew over me, probably the one which shot us down, I managed to wave to it. I remember lying back supported by the Mae West and I blacked out again. The next thing I remember was waking up in a hospital with strange voices speaking in a language I couldn't understand and I remember thinking in my confused state that they must be Matabele (Africans) talking to each other. I soon realised that they were talking German. I must have dropped off again or given an anaesthetic. The next thing I remember was waking up in a two-bed ward, with stitches down my chin and a bandage tied below my jaw and over my head. Also, a wound on my forehead required several stitches and I had a rather long wound approximately 6 inches long down the inside of my right knee into the gastronomies muscle. I could only take liquid through a tube or a spouted receptacle, I suppose because my front teeth had been shot away. I was able to use this gap without opening my mouth and I later realised the jaw bone [*sic*] had been broken approximately in the middle.

'The occupant of the other bed was a German soldier who had had an accident riding a motorcycle and had horrendous fractures in his leg bones. He had arrived there several weeks before me and was still there three months later as his wounds kept becoming infected, there being no antibiotics available at that time. I soon became aware of a German soldier with a large

SHOT DOWN IN A FJORD

Luger pistol on his hip. He was, I was told, my guard and was to prevent my escape, which was pretty ludicrous as I was almost incapable of even sitting up in bed. After a week or so, he was taken away.

'At the Stavanger Hospital, in which all the nurses were Norwegian, the top two floors were serviced by German doctors for German soldiers only and the bottom floor was for Norwegians only and under their own Norwegian doctors. I was, of course, given very special care by the nurses, particularly the sister-in-charge Sister Olina and Nurse Borga. I was warned to be careful of one other nurse as she was a quisling (traitor) and consequently pro-German.[1]

'After about ten days or so, a German soldier came to see me. He had been in the party which had picked me up from the sea. I was for the first time able to piece together what happened after I had passed out lying in my Mae West. A Norwegian motor boat with its owner on board plus eleven German Luftwaffe personnel (why so many was difficult to understand), picked me up some five miles off the coast of Stavanger. It must have been fairly late in the evening as I had been shot down around 2000 hours. My visitor said that once I was on board, I became very violent in trying to get up and empty my pockets of any papers I might have on me. A struggle ensued, with the Germans trying to restrain me, which according to him was very difficult in the small boat with so many on board. Also, he said I was very strong (must have been fit in those days). Apparently in the fracas, the paraffin lamp was knocked over and started a fire which could not be contained, so the boat was abandoned and soon sank. I was now in the water with twelve other people, pretty disgruntled I should imagine.

'I am not sure how the officials on shore were informed. My visitor said a sea plane from the air sea rescue base landed and picked me up, plus several of the Luftwaffe airmen. Being a fairly small, light float-plane it could only take a limited number of people, so my visitor and at least eight others were

---

1. Quisling, which is used in Scandinavian languages and in English for a person who collaborates with an enemy occupying force, is named after Vidkun Quisling, who in the 1930s, founded a pro-Nazi party. When Germany invaded Norway in 1940, Quisling attempted a pro-German coup against the government. From 1942 to 1945 he headed a pro-German administration. After the Second World War, Quisling was tried and convicted on charges of treason and he was executed by firing squad on 24 October 1945.

left and later picked up by another motor boat. They cannot have been very pleased with me, I imagine.

'My visitor had lost his watch and his practically new uniform had been ruined. So at least in some small way I had caused some losses to the German government, as the other ten must have had their uniforms ruined in some way by the fire and then sea water. Whether the Norwegian boat owner was ever compensated I never found out.

'On reflecting back to my crash into the sea and finding myself in the water, I am sure that Jesus was with me and pulled me out of the burning aircraft, which must have exploded on impact. Whether the torpedo was the cause of the fire, I never understood. Normally a torpedo only became active after it had been dropped and run for some distance for the nose cap to unwind and expose the detonator. I was incredibly lucky to have survived. My great regret was the loss of the three members of my crew. We had only been together for a relatively short time since leaving Chivenor and had flown on occasions on patrols in the North Sea and Norwegian coast. Stationed at Wick, which was not far from John O'Groats, I had little chance of meeting their parents. Fred Parkins was the only married member of the crew.

'I spent three months in Stavanger Hospital, during which time I had to undergo dental surgery to repair my broken lower jaw. This required me to be taken to the dental surgery in town. The first session lasted from 10am to 5pm, with no food of course and very little fluid. The dental surgeons, who were German, had to make two wire braces to fit my upper and lower jaw. These were wired to my remaining teeth. I don't know how many times my gums had to be anaesthetised with a local anaesthetic but it seemed like every hour or so. This I found very traumatic, plus the manipulation to align the two halves of the lower jaw. Eventually, leaving out all the gory details, the two wire braces were drawn together to prevent any movement of the bones during the healing process. At last, I was taken back to the hospital where I had a long sleep.

'The nurses brought cigarettes and books. I read the complete works of John Galsworthy's *Forsyth Saga*, also *Anthony Adverse* of a thousand pages. I had no news of home or my fiancée Doreen in England and no wireless. Although the German patient had a small one, he was not allowed to let me listen to it. But at one time he did tune into the BBC at the very moment Vera Lynn was singing "Don't know where, don't know when, but I know we'll meet again some sunny day". It was strangely a great morale boost for me, plus the prospect of being with Doreen some sunny day.

'Slowly, the jaw knit, but required from time to time fragments of bone and/or shrapnel to be removed as they surfaced. One of the temporary nurses whose name I have forgotten was connected in some way with the Norwegian resistance. She offered to help me escape to Sweden, which would have required travel over rough country. The idea was certainly encouraging; I asked what effect an escape would have on the nurses who looked over me. She said they would probably be shot or at the very least imprisoned. To her relief I think, I refused to allow this sort of punishment to be given to such lovely people. I would rather attempt to escape on my own, if possible, away from Norway, without having any civilians involved.

'The hatred of the Norwegians for the German occupying forces was something I had never experienced before. The courage and daring of the Norwegian resistance forces are legion and well documented in numerous books and films. So many lost their lives, as did their families, as reprisals by the Germans in an attempt to subjugate the civilians.

'Eventually, the German doctors saw no reason to keep me any longer in hospital, where I had been for four and a half months. With some emotion, my nurse saw me off under escort to Oslo. The journey was by train, guarded by two German soldiers. I was taken and imprisoned at Gestapo HQ in Oslo, a large multi-storey building in the centre of the city. This very building was later completely destroyed by a flight of precision-bombing Mosquitos of the RAF. Here I was interrogated by a Gestapo intelligence officer, in an attempt to gain any British information on the war. I gave him only my name, rank and number. He soon gave up as I think he realised that any information he might drag out would be ancient history as it was now four and a half months since I had been shot down. He spoke excellent English; he told me he had spent a long time in Singapore and had been a member of the English club there before the war.

'I recall him asking me what I thought would happen to Rhodesia after the Germans had won the war. I told him I didn't think they would win and things would be normal. He said, "We shall see" in a provocative tone, for at that time the Afrika Korps were having successes in the Middle East and on the Russian front.

'I spent only two days in Oslo and was then flown to Berlin via Copenhagen, under guard by Luftwaffe personnel. The aircraft was a Junkers

STORIES FROM THE STALAGS

Ju 52, a three-engined plane with corrugated fuselage, a very successful transport plane. My stay in Berlin was as brief as the stop in Copenhagen. Berlin seemed full of uniformed men and women, all saluting each other. There were so many varieties of uniform that my RAF uniform was largely unrecognisable to many Germans. Soon I was on my way by train to Dulag Luft (the Luftwaffe in-transit camp)[2] at Frankfort [sic] an der Oder. Here again I was confined for a few days and required to fill in a questionnaire asking a variety of questions, but as usual only name, rank and number were given. I wasn't pushed or threatened to divulge other information as were the recently shot down airmen.

'After two days, I was allowed to join other prisoners in the barracks. It was wonderful to meet up with all the air force crews recently captured, to be able to talk freely and have news of things in the UK. One was at first a little cagey as the Germans sometimes planted "stooges" in air force uniforms to glean any vital information from the conversations amongst the PoWs. Possibly the barracks were also "bugged".

'We were soon on our way across Germany to permanent PoW camps (Stalags)[3]. The journey was tedious and uncomfortable, but luxury in retrospect, as we later learned that many prisoners were transported in sealed cattle trucks for days on end, often with little or no food, or toilet facilities. Our intake from Dulag Luft was sent to Stalag VIII-B Lamsdorf, Ober Silesia, a large camp holding 14,000 army prisoners, mostly non-commissioned officers. There were about 1,000 RAF prisoners at Lamsdorf at this time because there were insufficient Luft (air force) camps. All RAF officers were sent to Sagan [Żagań] in western Poland. All non-commissioned air crew were incarcerated in a special security compound within Stalag VIIIB, completely separated from all the army or navy PoWs, virtually a prison within a prison. It was mooted that eventually we would be moved to Luft camps but we never did. After our arrival, only the odd RAF prisoner joined us, which was a loss inasmuch as news of home was very limited.

'Soon after my arrival, I met up with Phil Bridgeman, a Canadian observer from Calgary, and we became lifetime friends.'

---

2. The abbreviated name of 'Durchgangslager der Luftwaffe'. The main centre used during the war was at Oberursel, 13km north-west of Frankfurt am Main.
3. Stalag was short for Kriegsgefangenen-Mannschafts-Stammlager.

SHOT DOWN IN A FJORD

Bridgeman had been shot down over Bremen on the night of 4/5 September 1942 in a Lancaster of 61 Squadron flown by Pilot Officer Peter Clement Vellacott Joslin. Hit by flak over the Dutch coast, they were shot down by Oberleutnant Helmut Lent, the Gruppenkommandeur of II./NJG 2, and his radar operator Leutnant Walter Kubisch. Lent had at this point in the war been credited with 52 'kills', including 44 at night. Joslin and two of his crew were killed. Flight Sergeant James Cooper RCAF was listed as missing but human remains that were found many years later at the crash site near Warten, about 5 miles south-east of Leeuwarden are believed to be those of the Canadian rear gunner. Bridgeman, who had lied about his age to enlist in the RCAF, was flying only his second operation.

'Each barrack in the camp consisted of two long, rectangular buildings joined end to end by a wash house with showers (which only worked satisfactorily if the pressure was high enough) and cement wash basins which were built in. In the barracks there were three-tiered wooden bunks, housing 120 men and the other section the same. In total there must have been 7 or 8 such units. Inside, the furniture consisted of one table and two benches for ten men.

'The toilet facilities consisted of one large building completely separate from the barracks, situated adjacent to the parade ground. Built over a sump, the latrine was a 40-holer. Fortunately, it was never full at one time. There was no drainage; the fluid content was removed by a hand pump into a bowser-like vehicle drawn by a horse. The slurry was used for fertilising the agricultural fields in the area. This removal operation was done by the Russian prisoners under guard (a large Russian PoW camp was situated quite some distance from us). Phil and I collected cigarette "stompies" (butts) for the Russians, which were much appreciated as they saw no tobacco in their camp.

'The kitchens were outside our compound and were run by army PoWs. From the kitchens our daily rations were distributed to all the barracks in the camp. The normal daily routine was: 1. The arrival of hot to warm mint tea, usually awful and rarely drinkable, but it was useful for shaving 2. Soon after, the speakers erected on poles throughout the camp would be blaring out, ordering all prisoners to attend parade for the daily count. We had to form up in columns of five. This head count was a very serious matter for the German guards, to ensure that no one had escaped during the night. It was also an opportunity for the PoWs to annoy the guards, by moving about inside the ranks, so being counted twice. This caused much confusion amongst the Jerries. Their tempers were quickly inflamed and there was much shouting and waving of revolvers and threats of disciplinary action. The counting could on occasions, especially in the summer, take several hours. In winter it was often too cold to mess about for long. Of course, if any PoWs were missing, we had to remain on the parade ground until all the barrack rooms had been searched etc.

'After the count, rations would be issued from the kitchens. Black bread (one loaf to five), boiled potatoes for each set of ten men, which worked out to about 6–8 potatoes each, depending on size and rarely some margarine was also issued. At midday, plain non-descript "soup", which usually consisted of swedes and cabbage and sometimes small portions of horse meat, would arrive in large open-topped wooden barrels called "keebles" for distribution by each barrack leader, or "ration king" who ladled out the contents. Once the "soup" had been distributed, there would be a rush of men with spoons to scrape out all the remnants of soup stuck to the side of the keeble. These people were known as the "keeble scrapers", which became a somewhat derogatory description for anyone beyond the pale.

'One member for a week took on the duties of dividing the potatoes and bread into ten separate lots. Named cards were then "cut" and placed before each of the rows of potatoes and portions of bread. It was an essential factor to ensure that the food was distributed as evenly as possible. Tempers were easily aroused in some people if they thought they weren't getting their fair share. Hunger can produce some very distressing arguments and rarely, even fights. However, on the whole we made sure that in our section tolerance and friendship were paramount.

'There were times when the Red Cross parcels managed to reach the many PoW camps. These were a Godsend and were instrumental in saving many lives. Unfortunately, distribution was very erratic for long periods. Each parcel was shared between two. The Canadian parcels were very good, as were those from England and Scotland, but as the latter two were from rationed countries, they contained slightly less variety. The Germans punctured all the tinned food (jam, meat, condensed milk, soup, margarine, etc) to ensure we could not store it for escape purposes. The Canadian parcels contained tins of spam; a large tin of "Klim" [milk spelt backwards] that had originally held powdered milk, supplied by the Red Cross for the prisoners, and hard tack biscuits. The Scottish parcels always contained porridge oats.

There was also chocolate in all parcels. As can be imagined, these goodies were very quickly eaten up. Items like tea and sugar were made to last as long as possible. Canadian cigarettes were a boon to smokers and also to non-smokers as they became the main source of currency in the camp. Eighty cigarettes to one tin of "Klim" was the going rate.

'Medical and dental services were provided by captured doctors and dentists who worked in the Stalag hospital. They made the best of the limited facilities and drugs. Only on one occasion did I spend a few days in the hospital with a relapse bout of malaria. It was a change to get away for a little while.

'If one had toothache there was no chance of having a filling, unless prepared to wait for a year or so. Extractions, however, were done on a daily basis. All PoWs with toothache would parade in the morning at the dental clinic. The orderly sergeant would take your name and note the position of the aching tooth. This was passed to the British dentist (also a PoW), who then injected anaesthetic into the appropriate place. You would then go back into the line-up while the others received injections, thus giving the anaesthetic sufficient time to act. After several minutes your name would be called, the sergeant would, from his record, tell the dentist the position of the offending tooth and before you knew it the tooth was out. The dentist must have pulled out literally thousands of teeth and certainly was very expert. Very rarely there were cases when the wrong tooth was extracted.

'One of the various activities in our block was reading books supplied by the Red Cross. These were in great demand and all had of course been passed by the German authorities. My fiancée Doreen had sent through Rhodesia House a number of text books [sic] on biology, chemistry and animal management, all necessary for 1st year veterinary studies.

'Once the gates in the RAF compound had been opened, it was possible to join various study groups already active in the main camp. I joined a small veterinary class run by a New Zealander who had a degree in equine diseases and management. He had qualified in the United States but was not allowed to practise as his US qualification was not at that time recognised in Commonwealth countries. Also, the theatre centre produced plays and variety shows which were well attended. One of the leading actors was Denholm Elliott, a wireless operator/air gunner on 76 Squadron. On the night of 23/24 September 1942, his Handley Page Halifax took part in an air raid on the U-boat pens at Flensburg. The aircraft was hit by flak and subsequently ditched in the North Sea near Sylt. Only Elliott and two crewmen survived.[4]

'As mentioned previously, contract bridge was very popular and many a competition was organized. A Canadian friend, George Rodney and I usually managed to win many of these. The fee for entering was two cigarettes, so the first prize could mean up to one hundred cigarettes, the main source of currency in the camp. George Rodney was a pilot who had been shot down in his Kittyhawk fighter. In civilian life he was a professional baseball player. He suffered a horrendous wound to his right shoulder blade. Once it had healed, he started practicing pitching baseballs, day after day, until his right arm regained its former strength. After the war he returned to a successful career as a professional player.

'In the main camp was a larger open-topped reservoir tank filled with water to be used in case of fire. One morning a body in British army uniform was found floating in it. No one knew who it was. Most likely it was a German agent who was in the camp to report on escape plans and document forging activities and had obviously been found out by the camp escape committee.

'We were only allowed to write two letters (a small one-page form) and two postcards per month, which were heavily censored, so one could not say much but at least our families would know that we were still alive.

'Soccer games took place at fairly infrequent intervals. Also, a game of rugby was played, a South African team versus the rest. The match took place on the parade ground, which had not a blade of grass, but only rock-hard ground. Needless to say, very few rugby games took place.

'Another activity was "tin bashing", conducted mainly by budding tin smiths. It was incredible the number of articles these fellows could make: pots and pans, jugs, cups and ladles, all from tins from Red Cross parcels. Perhaps

---

4. Another famous actor, Donald Pleasence, who played one of the forgers at Stalag Luft III in *The Great Escape*, was a former PoW. In December 1939 Pleasence initially refused conscription into the British Armed Forces, registering as a conscientious objector, but changed his stance in autumn 1940 after the attacks upon London by the Luftwaffe. He served as aircraft wireless operator on 166 Squadron in Bomber Command, flying on almost sixty operational raids. On 31 August 1944, Lancaster III NE112, in which he was a crew member, was shot down during an attack on Agenville. He was captured and imprisoned in Stalag Luft I. Like Denholm Elliott, he acted in many plays for the entertainment of his fellow prisoners.

one of the most popular and ingenious was the "blower", a furnace-type contraption made from "Klim" tins, with a fan operated by a wooden wheel with a handle. This handle would force air through a fired enclosed grate on which was placed a little water and a type of fuel could be used. It would take less than one minute to boil 1½ pints of water. As can be imagined, it was very popular amongst PoWs as we had no heating facilities in the barracks.

'The bed bunks were made of wood, with the base lined with bed boards. We were supplied with palliasse mattresses made of straw-filled Hessian bags. The straw was removed and discarded as it was very dusty and prickly. The Hessian was laid over the bed boards and after a while one became hardened to sleeping on these. Bed boards were used to line tunnels and for fuel, so more often than not one had an incomplete set. They had to be so arranged to fit one's body, i.e., head and shoulders, hips and knees, with gaps in between. The Germans refused to replace missing bed boards. Many PoWs converted their bunks into hammock-like structures.

'Each barrack housed about 120 men. At times noise was a big factor but in time one became adjusted to ignoring the tin bashing, shouting, conversations, arguments, etc.'

Chapter 2

Young Winston

During the years we spent in the prison camp, our faith in God was important. We always had hope, believing we would come home. Some fellows had ideas about what they would do then, and others did not. I knew I wanted to be a rancher.

**Sergeant Winston Churchill Parker,
419 Squadron, RCAF**

Winston Churchill Parker was born in Calgary, Canada, on 31 July 1918, the elder son of English-born parents, Herbert Garfield Parker and Amelia 'Millie' Emily Churchill, a cousin four or five times removed of British Prime Minister Winston Churchill. Winston was just a baby and his sister was 2 years old when their father rented a farm with buildings in the Red Deer Lake District south of the city. The siblings were brought up to be proud of their English roots, so they went to gatherings and school wearing a tie, and English-style clothes. Winston loved the life of a cowboy from a young age. He studied tractor mechanics at college. At 21 and working for the Home Oil Company when the war began, he took a half day off work and joined the Royal Canadian Air Force. It was not a difficult decision. He had been greatly influenced by the flyer 'Wop' May, and the old Wapiti bombers that flew back and forth a few miles north-west of the farm intrigued him. 'Besides', he said, 'we had been brought up in the English tradition that if our country needed you, you volunteered.'

Winston went back home until he was finally called up in August 1940. 'In June 1941, we got our wings, graduated as aircrew, and were sent overseas on the RMMV *Stirling Castle*, a South African luxury liner, with about 150 airmen and several hundred army personnel.' Once he was categorised in England, he was sent to RAF Cranwell. Like his brother Geoff, Winston was a wireless air gunner. And soon he was flying ops on Wellingtons in 419 Squadron, RCAF at RAF Mildenhall in Suffolk.

YOUNG WINSTON

On his first leave, he went to London to visit his uncle, Reginald Parker, Prime Minister Churchill's personal chauffeur. Winston finally tracked down his uncle with the help of a sergeant at the front desk at Scotland Yard. 'He told me to look for a car with a specific number in a guarded area, protected by barbed wire. After I walked into the lot and started looking around, a Bobby grabbed me by the shoulder. I told him I was looking for a certain car number that belonged to the prime minister. Not buying my story, he marched me back to Scotland Yard, where the sergeant on duty confirmed he had sent me. Another Bobby offered to escort me to Number 10 Downing Street!'

Winston found Walter H. Thompson, Churchill's personal bodyguard, and his Uncle Reginald in a little office just inside. Churchill came walking through the foyer. 'My uncle stepped out and said, "Sir, I'd like you to meet the boy my brother named after you." Mr Churchill stopped and I was introduced.' The Prime Minister spent fifteen or twenty minutes in conversation with his namesake. Since he was one of the first to go through the British Commonwealth Air Training Plan, the Prime Minister wanted to know about that, as well as what young Winston had observed while crossing the Atlantic. 'After I satisfied his curiosity, the Prime Minister turned to my uncle and said, "Take Parker downstairs and show him the War Room. Tomorrow, bring me in and then take the day off to show Parker around London in my car." It was a great privilege to see the top-secret room. The walls were covered with large maps with different-coloured pins stuck here and there. The next day, as we drove around London the Bobbies stopped traffic and waved us through when they recognized Mr Churchill's car. That day, though, the only Winston Churchill in the car was me!'

On 22 February 1942, having been recalled from the USA where he was head of the RAF Delegation, Air Marshal Arthur T. Harris, had arrived at High Wycombe, Buckinghamshire, to take charge of RAF Bomber Command. Harris's concept was to break the German spirit by the use of area rather than precision bombing and the targets would be civilian, not just military. Such a concept two years before would have been unthinkable but Harris saw the need to deprive the German factories of its workers and therefore its ability to manufacture weapons for war. Mass raids would be the order of the day, or rather the night, with little attention paid to precision raids on military targets. However, Bomber Command did not possess the numbers of aircraft necessary for immediate mass raids. On taking up his position Harris found that only 380 aircraft were serviceable. Only 68 of these were heavy bombers while 257 were medium bombers.

The first target selected by Sir Arthur T. Harris was the Renault factory in the town of Boulogne-Billancourt just west of the centre of Paris, which was making an estimated 18,000 lorries a year for the German forces. It had been earmarked for attack for some time and it was set for the night of Tuesday, 3/Wednesday, 4 March. A full moon was predicted so Harris decided to send a mixed force of 235 aircraft – 89 Wellingtons, 48 Hampdens, 29 Stirlings, 26 Manchesters, 23 Whitleys and 20 Halifaxes; the greatest number of RAF aircraft despatched to a single target so far in the war. It was led by the most experienced crews in Bomber Command to bomb the French factory in three waves. The first wave was manned by fully trained crews followed by a second wave of medium bombers and a third wave of Manchesters, Halifaxes and Wellingtons equipped for 4,000lb bombs. The plan called for the massed use of flares and a very low bombing level so that crews could hit the factory without too many bombs falling in the surrounding town. There were no flak defences. All aircraft were to carry as many flares as their bomb loads allowed. The first wave was to light up the target, then bomb, and then drop its remaining flares to windward. The second wave was to the same so that the target would be well lit the entire time. Two separate groups of buildings were to be bombed with the aircraft of 3 Group aiming at the works on an island in the Seine and the rest at the main factory on the riverbank.

At Mildenhall Sergeant Winston Churchill Parker was on one of the eight Wellington crews of 419 Squadron, RCAF Battle Order that night and he and his crew came through safely. It was calculated that approximately 121 aircraft an hour had been concentrated over the Renault factory, which was devastated and all except twelve aircraft claimed to have bombed. It was reported that 300 bombs fell on the factory, destroying 40 per cent of the buildings. Production was halted for four weeks and final repairs were not completed for several months. A post-war American estimate said that the production loss was almost 2,300 vehicles. Just one aircraft (a Wellington) was lost but 367 French people were killed, 341 were badly injured and 9,250 people lost their homes.

By early April Parker had completed ten trips and was now a regular wireless operator–air gunner on Flying Officer Arthur B. Crighton's crew in 419 Squadron, RCAF. On the night of 8–9 April Art Crighton, who was from Calgary, got ready to take Wellington 'N-Nuts' (X3467) – better known as the 'Calgary kite' – off from Mildenhall for an operation on Hamburg but the Wimpy developed instrument trouble for this, the crew's thirteenth operation, and orders came through for Crighton to pull off to the side and take off as number thirteen. The crew wondered if this was a bad omen and indeed it was to turn out that way. Flight Sergeant W. Ralph MacWilliam, who was from Salisbury, New Brunswick, was attached to the crew as part of his training and flew as the second pilot. He reported seeing tracer rounds and heavy flak as the Wellington came over the coast near Wilhelmshaven. This was also verified by Sergeant Winston Churchill Parker but there was no immediate indication of any hits or damage from this enemy action. It was not for a half hour or more later before the port engine caught fire. Crighton, using the engine extinguisher, managed to put out the fire. Now running on the remaining engine, the bombs were jettisoned. Pilot Officer Ernest Richard Howard, a 20-year-old WAG (wireless operator–air gunner) of Longview, Alberta, disposed of the ammunition via the flare chute. With the lightened load they managed to climb another 10,000ft with the aid of the restarted port engine.

Approaching Hamburg, the starboard engine burst into flames and it too was extinguished and then feathered but the port engine then again caught fire and there was no fire extinguisher fluid left. Crighton tried to restart the starboard engine but was unsuccessful and it also burst into flames. He ordered the crew to abandon the aircraft via the front escape hatch. Ernie Howard, who had been at the flare chutes and tried to leave by the rear hatch, did not manage to escape and he went down with the aircraft, whereupon his body was recovered later. All the others – Crighton, Parker, MacWilliam, Flight Sergeant J.P. Paton, the wireless operator from Montreal and, Flight Sergeant Hubert Brooks, the navigator, bailed out safely. Brooks was born in the Peace River town of Bluesky, Alberta, on 29 December 1921. Following the Depression on the prairies in the 1920s the family moved east, first to Ottawa and then to Montreal, where Brooks received his (French-based) education and hockey training.

Sergeant Parker, who said later that there was an explosion in one of the fuel tanks after he had left the aircraft, stashed his parachute and then walked for about three hours down a railway track. However a little more than twenty-four hours later, he was picked up by the Volkssturm (German national militia) and held in a farmhouse. After processing at Dulag Luft, Parker and some of the other captive airmen entrained for Stalag VIII-B

(Lamsdorf) located in what is now Poland on the Polish–Czechoslovakian border. It was considered a tough, reprisal prisoner of war camp.

Flight Sergeant (later Wing Commander) Brooks, who was on only his second operation, did not remain a prisoner for long. After a few days at Dulag Luft, Brooks was sent to Stalag VIII-B, where, having exchanged identities with a soldier, he was employed on various work parties. On 10 November 1942, shortly after serving ten days' solitary confinement for his second escape attempt, Brooks was sent to a sawmill at Tost. In January 1943, with British Army Sergeant John Duncan in charge of the work party, Brooks got the job of lorry driver. Duncan had been captured at Sainte-Valéry-en-Caux on 12 June 1940 but he had escaped the same day and evaded for fifteen months in northern France, sheltered at Saint-Gilles-de-Crétot in Normandy, until he was arrested on 11 September 1941. He was held at a prison in Rouen until 1 December, when he was sent to Stalag VIII-B and served twenty-one days in solitary confinement cells in a Straflager (punishment camp) until 2 May 1942. While Duncan was serving twenty-one days in solitary confinement cells following his third escape attempt in September 1942, when he'd almost reached the Czech border, he met Brooks and they began to plan another escape.

Brooks' job as a driver enabled him to acquire two maps of Europe and large-scale maps of the Tost area as well as other items likely to be useful to any escaper. On 10 May 1943, Brooks and Duncan escaped by sawing through the bars on their hut window and cutting a wire fence. They made their way to Częstochowa, where they contacted the Polish underground at an address given to them by an airman at Lamsdorf. The two men stayed with the Armia Krajowa (AK) partisans, the Polish Underground Army, undertaking raids and assassinations against the Nazi occupation, until the arrival of Russian troops in early 1945. Brooks and Duncan left Odessa on board SS *Moreton Bay* on 7 March and arrived in the UK on 19 March. Brooks was one of only five RCAF members to receive the Military Cross for his actions and his award carried the longest citation of them all. An accomplished ice hockey player, he won a gold medal at the 1948 Winter Olympics in St Moritz.[1]

What must have immediately intrigued Parker's captors were his Christian names and the Germans were not slow to take advantage of the propaganda value. On 21 April a telegram told Winston's anxious family that 'Sergeant

---

1. See *Life and Times of Hubert Brooks M.C. C.D. A Canadian Hero.*

YOUNG WINSTON

Winston Churchill Parker was mentioned in a German broadcast on 20/4/42 as being a prisoner of war.'

'Eventually, we had 135 men to a billet, even though the billets weren't big. Prisoners slept on and under tables, wherever there was space. The cement floors were so cold our feet literally froze in our leather boots. We were issued clogs to wear around the camp.

'If a rainstorm came, we'd get our soap and whip outside to bathe. We were very happy when some chap would get lousy, because the Germans would take our whole billet down to the delousing area. When we stripped off, our bundled clothes were put through a cyanide gas treatment. When we came out of the shower, we would lie down to avoid the deadly cyanide gas fumes, and unwrap our clothes at arm's length to get dressed.'

Every day, the prisoners received a ration of potatoes, a small slice of black bread about an inch thick, tea made from mint, and soup. Sometimes the soup wasn't too bad; other times, it was terrible. The daily German ration wasn't enough to keep the prisoners going.

'We relied heavily on the Red Cross parcels filled with vitamin-fortified foods. When they came in, we were reasonably healthy and felt pretty good. When they didn't, we didn't feel good. If it hadn't been for the Red Cross, we wouldn't have made it.'

The prisoners were permitted to send one letter and two cards home every other month. While they could receive all the letters sent by their family and friends, they were allowed only four clothing parcels a year. That was a highlight in their dull, monotonous lives.

Cigarettes were the camp currency. Although Winston didn't smoke, he used them for barter, once trading packages for three cobs of fresh corn.

Some of the prisoners who were trained as radio technicians constructed a contraband radio that picked up the BBC. The news was copied down in shorthand and passed along by word of mouth.

During the attack on the German-occupied port of Dieppe, France, in August 1942, Canadian troops captured some German soldiers. Allegedly, the Canadians bayoneted some of the Germans so they would never fight against the Allies again. In retaliation, all the PoWs who had been serving in the Canadian army were tied up with ropes. According to Winston: 'Not long after that, a bunch of Canadian prisoners were put in a compound not far from us in Stalag VIII-B. Their wrists were tied with cords. We would holler across the fence to them, kind of laughing and teasing, saying, "They'll take them off for you on Christmas Day!" But our smiles faded when the Germans decided that aircrew would be tied up, too. The cords were so tight they constricted the circulation in our hands. Some weeks later, a truck that drove into the compound dumped thousands of handcuff sets. The guards took off our cords and manacled us with handcuffs with 12-inch-long chains. Ironically, they had been manufactured in England. While the Germans did take the cuffs off for Christmas Day, it was eleven months before that order was rescinded.

'During the years we spent in the prison camp, our faith in God was important. We always had hope, believing we would come home. Some fellows had ideas about what they would do then, and others did not. I knew I wanted to be a rancher.'

Winston recalls that when a prisoner in the camp died, he would be given a military funeral at a little cemetery out in the woods. He remembers how very, very cold and miserable it was when 'The Last Post' was played at some of those services, and how hard it was to turn around and leave a comrade there.

'We had to find ways to kill time and stay healthy. We walked many, many laps around our compound, and did push-ups. We read as much as we could. Whatever material came in, we thumbed through it until it was worn out. An Australian pilot, who was a very good bridge player, taught some of us how to play. I still play bridge once or twice a week.'

After several years in the prison camp, Winston came down with pleurisy. He was sent to Lazarett, the camp hospital. Unfortunately, a prisoner in the next bed was very ill with malaria, and Winston contracted it. He lived with bouts of malaria on and off thereafter.

As the Russian armies neared Stalag VIII-B, the Germans moved their prisoners into columns of men, numbering approximately 1,500, and sent them walking westward on 22 January 1945.

'We marched 35km at a pretty fast pace the first day, testing our limits. They gave us some shorter marches and occasionally, we'd have a day's rest. We got so very little to eat that we literally were starving. Some nights, the Germans would bring in big tubs of soup or a ration of bread. Other nights, we were fed nothing. There were no more Red Cross parcels or mail. We sometimes were herded into brick kilns or big sheds filled with straw at night. Other nights, we slept in the open.

'In mid-February 1945, we were marching fairly close to Dresden when we saw more aircraft than we had ever seen in our lives coming over, flying low. During the raid, the German guards ordered the prisoners to lie down in a field and kept their guns trained on them. For nights afterward, they could see the glow of the city of Dresden burning on the horizon.'

When the British would make raids at night, they invariably would drop bombs where Winston and his fellow prisoners had slept the night before.

'It gave us great comfort to tell each other: "They know where we are." Then one night, the British dropped bombs too close to our column, and one or two of our fellows were killed. I was just shaken up.'

Winston and his comrades marched south-west of Hanover. There, the Germans turned them around and marched them back in the direction in which they had come. By that time, as many as six to eight PoWs didn't get up each morning. They had died in the night.

The march from Lamsdorf went all the way west to Minden on 20 January 1945, and then eastward again to a point east of Hildesheim on 11 April 1945. That was the day their cruel march ended. 'On 11 April, we awoke to find the German guards had fled. The next thing we knew, American jeeps and a couple of tanks came rolling toward us. We were no longer prisoners of war!

'We had spent nearly three months on the road and travelled over 1,000km, one of the longest forced marches of World War Two. It has been called the Death March.'

When Winston reached an English hospital, he weighed only 98lb. A nurse, who was caring for him, asked if she might have what was left of his boots, and he happily obliged. Early in July 1945, when the SS *Île de France*, the third largest ship afloat, sailed for Canada, he was on it.

'I got back to Calgary in mid-July and my family met me at the CPR Station downtown. Jessie recalls that I was thin, drawn and pale. They were anxious to hear about what I had gone through, but I didn't want to talk about the war. I wanted to try and forget it.'[2]

---

2. Adapted from *Saddles and Service: Winston Parker's Story,* told to Elaine Taylor Thomas. Used with permission.

Chapter 3

No Particular Courage

We did not know, we could not know that within two hours some of us would die, violently. Statistically, we were aware that there was at least a 5 per cent chance we would not return that night or any other such night, but we refused to admit it, even to ourselves. A one in twenty chance tonight did not necessarily mean a certainty by twenty such nights. It happened to others, so we persuaded ourselves; we believed, or pretended to believe, we were immune, even though, privately, most of us were scared of what lay ahead. Even if we had known, there was little anyone of us could do except report sick and it was too late for that now. It would be unthinkable to desert comrades with whom work and pleasure had been shared. Besides, any action deliberately taken to avoid participation would result in disgrace.

Sergeant Harold 'Harry' Church, the 21-year-old navigator on 21-year-old Flight Lieutenant Norman Henry Carfoot's crew on 49 Squadron at Fiskerton, a few miles east of Lincoln, recalling the events of the night of 3–4 November 1943 when the target was Düsseldorf for only their second operation. See 'No Particular Courage' by Harry Church in *Flights Into History: Final Missions Retold by Research and Archaeology* by Ian McLachlan.[1]

'On the evening of 3 November our crew of seven stood by the huge undercarriage of our Lancaster, "E-Easy", flies open, ready for the ritual urination before climbing into the aircraft's dark and narrow interior. As well as fulfilling a superstitious need, this was a very practical thing to do, as there would be no other reasonable opportunity for several hours. This was

---

1. Sutton Publishing, 2007.

the seventeenth "op" for most of the crew, although the great majority of them had been undertaken with another squadron before being posted to this special one. "Op", short for operation, sounded more casual, less ostentatious, than the American "mission". We had only thirteen more to do after this one to complete our tour. The commanding officer, Wing Commander Alexander Annan Adams DFC, inevitably known as "Triple A", enjoyed flying "E-Easy" and usually did so when he selected himself for operations.

'After the briefing we were then ready for transport to the dispersed hard standings. We were usually driven out by a pretty young blonde WAAF [Women's Auxiliary Air Force] called Vi who was always very quiet on such occasions, though usually happy and talkative, particularly when she collected us on our return. Once airborne, the usual drills were followed. After crossing the coast, the air gunners tested their Brownings with a short burst to ensure efficiency and readiness.

'"Enemy coast ahead" announced Flight Sergeant Steve Putnam, the bomb aimer, over the intercom. Aged 21, Steve was a Canadian from Winnipeg, who had almost completed his pilot's training in Canada when he was advised to transfer to a bomb aimers' course. He spent most of his time in the nose of the aircraft and always carried an empty milk bottle, in case he needed to urinate. That particular part of his anatomy which relieved the need became stuck in it on one occasion, during a long flight, much to the glee of the rest of the crew.

'Now we were over hostile territory, not that we had been particularly safe from fighter attention over the North Sea. Now we would have searchlights and flak to deal with too. We were becoming used to this, gaining more and more confidence with each op, but we knew we could not afford to become over-confident or careless. I remembered the first one; after the target had been confirmed and the time of take-off approached, I had felt very unwell and had almost persuaded myself that I was unfit to fly, that I would be a danger to the rest of the crew and ought really to report sick. It had taken a great deal of will-power to convince myself that I was not really ill, just scared stiff. After that, it had been a bit easier. The waiting was the problem; once in the aircraft, all the crew members had their specific tasks to perform and involvement with the job in hand left little time to think of other things.

'Then the first attack came. "Enemy fighter to port," called Flight Sergeant Dave McCarthy List, the 22-year-old rear gunner, and his Browning guns began to chatter spitefully at the intruder in their air space. Dave came from Newcastle in Australia when aged 21. Sergeant Wilfred Henry Marson, the mid-upper gunner, joined in and the enemy broke off to choose another target. He was the baby of the crew at just 18 years old, having falsified his age in order to volunteer at the age of 17. The two gunners had sent a twin-engined German fighter, a Ju 88, spiralling down in flames on one trip, much to their delight and the relief of all.

'"Window" was ejected and then, spot on the ETA, the target loomed ahead. It could hardly be missed. Myriad searchlights probed the night sky and occasionally an aircraft was caught in the interlocking beams. A blazing bomber spiralled down in flames, while another suddenly exploded. The crew of that one did not have time to suffer. Innocuous looking but deadly white puffs, like balls of cotton wool, blossomed around us: as expected in "Happy Valley", the flak was heavy tonight. The cotton wool puffs were close now and "E-Easy" rocked, as if in protesting at the intrusion. Then began the run-in; straight and level. Now came the really hairy half-minute or so.

'After the bomb aimer had released the load, the aircraft would leap, owing to the sudden loss of weight, but it would be necessary for the pilot to stay as straight and level as possible until the camera had done its job. The resultant photographs would indicate the accuracy of the bombing and also give valuable information as to probable damage when they were analysed by the experts. For that reason, Bomber Command pilots had been recently instructed that they must not weave over the target.

'Bomb aimer to pilot, left, left – steady, right, – steady … steady … bombs gone.

'Simultaneously and before I could enter that fact and the time, in my log book we were coned by searchlights. The interior of "E-Easy" was starkly illuminated. Norman threw the aircraft into a dive, turning violently to port at the same time. The searchlights pursued "E-Easy" relentlessly and the flak increased in intensity. The aircraft shuddered like a wounded beast as the anti-aircraft shells exploded; in the harsh light it was obvious that the starboard wing had been damaged. The flak stopped suddenly, but the crew knew the likely consequence. Sure enough, Dave announced, almost conversationally, "Ju 88 to starboard – dive, dive". The gunners' Brownings burst into action. But they were already diving. Norman fought for control. Then came disaster; our gunners' fire had no effect on this occasion. I escaped death by inches as tracer bullets appeared lazily across my vision from left to right. This illusion of laziness was caused by the fact that tracers were regularly spaced among the equally deadly other bullets in order to help the gunner direct and correct his fire.

'The port wing burst into flames. Sergeant "Jock" Mason, the flight engineer, made valiant efforts to divert the fuel supply to a different wing-tank. "Jock" was a typical Scot, dour, down-to-earth, good at his job and reliable. He had reached the ripe old age of 22.

'Norman's calm voice was heard over the intercom, checking the well-being of the crew. No reply came from the wireless operator, but we others reported in, one by one. Inevitably, the dreaded "Abracadabra, Jump, Jump" order was issued, calmly, by the pilot.

'"Skipper, I can't get out," called Dave from the rear turret.

'"The navigator will come to help you," said Norman reassuringly, as if such a minor problem would soon be solved.

'I drew the blackout curtain behind me and was about to move when Dave announced, "I'm OK now, Skipper". I could not help my vast relief that I would not now have to struggle to the rear of the blazing aircraft. Relief turned to shock as I looked to my left and saw "Hank" Wood the wireless operator, a 20-year-old Londoner, or what remained of him. The bullets that had passed across the navigator's table had not missed Hank, who was now quite unrecognisable. The shock was even greater in that I had never before seen a dead body, even one that had passed away peacefully.

'By this time Norman had managed to pull the Lanc out of its steep dive in order to enable his crew to bail out. Norman was an outstanding pilot but he knew before he flew that due to his size, he would never be able to escape through the hatch if they were hit. He held on to the aircraft as his crew bailed out. Had he been unable to do so, our evacuation would have been almost impossible. I quickly reported Hank's fate, clipped on my parachute, removed my oxygen mask and moved to the escape hatch in the nose. As I passed Norman, still fighting the controls in order to keep the aircraft as steady as possible, my pilot, Skipper, friend and colleague briefly took one hand from the controls and waved goodbye. "Greater love has no man ..." – we both knew that Norman had no chance of survival. He held on to the aircraft as his crew bailed out. It exploded shortly afterward. Reaching the nose, I saw that the hatch had been removed and Steve and "Jock" had gone.

'"E-Easy" was now burning fiercely. I dived out. As the chute opened several seconds later, I saw our aircraft below and in front, plunging earthwards in a ball of flame. A minute or two earlier I had escaped death by inches, now I had survived by seconds – but I had thoughts only for Norman, Hank and any others of those close friends who could not escape the inferno.

'I drifted down. The fall seemed unending; it must have taken at least 30 minutes. Then I saw clouds below and suddenly with no warning I just stopped, standing upright! The chute collapsed around and on me.

'Orientating myself by the Pole star, I trudged south, hoping to find a copse or wood to hide in until any probable search had been called off. However, after a few hundred paces I climbed over a low bank and found myself on a narrow road, along which I walked. By now the moon was shining brightly and I was able to identify what looked like a village ahead. Deciding to bypass it, I prepared to take to the fields again, but before I could do so, heard footfalls and a man's voice called "*Gute nacht*". Although a few German phrases were posted in the Mess for such an eventuality, I now wished I had learned to speak the language better. However, the meaning was obvious, so I returned the greeting as best I could. One small hurdle had been surmounted. Jumping another bank, I crossed another field and – my luck was in – saw trees ahead. Approaching, I found it was indeed a small wood in the corner of the field. I entered, pushing my way through bracken and bushes and sat down. I would wait until midnight, when all should be fairly quiet, before resuming the journey. Looking at my navigator's Omega watch, I could see well enough that the time was 2125. "What a lot has happened in a few hours," I muttered to myself. I thought again of my friends, who had so recently died. Hank was dead and Norman could not possibly have survived; of the other four, how many had been as fortunate as I?[2]

'0200 I saw a bridge spanning a railway. As I began to make my way to the centre of the bridge, I quickly realised it had not been a wise decision. "Halt, who goes there?" were not the words actually spoken, but the commanding tone made the meaning quite clear. I turned to run, but the sound of a shot dissuaded me and I halted. I had been lucky on three occasions – to avoid death four times in a few hours was too much to hope for. Two soldiers approached; rifles at the ready. One soldier appeared elderly, the other young, in the light of the torch that one held.

'"*Englander terrorflieger*," the older man declared. "*Schweinhund*," said the younger. Unwisely, I retorted, "*Hitler ist scheisen-hausen*". For my pains

---

2. Apart from Church only Sergeant 'Jock' Mason and Flight Sergeant Steve Putman survived to be taken into captivity.

I received a spiteful blow on my knee from the butt of the youth's rifle; the natives were not at all friendly and it seemed that my all-too-brief attempt at escape was over, at least for the time being. It was difficult to realise that I had been captured – or "in the bag" in RAF slang.'

***

'In Dulag Luft at Oberursel I told myself there was no point in dwelling on the past, and it was certainly futile to feel sorry for myself in my present predicament. "It can only improve," I told myself firmly.

'A week later nine of us were escorted to the railway station at Frankfurt and bundled into a carriage, escorted by two armed guards. The train, carrying passengers in other carriages, travelled eastward for hours, at first in daylight. We were not in the right frame of mind to appreciate the wonderful scenery. Darkness fell, the train stopped at a station and water was brought. It tasted better than the acorn coffee! Still the train rumbled on, until, during the night, we reached the end of the journey. There were no lights to identify the name of the station, but someone outside shouted "Leipzig". Jock, Steve and I remarked ruefully, "We were over here a couple of weeks ago."

'By this time deprivation of food and drink had begun to befuddle us prisoners. We had little idea of time and distance and were almost in a stupor; even our eyesight was affected. We did vaguely remember being herded into a cattle truck, which was already partly filled with civilians, male and female, young and old. One of the airmen spoke German fairly well and learned that they were Jews. The conditions were most unpleasant for all; the cattle truck itself was not an ideal means of transport and the crowded conditions provided little or no opportunity to sit. The journey seemed never-ending and became more and more uncomfortable as time passed. We airmen were sorry for the Jews more than we were for ourselves and we were certainly sorry enough for ourselves. All things eventually come to an end, and eventually the train stopped. We airmen were selectively removed and then herded, shuffling, along a narrow road with fields on either side. Some stumbled and were prodded to their feet to continue. This road continued for several miles until we saw a large rectangular enclosure, fenced with double coils of barbed wire to a height of about 10ft, with sentry boxes at each corner and others spaced along the sides. The enclosure itself was approximately 200–300 yards square, with a formidable gate at the end of the road, guarded by sentries with rifles. Outside the camp were acres of bare fields on all sides; there were no trees, hedges or vegetation of any kind. We would discover later that nor were there any birds, which always seemed strange. The interior of the camp was similar in that there was no vegetation, just a great number of large wooden huts, grouped in separate compounds, together with a small, detached section containing more solid administrative buildings and German quarters.

'Once inside, the nine of us were taken to a brick building, where we were told to strip, then ordered into a room in which there were a number of shower points along the walls. The welcome showers were turned on for far too short a time, but sufficiently long for us to clean ourselves with the aid of the soap provided by the Red Cross. After drying ourselves we dressed, unfortunately having to don again our dirty clothing. Then we were escorted to another room, where our heads were shorn, almost to baldness. We were, by now, so tired, hungry and thirsty that we could not have cared less. Finally, carrying our precious soap, razor, mug and spoon, we were escorted, none too gently, to our living accommodation. This consisted of a large wooden hut, about 80ft long by 30ft wide; into this space were packed almost two hundred bodies, all airmen. Our new home was numbered 57. Most of the available space was taken up by double rows of bunks, about 6ft long and 2ft wide, in three tiers, so that a floor area of 72 sq ft could accommodate 18 bunks. Narrow gangways between the double rows provided access. Straw palliasses adorned the bunks, and that was all. Apparently, our captors considered that their "guests" would not need luxuries like blankets, as sufficient body heat would be generated to keep them all warm. The remaining floor area, about 10ft wide and running the length of the hut, was adorned by a few trestle tables and wooden benches, enough to seat perhaps forty. Simple arithmetic showed that when the inmates were confined to the hut, only one in five could sit at the tables, while the remainder had to lie on their bunks. Sitting on the bunk was almost impossible, except for a dwarf or a contortionist, as the headroom was very limited. There was nothing else in this palatial apartment; no chairs, no lockers. Indeed, the latter were hardly necessary, as no one had possessions, apart from a small Red Cross cardboard box each. There was a tortoise stove near the end of the building, but as there was hardly ever any fuel available, it was almost superfluous! Beyond this a doorway, with no door, led to a narrow-tiled area, along the walls of which were rows of metal troughs with taps at either end, providing running water for ablutions, drinking and the washing of small items of clothing; needless to say, the water was cold: only sissies would need hot water! There were also four elementary urinals. Into this, then, our new abode, stepped the nine of us.

'All this lack of luxury was not apparent at first, for we were greeted warmly and each given the inevitable cup of acorn coffee and a slice of stale black rye bread. We did not realise at the time what a sacrifice this was, for the daily issue to each PoW at the camp was an eighth of a loaf per day, while a ration of nearly 4 ounces of margarine was issued weekly. It would have been difficult to weigh and distribute a daily ration! The coffee was certainly not plentiful. A bowl of watery soup formed much of the rest of the daily allowance. A few ounces of potatoes, fish paste, vegetables (mostly dried), millet or barley and about an ounce of cheese, our "entitlements" for the week, were issued to the cook-house, which was staffed by PoWs, and incorporated into the sparse diet. An infrequent allocation of meat was welcome, even though it was not prime beef or pork. In fact, it was probably horse or dog. Inmates tried to forget that cartloads of dead dogs were delivered to the camp each week. Fruit was never available. The occasional arrival and issue of Red Cross parcels, however, did alleviate hunger and saved many from near starvation. Unfortunately, the receipt of such luxuries was far from regular, and one issue a month was the most that could be hoped for. We new arrivals had yet to experience the longing for the arrival of the next delivery and the excitement of the receipt of the food the parcels contained.

'Jock, Steve and I were allocated three of the few vacant bunks, on which we flopped down and slept and slept. When we awoke, the first to greet us was Ivan, a navigator from our own squadron, whose aircraft had failed to return from an operation in October. Ivan had been the only survivor. News was exchanged and the three of us learned more about the camp [Stamalager 4B Mühlberg, a small German town located at the River Elbe approximately 80km north-west of Dresden. One of the largest German PoW camps that existed here between 1939–1945, in total approximately 300,000 prisoners from over forty nations passed through. More than 3,000 mostly Soviet PoWs died there]. Apparently, it had been built as a transit camp only, but no one ever seemed to be transferred to a more permanent one. As a transit camp it was not inspected by Red Cross representatives, so the rules of the Geneva Convention could be conveniently "bent". There were five compounds: one for RAF personnel, one for British Army prisoners from the North African campaign, transported via Italy; one for other western Europeans; one for

Russians; and one for Polish Jews. It was rumoured that many of the latter had been gassed or executed and that over three thousand of them were buried beneath the soil of one of the compounds. It was said that a total of about twenty thousand prisoners were held in the five compounds. The Russians' and Jews' compounds were inaccessible from the others, but inmates of the other three were able to communicate during daylight hours on the occasions they were allowed to leave their huts. The area within the confines of the main fence was surrounded on all sides by a low wire, beyond which one would pass only at the risk of instant lead poisoning from the machine guns of the guards situated in sentry boxes perched high over the outer fences at intervals of about 40 yards. These twin outer fences consisted of intertwining rolls of barbed wire, to a height of about 10ft. It was evident that our captors didn't want their guests to leave!

'The RAF compound contained eight huts, all of the same size and each accommodating nearly two hundred airmen, ranging in rank from sergeant to warrant officer. Many of these airmen wore wooden clogs, issued to replace their old-type flying boots that had been lost in the clouds. The compound itself was a rectangular enclosure about half the size of a football pitch. The inmates were generally permitted to leave their huts during daylight hours and take exercise by walking around the perimeter, and to make use of one of the four communal lavatories in each compound, sited close by the fence. These were hardly the epitome of luxury, containing two facing rows of ten wooden seats, with the necessary apertures. Almost needless to say, the sanitation was elementary; the results of users' labours, so to speak, dropped directly into a long trench below. The trenches were emptied regularly, via openings in the exterior walls, by a group of Russian prisoners, escorted by guards, and then removed from the camp by cart. Fortunately, the lack of food ensured that a visit to one of these edifices was necessary only infrequently; once or twice a week was usually sufficient, unless the intake of food well past its "best by" date prompted urgent visits. However unsavoury it may seem, this description of the facility is necessary, as it was to become a focus of attention later.

'Life in the camp became a boring routine. During inclement weather and in the evenings, there was absolutely nothing to do, except wait and long for the daily issue of stale black bread and vegetable soup, brought to the entrance of the huts for the inmates to distribute. As bunks occupied most of the available space, a system was evolved to ensure that all had the occasional opportunity to sit on a bench. Fortunately for those who remained reasonably alert and optimistic, there were some who stayed on their bunks all day and every day, except to collect their rations. On the increasingly rare occasions that Red Cross parcels arrived, even these depressed airmen shared in the excitement. The parcels, containing such luxuries as tinned meat, usually "Spam", dried milk (labelled "Klim"), condensed milk, tinned jam, tea and biscuits, were distributed and gloated over; the contents were examined and re-examined and decisions made as to what to eat first. Often three or four particular friends would share parcels, so that an opened tin of meat lasted the group two or three days. Although it was a great temptation to eat all of a parcel's contents in a few days, most airmen made them last at least a week. Some empty tins became drinking mugs, while others were carefully and laboriously fashioned into plates. Nothing was wasted. On one occasion a Red Cross issue contained packs of cards and books, enough for four packs and six books for each hut in the RAF compound. Those occupants of Hut 57 who were fortunate enough to be able to read at least one of the books enjoyed the temporary escapism, while bridge players made good use of the cards during most waking hours. I played a lot of bridge and read *Alice in Wonderland*!

'The other great excitement was the arrival of mail from home, which was collected by the senior officer in each hut. Jock, Steve and I had to wait almost three months for our first letters. Only then did we learn that our parents had been informed of our safety at the beginning of January, nearly two months after we were reported missing. We realised how traumatic the wait must have been for our parents, wives and fiancées, and felt very sorry for the families of the rest of the crew who had not survived. As the letters were censored, the news received was confined to family matters, but the receipt of the letter mattered more than the content. Writing letters to our nearest and dearest was more of a problem. Usually a postcard was issued, irregularly, but not more than once a month. With pencils provided by courtesy of the Red Cross, we prisoners wrote our messages on the postcards. We could not describe the conditions in which we lived: not only would the German censor obliterate any such references, but also, we felt there was no point in burdening those at home with further concerns as to our welfare. Therefore, most cards, and the occasional letter-sheet, contained cheerful comments, without actually saying or implying that our treatment was of a satisfactory standard. One particular incident did give us the opportunity to assure loved ones that all was well. One of the inmates, a Belgian who had joined the RAF, had been a hypnotist in civilian life. One evening he consented to give a performance, which was truly amazing. Subjects leaned over to impossible angles, sat without chairs and became inebriated on water. Letters home were then able to include, without actually lying, the comment that "We thoroughly enjoyed a concert". No doubt some recipients thought the prisoners were having a comfortable time, and had no wish to escape. They could not – and should not – know of our deprived conditions or that escape was constantly in the thoughts of most of the incarcerated airmen, second only to the need for food!

'Christmas 1943 came and went. It was a non-event in terms of any kind of celebration, other than the event itself. Extra food and drink were conspicuous by their absence, although our thoughts naturally turned even more to home. Shortly after this Ivan received his first letter from his parents, mentioning that Alan, his twin brother, had recovered from the necessary twenty-five visits to the lavatory. Although the German censors must have been puzzled, the comment was not obliterated. As Alan was also a navigator on another Lancaster squadron in Lincolnshire, Ivan concluded that he had returned successfully from that number of operations over Germany, with five more to do before a welcome and deserved respite. However, Ivan was not thrilled with the news that his twin had almost completed his tour, for only on the previous evening he had made a point of coming to me to voice his concern. He said that he knew without doubt that Alan had, just at that very moment, been killed!

'I did my best to reassure him, but to no avail. Ivan knew, and that was that. Astonishingly, Ivan was right: later he learned that Alan had indeed lost his life, on his thirtieth and last operation, on the very evening that Ivan had had the premonition, or perhaps telepathic message. I had heard, or read, somewhere that identical twins usually shared experiences, even when apart. This occurrence was surely proof that such telepathy existed. I was saddened by the news. I had completed most of my training with the twins, from Initial Training right through to our postings to squadrons some 18 months later. It was only at that stage that authority had decreed that the twins must serve on different squadrons. It was probably a wise decision. Neither twin had made any comment to me, but I could speculate as to their feelings had they been on the same squadron and one had stayed at base when the other was flying on ops. It must have been traumatic for their parents, too, having both their sons in Bomber Command. They were two fine young men, full of fun. During our stay at Scarborough, they had shared the same girlfriend for two weeks. Alan would go out with her one evening, report to his brother where they had been, and then Ivan would take his place on another evening. The aim of this exercise was, of course, to attempt to fool the young lady for as long as possible. They managed two dates each before they were dismissed with dishonour! Almost inevitably they were nicknamed Castor and Pollux (the heavenly twin stars).

'The lavatories in the compound were close to the inner fence and the contents were emptied regularly by Russian prisoners who scraped the effluence through apertures along the outside of the buildings. Moreover, the guards never bothered to enter those palatial premises or to check comings and goings. These facts prompted considerable thought. Given the necessary tools and ignoring the unpleasant surroundings, a tunnel could be dug from beneath one of the lavatory seats, under the fences to the field beyond. It had to be assumed that the field would contain growing crops by mid-summer and that these would be tall enough to hide escaping prisoners from the traversing searchlights after the barbed wire fences had been negotiated.

'Although in our particular camp there were no means of providing false documents or civilian clothes, the optimists among us were convinced that once out, other difficulties could be resolved. Plans were made. The occupants of the hut would need to be told and involved. Every airman would be asked to contribute bed-boards to help prop up the sides and roof of the tunnel. The bed-boards were about 2ft long and 4 inches in width, so about 500 would be required for a tunnel up to 60ft long. The soil was soft, particularly at the beginning of the tunnel, so there was no great need for digging tools any more sophisticated than empty tins from Red Cross parcels. Dispersal of soil presented no insuperable problem; it could be dumped in the other apertures or "filtered" through trouser legs on to the compound.

'Sergeant "Jock" Mason, the flight engineer on my crew when we were shot down, and I were involved from the planning stage, as were ten or a dozen others. Who else should be included? If possible, it would be wise to confine the knowledge to those who had to know; the more people that knew of the proposal, the greater the chance of a leak. As it was, there was no way of telling whether an infiltrator had been planted in order to learn of such plans.

Prospective escapers could make their way, individually, to the building in the evening, before nightfall. After all the others had left, they would have ample time to negotiate the tunnel, break through the soil above and begin their journey to freedom before their disappearance was discovered. Once out of the camp, they would travel in pairs, but it was left to each pair to decide on their preferred route.

'Jock and I agreed we would travel north-west along the east bank of the Elbe, and attempt to reach Lübeck on the north coast. We had no maps, but estimated the distance to be some 200 miles. At least following the Elbe would ensure we were going in the right direction. I remembered from my Mercator charts that Dessau and Magdeburg were on the proposed route, with Berlin to the east. There should be few other large centres of population. Perhaps we would be able to board a boat travelling to Sweden? The Lübeck–Sweden escape route had been one of those suggested by the intelligence officer in lectures on escape procedures back at base. A major problem was the lack of any disguise, but we could do nothing about that at this stage. Stealing clothes was a possibility, while purloined bicycles could provide transport.

'However, there were still difficulties to be overcome before the break-out. We would need to ensure that the chosen lavatory seat was not used during the excavation. We would have to contrive a means of keeping our clothes reasonably clean to avoid suspicion both while the tunnel was being dug and for the period after the escape. We could dig in the nude, but how would we clean ourselves afterwards? The issue of seat use was soon resolved: the chosen latrine block was the nearest to the fence and we were confident we could contrive a method to prevent people using the chosen seat, whether or not they were aware of the digging going on below. The last seat in the line would simply be "damaged" in such a way as to persuade men to avoid sitting on it. No one would wish to risk splinters in the rear! The problem of clothing for the digging was difficult, but eventually a possible solution was found, albeit a risky one. At least two pairs of overalls would be required, one for the digger at the tunnel face and one for the person transporting the soil back to the beginning of the tunnel. With only two airmen working in the tunnel at any one time, the operation would take a long, long time – but time we had in abundance.

'It so happened that wireless operator Jim Hobbs, one of the instigators, was quite fluent in the German language, having spent several holidays in the Black Forest area before the war. Jim had discovered that one of the guards, who had been wounded on the Eastern front, lived in that district and he had cultivated his acquaintance, with the obvious ulterior motive of bribery. The occasional gifts from home of cigarettes, using the Red Cross facilities, were used for this purpose, as they were greatly prized by the captors, some of whom were not averse to exchange when it involved little risk. In contrast to the coarse half-filled, noxious weeds they smoked, even in 1944, British cigarettes were indeed nectar. It was decided that Jim would attempt to procure the overalls from this source, pointing out to the not over-intelligent guard that they were required for use in cleaning the floor of the hut with the two brooms provided for that purpose. After all, the airmen's uniforms were all we had and they were scruffy and dirty enough already. Once obtained, the overalls could be smuggled to and from the latrine block under our uniforms. Jim would begin negotiations when the opportunity presented itself, so that the overalls would be accepted as commonplace. Most potential difficulties now appeared to have been overcome, although there were many minor points still to be considered. These could be left to a later date, however, when the participants had been chosen and all the details finalised. It was decided that the digging would commence in May 1944, when there would be longer hours of daylight.

'During the early spring months plans for the proposed tunnel were complete. After much deliberation it was decided that twenty should be the maximum number to make the initial attempt. If all went well, others could follow, until the absences were discovered. The plotters and diggers would go first. Occupants of the hut who wished to be involved drew lots for the remaining initial places. Jim had negotiated for and procured not two but three sets of overalls from the guard. The overalls and brooms were on constant display; the hut had never before had such clean floors. The vital bed-boards had been promised readily, in spite of the fact that the bunks would be even more uncomfortable without them. The lavatory seat had been deeply scored and inspections showed that it was no longer in use.

'The Russian detail had evidently not noticed or didn't care that they had nothing to extract from under the last aperture in the line. Work on the tunnel began in early May, and a routine was soon established. The first two diggers of the day would saunter to the latrine, with overalls under their uniforms and empty cans in their pockets. Another airman would follow, to act as look-out. After about an hour the first workers would be relieved by two more would-be escapees, who would change into the overalls while the two finishing their shift changed back into uniform, taking with them in their tucked-in trouser legs the soil they had excavated, to be shaken out in the compound. The look-outs were also changed frequently. The last pair to dig before the evening confinement took back the overalls. Transporting the bed-boards to the scene of operations was left until twilight, so that stiff-legged prisoners would not be so readily spotted by guards in the towers or patrolling the compound.

'The first few days of digging were extremely unpleasant, as the first foot or so of soil removed was liberally mixed with excreta. However, it had to be done. The work was shared and the going was fairly easy. The diggers soon became accustomed to the use of the tin cans as tools and quickly evolved an efficient system. The "topsoil" was scattered beneath the other lavatory seats, until the hole became deep enough and wide enough to insert bed-boards vertically to support the shaft. Then the construction of the horizontal tunnel began, sloping downwards slightly for the first few yards, until it was estimated to be about 4 ft below the surface of the compound, leading towards the fences. After each few feet of construction vertical bed-boards were inserted, with a horizontal board pushed, banged and persuaded into place above each pair. Mistakes were made and minor collapses occurred, but novice diggers gradually became more proficient as we progressed, slowly but surely, towards our objective. Slowly was the operative word, as the method of execution, the need for secrecy and the tools available were not conducive to speed and efficiency. No doubt one man with a modern machine and an efficient support system could have constructed a much safer and neater tunnel in a few hours. Our masterpiece, it was estimated, would take weeks, if not months, at the initial rate of about 2 ft a day, on those days when it was safe to work. As the tunnel became longer, the excavation, transportation and removal of soil would take more time. Still, we had nothing else of importance to do; although the conditions were claustrophobic, the tunnel diggers did have the satisfaction of knowing they were "digging for victory", so to speak.

'Those who have never had occasion to dig an elementary tunnel, 2 ft wide and 2 ft high, with nothing more sophisticated than tin cans, wriggling forwards and backwards in a claustrophobic space, in a fetid atmosphere, cannot possibly understand what the experience is like. Those few of us who have had occasion to do so were probably slightly mad! Of the twenty original volunteers, some withdrew, either from illness or claustrophobia, to be replaced by others. The work continued, albeit slowly.

'By the middle of May it was estimated that a total length of about 50ft would be sufficient to ensure that the exit would clear the barbed wire fencing and take us safely into the field beyond, but only just. The crop growing in that field was watched anxiously and soon identified as wheat. By mid-June it would be tall enough to hide crawling bodies. Searchlights constantly swept along the outer fences after twilight, so it would be a tricky operation for the escapees to run, one by one, across the frequently lit area, before reaching the haven of darkness. Each such dash would need to be timed to coincide with the brief dark intervals between the sweeping beams.

'One reason why we felt it necessary to shorten the tunnel was one that had not been thought of! After only a few days of excavation, the interior of the tunnel began to darken, so that the job in hand became more and more difficult. Some form of lighting was necessary if the diggers were to see what they were doing, and indeed to maintain a straight line. One wag suggested we should beg, borrow or steal a searchlight, but this was ill received, while a shortage of glow-worms precluded that form of illumination. It was soon decided that Jim Hobbs's bribable guard should be approached with a view to obtaining a few candles and a box or two of matches. The need could be explained easily. The lights in the huts were turned off after dark and it was sometimes necessary for an inmate to visit the urinals during the night. How much more considerate to others it would be to do so without making a noise in stumbling towards the objective. So, in exchange for a packet of cigarettes, candles and matches were obtained.

'Progress continued, but even more slowly as the tunnel lengthened. Fortunately for the purpose in hand, we diggers were all very slim, even skinny, because of the meagre diet, but even so the laboured crawling to the work-face, empty tin in hand, and the even more laboured crawling backwards on knees and elbows, with a full tin in each hand, was a time- consuming procedure. Our target was to clear 2 ft per day. That does not sound very much, nor is it, until you realise that the soil dug out and transported amounts to 8 cubic ft. A medium-sized can holds about 45 cubic inches, so it was necessary to dig out and transport about 300 cans-full to reach that daily target. It was also necessary to dispose of the soil. This then, was a further reason to shorten the tunnel, as the labourers became even wearier and output decreased. Another fact that had not been considered was the shortage of fresh air as the tunnel became longer. In spite of the increasing difficulty, the tunnel lengthened by about a foot per day and spirits became higher. Optimists estimated that an upward shaft could be excavated by mid-June, while the more cautious reckoned that the end of June was a more realistic target.

'During the first week of June, when it was calculated that the tunnel had reached a point somewhere below the first rolls of the outer barbed wire, the Germans demonstrated their childish sense of humour and their capacity for deceit. One fine morning, when the first shift had begun their labours, the look-out was surprised by the rapid arrival of an armoured truck, from which descended, equally rapidly, several guards armed with rifles, bayonets fixed. Four invaded the privacy of the privy, while two remained on guard outside. The two labourers in the tunnel were invited to come out, somewhat impolitely, prodded to the waiting vehicle, and taken away. Other prisoners did not see them again, but it was hoped they had been transferred to another camp no worse than this one. It was known, although no one seemed to know how it was known, that a camp only a few miles north was a concentration camp, mainly for Jews. Surely the two would not have been transferred to that place?

'The occupants of Hut 57 were then paraded and informed, rather smugly, that the Commandant and his officers had known of the existence of the tunnel since the first soil had been removed, but as he had no wish to spoil the prisoners' enjoyment, they had been allowed to continue. Now he intended to give them the pleasure of filling in the tunnel again, using the available contents below the seats of the remaining lavatories. Of course, they could decline – but if they did so it was regrettable that no food would be made available until they agreed to his suggestion. The inmates of the hut, who nevertheless decided that a short period of unpleasantness was vastly preferable to further deprivation, did not appreciate this infantile sense of humour. Thus, the tunnel was filled in, very sportingly, by several airmen who had not been involved in the excavation, but who took the view that enough was enough for those who had participated. Surprisingly neither the commandant nor his officers took any further disciplinary action against the occupants of Hut 57. There was little point in speculating how it had all gone wrong. Had the guard reported the bribery in obtaining overalls and candles? Had the comings and goings from the latrines had been noted? Had a German in RAF uniform been planted in our hut? Those seemed to be the main possibilities. It had to be admitted that the captors had at least ensured that several of their troublesome charges had been kept out of further mischief for a while. Our disappointment was great, to say the least. All that work – and hope – for nothing. However, we realised that we must not allow ourselves to become too despondent; despondency could lead to despair, and that must be avoided at all costs. After all, we had caused considerable trouble to our captors. We also reflected that a successful escape from the confines of the camp would have been only the first of three difficult stages; the long journey through Germany would have been extremely hazardous, as would egress through any of the closely guarded borders.

'Other attempts to escape were made by those in other huts. One hopeful warrant officer concealed himself in the refuse being taken from the confines of the camp by escorted Russians, perhaps inspired by the efforts of Hut 57. Although he did manage to escape from the confines of the camp and then from the cart, he was soon recaptured, possibly because of the less than delicate perfume he emitted. His courage in taking this extreme method was much admired, although close proximity to his person was avoided until he had washed his clothes and himself in the cold-water troughs provided in the hut. Two other airmen exchanged clothes and sleeping quarters with privates from an Army hut. These privates were occasionally sent out of the camp on escorted working parties, labouring on the adjoining fields, so there was always the possibility that an escape could be effected. Alas, no opportunity arose, and after a week or so the pair returned to their original hut and their friends. They consoled themselves with the memories of fresh air, fresh surroundings and some food purloined from the crops in the fields in which they had worked.

'It was around this time that the Camp Commandant informed us, via the senior British officer, that the German High Command had issued orders to the effect that future escapees, from any camp, would be shot when captured. This was the reaction to a recent mass escape from Stalag Luft III, about which we had heard from new arrivals. This edict was rather discouraging, but we rejoiced at this sign of panic among our hosts; escapes and attempted escapes were evidently causing them much trouble.

'Life at the camp continued its boring routine. Inmates had to will themselves to walk round the compound as the shortage of food made them weaker, knowing that some exercise was vital in order to remain reasonably fit. Two circuits were usually enough for most. Part of the routine was a daily parade of bodies, usually around breakfast time. (Breakfast time it may have been, but there was certainly no breakfast at that time. The first and only meal would not be available until midday.) At this daily assembly the occupants of each hut were required to line up in five rows in the compound, prodded by dangerous-looking bayonets, in order to be counted. It was surprising how a group of well-drilled servicemen could be so awkward in such a simple exercise! It was also surprising how difficult it was for the German unteroffiziers (non-commissioned officers) to count up to two hundred! Any slight disturbance in the ranks or another distraction would result in a recount. Unfortunately, the "goons" possessed no sense of humour, at least not one comparable to ours, so they often gained their revenge. Thus, on particularly cold and frosty mornings the inmates of a specific hut would be kept standing for hours, while two or three German soldiers searched their hut for anything that ought not to have been there. Nothing was found, as there was nothing to find, but some of the captors did have the annoying habit of scattering the airmen's few possessions – mugs, tin plates and carefully preserved contents of parcels – causing much annoyance and re-sorting after the interminable parade. Strangely enough, the soldiers did not attempt to steal the contents of the parcels. It became a point of honour not to collapse from cold or hunger during such occasions, and surprisingly few did. Apparently the unteroffiziers did not like their smart uniforms to get excessively wet, so, happily for the airmen, such lengthy parades were confined to dry weather. Even then the "goon-baiting" continued; the prisoners would not allow their captors to relax.

'Another relief from routine was provided by occasional visits to the showers. These excursions were most welcome, for after about a month the odour of almost two hundred young men in a confined space did become rather offensive, although, given time, one can get used to anything. On these infrequent occasions the occupants of each hut were escorted from the compound to the brick buildings that contained the showers (the same buildings that the nine of us had been taken to back in November). Unfortunately, the prospect of the cleansing process was somewhat spoiled by a rumour that the brick building also contained the gas chamber used for the Jews reputed to be buried at the camp. However, we were reassured by the knowledge that, so far at least, all RAF personnel had returned safely to their huts after showering! New occupants of the huts soon learned the routine: as the showers were blissfully warm, it was the practice to undress and drop one's clothing at one's feet, to be washed also.

'Then, when the typically efficient warm air was produced to dry the bodies, the clothing was also dried, albeit only partially. Our captors did have the decency to leave both the showers and the hot air running for some time. In retrospect, the infrequency of the showers was understandable. Even if the facility were extended only to those who were neither Russians nor Jews, there were still 10,000 or 12,000 people using the showers. Presumably there was some sort of roster.

'Inevitably, in a camp of that size, there were illnesses and deaths. Only the less serious cases could be dealt with in the small basic hospital, which was mainly staffed by British and other European prisoners who had had medical experience during or before the war. Of course, nothing could be done for those suffering from malnutrition; a problem that affected all the inmates of the camp, but minor operations could be performed. A captured British medical officer was available for dental work, but unfortunately for the patients any urgent initial treatment was a painful experience, as no anaesthetics were available. Needless to say, only those in constant pain asked to be escorted to the dental surgeon to have a tooth extracted; there were no facilities for fillings. No medical facilities at all existed for the Russians and Jews: if they were ill, they were ill, and if they died, they died. Cartloads of deceased and naked prisoners were often seen leaving the camp, piled one on top of another.

'News of the progress of the war filtered through as new prisoners were brought to the camp. These irregular arrivals were our only source of any information, as of course there were no radios or newspapers. In the middle of June, a fresh batch of captured Allied airmen brought the glad tidings of the successful landings in France after the D-Day operations. Spirits soared and "goon-baiting" intensified. Although no one was optimistic enough to think that the war would be over in a few weeks, at least the end seemed to be in sight. Then, gradually, more and more American Flying Fortresses were seen in the skies during the day. On one occasion Allied fighters strafed the camp; the toilets at the end of Hut 57 were hit, but fortunately no one was hurt. Evidently the camp was mistaken for an army barracks.

'Now, at least, there was something to talk about. When a group of young men are confined to a small space for months and months, with no news of the outside world, no experiences of any kind to relate, no line-shooting to do, and no conquests to describe, stimulating conversation does become difficult, if not impossible.

'One fine morning the first few to leave the hut for their daily exercise walking around the compound came dashing back quickly, exhorting all to come and look outside. Soon most of the occupants of Hut 57 and other huts too were lined up along the inner boundary wire, gazing longingly across the adjoining field. It was truly a sight for sore eyes. A solitary German woman, young and buxom, was hoeing 200 yards away. Perhaps such intense interest was understandable, as many of the inmates of the camp had not seen a woman for two or three years! Some of the airmen stayed a long time, just looking, until the young woman was approached by a man, probably the farmer, and led away from the ogling stares. One effect of the advance of the Allies across France was the increasing rarity of Red Cross parcels to augment the diet of bread, soup and acorn coffee. Even the issue of bread was reduced to one loaf for ten inmates. Those who shared each loaf would gather round the day's sharer, who would divide the bread into ten portions, as equally as possible. A roster ensured that turns to choose were in strict rotation, the sharer taking the last piece. He then had the privilege of first choice the following day. It was sad, even demeaning, that such measures had to be taken, but every crumb was important to hungry young men. Hunger became an obsession, so that we thought of little else, yet our sense of comradeship was so deep-seated and highly valued that there were few quarrels over the division of rations, or indeed about anything else.

'During the summer months of 1944 the attitude of the German officers and guards had remained arrogant, but gradually we noticed a change. Fewer rifle butts were viciously used by the younger guards who had previously been only too willing to vent their spite on those who had dared to oppose their idol and leader, Herr Hitler. The more mature guards had always been more amenable, and they became even more so as they realised that eventual defeat was much more than a remote possibility.

'One day in early autumn I received, through Red Cross channels, a present from Olive, my girlfriend back home. I had had cigarettes, also through the Red Cross, from her before, as well as from parents, other relatives and friends; while they had been much appreciated, this present, a blanket, was prized indeed. I could now take off my uniform blouse and trousers at night, and keep reasonably warm. Wearing the same uniform day after day, night after night, for almost a year was not only uncomfortable but extremely unhygienic. Rolled in my new blanket, even the straw mattress was more comfortable. I was the envy of many!

'By this time most inmates had become inured to the discomfort and the lack of belongings. Those who have never gone without the basic requirements do not and cannot imagine life without them. Taken for granted are such needs as a change of underwear and socks, a spare handkerchief, comb, toothbrush, soap, flannel, razor, scissors (for nails and haircuts), towel, toilet rolls, sleeping apparel, sheets, a bed, a chair, hot water, cutlery, newspapers, books, radio, and of course a cup of tea with milk and sugar. The prisoners could not, however, become used to hunger. As hunger increased, so energy decreased. A plain white slice of bread, preferably with butter and cheese to accompany it, became a daydream to savour; luxuries such as meat, fish, fruit and vegetables were not nearly so important as that plain white slice of bread!

'As energy decreased, health deteriorated. Many confined themselves to their bunks for most of the day as well as during the night. Fewer and fewer took any exercise. Some died and were taken out of the camp for burial. New arrivals brought further news of the Allied advances on all fronts. Even these glad tidings failed to inspire many for whom food, food, food, was the only concern.

'Christmas 1944 was just another date in the calendar. Although no calendars were available to the prisoners, the days were counted so that the date was always known. Early 1945 was extremely cold. The meagre ration of fuel for the tortoise stove in each hut was completely discontinued; our one consolation was that the Germans were also suffering the same shortages as their resources became more and more depleted.

'Soon the first American airmen arrived at the camp, and they were in a sorry state. Many had dysentery, which spread among the existing inmates. More prisoners died and their bodies were taken away. It was better not to think of the poor Russians and Jews, who were even less well treated. It was reported that an Alsatian dog had been put into one of the Russian huts to quieten the noisy inmates; the next morning its skin and bones had been found outside. It was also reported that retribution was swift and severe. There was no way of telling whether the story was true or invented.

STORIES FROM THE STALAGS

'The coldness intensified, as did hunger; the days seemed interminable. However, the now rapid advances of troops from the west and now from the east did begin to cheer us, and we began to be more optimistic that release from our tribulations was imminent. Then, one day in mid-April, as the weather improved, all British and American prisoners, some 5,000 or 6,000 in total, were paraded in a single compound. The Commandant, who spoke English, addressed us through a loudspeaker. He announced that he had received instructions from the German High Command that all prisoners of war were to be executed. This was very distressing news to the assembled airmen and soldiers, but before we had time to realise that such an announcement was quite unnecessary, as a mass execution could be carried out without any such warning, he paused, then went on to declare that he had no intention of obeying this order. He trusted that his clemency and humanity would be remembered, if and when the American or British troops liberated the camp. Those gathered there that day cheered, not because the Commandant had been so lenient, but because liberation must now be close and the war in Europe almost over. For the next week or so the guards continued to guard and the searchlights to search, but it became obvious that almost all the German captors were now completely demoralised. In most, arrogance was replaced by attempts at comradeship, which we rejected of course. A few still refused to believe defeat was near.'

A crowd was there when he stopped his crate.
'Where am I?' he asked, 'It sure looks great.'
'Why where,' they asked, 'Were you heading for?
'This my boy is Stalag Luft IV.'

*****Willie Green's Flying Machine*****

'St George's Day, 23 April 1945, was a date to be remembered for the rest of our lives,' wrote Harry Church in Stalag Luft IV. 'In the very early morning the sound of exploding shells and machine-gun fire was heard throughout the camp. Prisoners awoke and warily opened hut doors. No guards, no accompanying dogs, were to be seen. The whole camp appeared to be deserted; there were no searchlights operating and the sentry boxes were unoccupied. Still, we wondered what could have happened. Then the outer gates were flung open and a troop of Cossacks rode through, armed to the teeth with revolvers, rifles and swords festooned around them and with hand grenades on their belts. Among them were a few young but tough-looking young women! They were singing loudly to the recognisable tune "Song of the Plains". The locked gates to the Russian compound were contemptuously broken and those imprisoned therein flooded out in greeting. In spite of their dreadful physical condition, they were herded out, presumably to join the advancing Russian army, of which the Cossacks were in the vanguard. The gates to the Jewish compound were also broken. Nothing was said to the remaining prisoners and we were left to our own devices, while the mounted troops departed.'

Chapter 4

Lamsdorf and Beyond

After the disastrous raid on Nürnburg on 30–31 March 1944 the German night-fighters were largely given a three-week respite before the next big raid, though Aachen was bombed on 11–12 April by 341 Lancasters and eleven Mosquitos of 1, 3, 5 and 8 Groups. The raid was accurate and caused widespread damage in the centre of Aachen and in the southern part of the town. Nine Lancasters FTR (Failed to Return) – one being Lancaster II LL639/R on 514 Squadron at Waterbeach, which was shot down, probably at 2315 hours 10km West of Roermond, by a Bf 110 flown by Unteroffizier Hans Fischer of 12/NJG1. Twenty-seven-year-old Pilot Officer Noel William Faulkner Thackray RAAF and Flight Sergeants John Russell Moulsdale RAAF, the 32-year-old air bomber, and Reginald Ernest Bromley RAAF, the 28-year-old rear gunner; Sergeants' Patrick 'Jock' Hughes, WOp, and Clive Walter Banfield, flight engineer; and Flight Sergeant Clement Herbert Henn RAAF, the 22-year-old mid-upper gunner, were all killed. Sergeant Edward Humes, navigator, was the only survivor. 'Thack' Thackray left a widow, Phyllis Mary of Surrey Hills, Victoria, Australia, as did John Moulsdale, whose wife Ethel Jean lived in Collie, Western Australia. Reg Bromley's wife Joan Veronica Bromley lived in Punchbowl, NSW.

Sergeant Edward Leo Humes

'On 11 April 1944 our target was to be a fairly easy trip to Aachen, perhaps our shortest flight over Germany. The usual preparations were made and in the early evening we set course for the target hoping to return well before midnight. All went well and we dropped the bomb load over the city and set course for home.

LAMSDORF AND BEYOND

'Disaster struck! The port outer engine caught fire. It seemed that we had been hit by flak, as none of the air gunners had sighted enemy aircraft. Noel ordered us to prepare to abandon which meant that all secret equipment and navigational and wireless codes had to be destroyed. Gunners had to leave their turrets and all had to head for the escape hatches, except of course for "Thack". For a few moments we flew on. Clive was doing his utmost to extinguish the blaze and believed that we would be able to continue. The blazing engine fell away. The end was near, as the pilot could no longer keep control.

'Abandon aircraft!

'Jack answered at once. "Reg" reported that his turret would not operate. "Jock" said that he would try to help Reg and Clem responded that he too would move to help with the rear turret. Clive was not at all pleased that we were to abandon. As for myself, I headed for the front escape hatch passing both Clive and "Thack", who was still at the controls. As I reached the top of the steps, I was astounded to find the escape hatch open, but Jack's parachute pack was still in the container. There was no sign of him!

'I had no time for further thought, for at that moment the nose of the plane dropped and I found myself trapped by my legs. To this day I do not know what was preventing me from leaving the stricken aircraft. What was I to do? Without any further thought, I pulled the ripcord. I felt a sharp pain in my legs but to my great relief, my 'chute pulled me clear of the aircraft. I drifted towards the earth, but could see nothing nor could I hear a sound. I prayed to almighty God for his help and cried out for my mother. All this had happened in seconds.

'I assumed that I was drifting downwards but could not be sure where I was going to land. Crash! I had landed in undergrowth but where? I did not have the slightest idea. Minutes passed, I could feel that my uniform was in tatters and that I was bleeding profusely. Strangely I felt no pain. I heard movement and immediately began crying for help, but was warned to be quiet. Obviously, it was not German soldiers in the immediate vicinity. Helping hands picked me up and untied my Mae West; I had responded to training and had by instinct got rid of my parachute silk on hitting the ground. When I awoke, I was lying on something very soft, but could not see what it was. My right leg gave me a lot of pain and I ran my hands over it. It seemed to be a peculiar shape. Gradually my hearing improved and I could hear voices in what seemed to be prayer. As yet, I could not see where the sound was coming from, but realised that I was being addressed in English. A doctor had been called and he was advising me that there was nothing he could do to treat my wounds, but that he would make me comfortable until the Germans arrived. A couple of pieces of wood from the garden fence were used to make splints for the leg that had sustained a very bad fracture. My face and hands were washed clean of blood that had come from multiple scratches. After making me comfortable and allowing me to sleep for the remainder of the night the Germans were called. As soon as they arrived the atmosphere changed. What had been a quiet room now became a very noisy area indeed. I was to be taken away by them, but it appeared that the family would not permit the enemy to move me from the sofa on which I was resting. Finally, I was carried, still on the sofa, to the waiting lorry.

'Somewhere around teatime, my guards deposited me at a hospital staffed by German navy personnel. I was well scrubbed and put into a nice clean bed. A meal of black bread, cheese from a tube and the foulest-tasting coffee was given to me. All the time I was eating, sailors wandered by to take a look at the English captive.

'My next real visit was from a medical officer, who explained that there would be a need to operate on my leg in the next few hours. He was quite friendly and was in no way what I had expected. Maybe this was part of the softening-up process I had been warned to expect in those briefing sessions in training. Sometime later I was taken to the operating theatre and knew no more until I woke up in a private room with a large picture window on the left and a pair of doors to the right of my bed. There I lay, with my leg in traction but with no sign of a plaster cast. A large iron framework kept the sheets from weighing on my legs. Looking further to my right I saw a German sailor standing guard inside the doors and beyond him another sailor, both with fixed bayonets! I was told afterwards that these guards were there to keep Belgian people out, for there was no way I could possibly escape.

'What lay ahead of me? Meals were delivered on time and once I had become used to the black bread and acorn coffee, the rest of my diet was quite pleasant. Strangely enough, I felt very little pain and I was able to see quite well. After a few days my Rosary was returned to me and it transpired that one of my guards was a Catholic. Now we had a talking point, but he was not particularly interested in teaching me German, but wished to improve his English so that he would be able to converse with English citizens when

Germany defeated England! Sign language was used more often than words in the first instance, but we got along very well indeed.

'At first, time passed pretty quickly. When night fell, I would listen for the sound of allied aircraft passing overhead and try to work out where they might be going, by working out the time that elapsed between the inward and outward journey. Sometimes an airman would be brought in to occupy the second bed in the room and I would become updated with the progress of the war. Sadly, there was seldom a time when any of these new aircrew members stayed longer than one day. As the weather outside improved I began to yearn for a move to somewhere among English-speaking prisoners. I was aware that there were no prisoners from the allied forces in the hospital in which I was being treated.

'Early in June, fighter activity began to increase quite dramatically and the air raid sirens were often sounded. Each time this happened my guards disappeared and I soon found out that part of their duties was to man part of the air defences. I cannot remember the date, but one evening, I noticed that the night sky was rapidly illuminated with brightly coloured flares. This could only mean one thing – the area was to be the target for that night!

'I was right. Sirens wailed and anti-aircraft guns blasted away at the allied aircraft. Soon, bombs began to fall and I heard explosion after explosion. Surely, I was not going to be a victim of action by the RAF? Soon I had my answer for my bedroom shook and glass windows broke. The noise was horrendous and because of my situation, I could take no action whatever to hide away or to reach shelter. Just as I pulled the bed sheets over my head, I felt an almighty crash and wondered what the outcome of this was going to be. Gradually the noise subsided and soon I was able to risk turning down the sheets. The window and doorframes were lying across the cage that protected my legs and I saw searchlight beams and ack-ack bursts. The ceiling had collapsed! I was alive but terrified. What would happen to me now? One of my guards visited to check on my condition, but it was some hours before I was made aware of the extent of the damage caused by the raid. My room was reasonably sound when compared to the rest of the hospital.

'As the morning passed, I could hear the sound of rescue crews moving about the hospital grounds. Now and then, there would be an almighty crash as a building toppled. Fires burned brightly and soot fell, making my once white bed linen look very dirty indeed. I thought for a time about the times when I had been bombed back in England and how enemy fighters had attempted to destroy the barrage balloon sites on which I served, but I am afraid it gave me little comfort. There I had been among friends, but now I was among enemies. How would they react to the night's events? I was soon to find out.

'From the background of soot and smoke, there appeared the figure of one of the surgeons who had cared for me over the previous weeks. His apron was bloodstained and, in his hand, he held a scalpel, likewise covered in blood! What was he going to do to me? He soon put my mind at rest and after referring to the air raid being carried out by my friends, he told me that although I should be in traction for a further four weeks, there was nothing that could be done but to remove the pin and other items and transfer me as quickly as possible to another hospital.

'No sooner said than done! I just had to grit my teeth, hold tight and the job was done. A lorry was drawn up to the ruin and a stretcher was brought from somewhere and I was loaded aboard for my journey, no guards this time. Off we went, sometimes dodging the potholes, but more often than not there would be an almighty jolt as we hit what I presumed was a crater. Suddenly the stretcher left the floor of the vehicle and I was deposited on to the boards. I felt more pain than I had felt since leaving the aircraft, but try as I may, I could not get the attention of the driver. Another gritting of teeth until we reached our destination, which turned out to be a "Rest Home" for German officers.

'I got little sympathy and was informed that there was not the facility to deal with my new injury, which was a refractured femur; the fall had undone the work that had been done. Soon, I was on my way again to another hospital, somewhere in Brussels. I was hungry, dirty and in quite some pain, but at last I reached my new home. The hospital sister was not at all pleased at the state I was in. She was unaware of what I had been through and commented that surely no soldier would set out on a mission in the dirty state that I was in. "Stand up and follow me to the bathroom," she said. Only when I had convinced her that my leg was broken did she realise the predicament I was in. Immediately her attitude changed. She became an angel and remained so for the rest of my stay.

'Now spotlessly clean, I was placed in a bed in a barrack room along with twenty or so captured allied aircrew and learned that I was in an annexe to a German military hospital in the centre of Brussels. They were not too happy to hear that I had been captured several weeks earlier and thus could not give news of the allied advance through France. To be honest, I was pleased to know that our forces were on their way. My next information was that I would have twenty-four hours to talk about my predicament and then the subject would be taboo. My "Angel" returned to prepare me for an operation on my right femur.

'She explained the whole process and commented on how lucky I was going to be to have a leading surgeon carrying out a recent technique, to put my bone together again (I have since learned that the procedure was known as "The *Kuetschner* Nail Method"). Off we went to the theatre and the surgeon began his task. He was far from happy when I yelled with pain! I had felt his scalpel cut into my upper leg! Initially he did not believe me, but quickly realised that the spinal anaesthetic had not done its work. At once he took steps to remedy the matter and my next memory was that of waking up in bed, again in traction and being cared for by a young lady in white. Was I in heaven? No, I was back in the PoW ward.

'The following morning, the operating surgeon came to check on my well-being and to apologise for the slip up of the previous day. He told me that the operation had gone well and that I would be in traction for approximately twelve weeks. Where had I heard that before? Now I was able to learn about my fellow prisoners and to catch up on the progress of hostilities.

'My colleagues were from all parts of the Commonwealth, USA and France and there was even a prisoner with Russian nationality. Their injuries were of many kinds. Severe burns, broken limbs and some had limbs that had been amputated. I was only a small player.

'Many and varied were the tales my fellow patients had to tell. One especially, bears repeating. After the aircraft had been hit, the radio operator had moved to leave his position when the aircraft broke up and he was left hanging from a piece of wreckage, but he was still wearing his helmet with the intercom plug connected. His parachute opened and pulled him from the aircraft but not before he had removed the plug. Suddenly the headset gave way and the cord caught in the lines of the 'chute. He landed unable to move. He arrived at the hospital fully conscious and able to speak but it was quite a few weeks before he was able to use any of his limbs. Part of his recovery programme was to attempt using a concertina. The last time I saw him, he was still struggling.

'Each new arrival brought news of the progress of Allied forces; often their stories were very much different from the propaganda given out by the

German radio and the tales told by the staff of the hospital. The weeks passed quickly and as August approached, the sound of heavy gunfire increased. The news from Belgian workpeople was that the allies were now close to Brussels. Each day we waited for good news but it seemed to us that movement had come to a halt. Perhaps the forward push had ceased or the powers that be had decided to by-pass the capital. On the 6th September, we had a visit from the senior officer of the hospital staff. He was ready to leave us in the hospital if the senior British officer would sign a document stating that we had been treated well during our captivity. We were overjoyed and were 100% ready to agree! The day passed agonisingly slowly and the night was full of the noise of artillery fire. There was nowhere for us to find shelter so we hid our concern by singing the tunes of the time.

'As dawn broke, the sound of gunfire decreased and the sky was red with flame. Surely, we would be recaptured in an hour or two! The doors of the annexe burst open and a number of German troops appeared. To our horror they wore the uniform of the SS. Thoughts of being recaptured were dashed as the officer in command refused to accept the document signed the previous day. The walking wounded were ushered away and the bedridden lifted into wheelchairs. I was released from my traction, given a set of crutches and told to make my way to the bus, which was waiting. I soon had the knack of using crutches for the SS were in no mood to hang about. When it was clear that there were no other Allied prisoners left in the hospital, the bus moved off and we turned into the main square where we saw the Palais de Justice burning fiercely. There seemed to be thousands of troops moving about and heading out of the city. Slowly, yard-by-yard, we passed among the crowds and at last reached the road signposted "Venlo". We were on our way to Holland but much was to happen before we reached our goal.

'The roads were packed with retreating German troops and fleeing Belgian citizens. Every available type of transport was being used to leave the capital and there was barely enough space to pass that which had already broken down. Dead animals littered the roadside. Horses lay with their feet in the air, dead either from attack from the air or just sheer exhaustion. Broken down vehicles littered the highway, their owners frantically seeking alternative means of escape. This was organised retreat? Suddenly, above the din, we heard the sound of fighter aircraft and then recognised the planes as Typhoons, not only that but our Senior British Officer made us aware that they were from his own squadron!

'Within seconds the pilots began their attack on the fleeing troops and it was plain that we were not to be spared. The bus stopped, but our guards would not allow us to dismount and seek shelter. They were armed and we were not but the SBO took his life in his hands and hurled himself at the nearest guard who immediately dropped his rifle and, together with his colleague, left the vehicle. We helped one another off the bus and headed for farm buildings nearby. The pigs were hastily evicted and we took their places. The sty was strongly built and we felt a good deal safer. Three of the walking wounded decided that this was an ideal opportunity to attempt an escape.

'I know for certain that one, Sergeant W. Durland was successful, for his story was told in the records of 514 Squadron, which was my own squadron. I have not heard the outcome of the others who made the attempt. At last the aircraft broke off their attack and we were ordered to re-board the bus, which was undamaged, and we noticed that there was no Red Cross insignia, Squadron Leader Brannigan was not too sure that a red cross would have made very much difference to the attack, as the bus was slap in the centre of the fleeing convoy. Slowly we moved on again.

'The damage wreaked on the fleeing army was horrendous and one could only feel pity for the wounded and dying, as each person in the convoy seemed bent on one task – to reach shelter and perhaps safety. As the day drew to a close, we felt a little safer, for we were aware that fighter aircraft would not operate in the dark and bombers would be too expensive to use against targets such as a fleeing convoy.

'It was quite dark when we drew into the suburbs of Venlo, but we now came under attack from Dutch citizens who thought that we were German soldiers being carried away from the front line. Fortunately, no great damage was done and at last we were deposited at a convent near the centre of the town. Our first thought was: "When are we going to get something to eat?" and then we became puzzled as to why we had been taken to the very top floor of the Convent.

'The second question was answered by the Mother Superior, who informed us that the senior German officer in the town did not want the responsibility of looking after us; perhaps if we remained hidden on the top floor advancing German troops would pass us by. You will remember we had heard a similar tale before.

'For four days we remained hidden. We had reasonable food and excellent facilities. Perhaps this time we would be recaptured. It was not to be. On the morning of the fifth day one of our number decided to investigate the troop noises in the street below. Sadly, his appearance on the balcony was noticed by the civilian population below. They waved and he acknowledged their greeting, but was spotted by a soldier who was passing by. It had to be a member of the SS! Within minutes, we were taken into the grounds of the convent and I believe that the others felt as I did, we were going to be executed! To our great relief, this did not happen. A few hours later we were put aboard railway wagons to be transported into Germany.

'At the railway station, we were kept strictly apart from the civilian travellers who were boarding trains for various parts of Germany and we were ushered towards a row of cattle trucks standing in a siding. The doors at the side of the trucks were open and we could see barbed wire, which was stretched across the width of the truck separating the interior into two sections. On the left were a number of palliasses and to the right a cast iron wood-burning stove and three bunks. We realised that this was to be our mode of transport for the next leg of our journey.

'The guards occupied the section with the stove and we were to travel in the other section, but where we were heading, no one would tell us. We came to the conclusion that our trip was not going to be a long one, for there was no food or drink aboard. The doors slammed shut; we heard the locks on our side being closed and then we were on our way. There were eight of us and three very old men acting as guards. It was very dark and the soldiers had no wish to converse just yet but as we moved into the countryside, we learned that the men were really "Home Guards" and were terrified of authority and for some reason, equally terrified of us. We had been classified as dangerous prisoners!

'Uncomfortable as it was we gradually fell asleep, only to be woken up by a string of German oaths and the sight of one of the guards frantically trying to beat out the flames coming from his very long ersatz overcoat. He had got too near the stove, which was now glowing in the dark. His companions came to his aid and soon all was quiet, except for the injured guard, who was now afraid of his fate when he came to the end of his journey and would have to report the incident. There was nothing we could do to help treat his burns, for we were separated from him by the barbed-wire screen. As evening approached, the following day we pulled into a siding and the doors were opened. We had not travelled far as we could hear voices calling, "Düsseldorf! Düsseldorf!" – this was our destination.

LAMSDORF AND BEYOND

'We dismounted and after a few moments, our party was separated into two groups, the RAF to one side and the USAAF to the other. The American section was put aboard a bus and immediately moved from the station. We never saw them again. As for us, we boarded a truck and moved out of the city. The journey to our destination did not take very long and we eventually stopped at a camp which we soon realised was a Workers' Camp.

'It was divided into four compounds, which housed French, Italian, Polish and Russian citizens who were forced to work in the locality. Our quarters were to be in the French section and a few hours after our arrival, we were allocated three Russian prisoners to serve our every need. It was not too long before we realised that there was a definite pecking order at the camp.

'After the Germans, the French were the pampered race. The Italians came next followed by the Polish inmates and a very long way behind came the Russians. Germans did not stand guard over the Russian compound, they left that to the Polish group and the Russian group provided the guard for the Polish compound!

'At this stage we found it very difficult to comprehend the attitude of the Germans towards the Russian and the Polish people, after all, we had not been subject to the rule of the Nazi regime and as yet, had met none of the cruelty meted out to the races they, the Germans, had conquered. Not many days were to pass before we saw examples of such cruelty and it was with disbelief that we saw Russian captives digging holes in the ground, into which they placed their dead comrades.

'At least the Polish dead were given a decent burial service and had fellow countrymen saying a prayer or two at the graveside, and in some cases placing a small wooden cross to mark the spot where the internment had taken place. Why were there so many deaths among these two races? The Russian captives would be given food only if they carried out a day's work and this explained why they were so eager to be our "servants". The food we gave them was perhaps sufficient to keep them alive for a few days longer and even to build up their strength to resume the work they were ordered to carry out for their German captors, so obtaining further rations.

'It was so sad to witness the actions of these poor creatures when they scrambled for a cigarette end, a crust of bread or any other morsels discarded by us. They took enormous risks to find a hole in the barbed wire, through which they'd visit our quarters and offer to carry out the most menial tasks for a very meagre reward.

'Our next concern was more to do with ourselves. We seemed to be receiving rather a lot of French Red Cross parcels and the British parcels were turning up in the French section, but were issued to French workers. Really it was the shortage of English cigarettes and chocolate that triggered the enquiry.

'The British Red Cross parcel was superior in every way to the French one and the contents much greater in both calorific value and for the purposes of bartering. At the meeting we held with the French quartermaster, we discovered that the French believed that, as they were used as workers by the Germans, they were entitled to the better products in the British parcel. It must be noted here that Senior NCOs and Officers were not obliged to work for the enemy and very rarely did so.

'The plight of the other inmates in the camp was not considered by the French. The atmosphere was somewhat strained for the next couple of weeks and I think both sides were happy when it became known that the RAF were to be moved on, again no hint of our destination was given.

'The day of our departure arrived and I was asked by the Medical Officer in the camp to forego my crutches and use sticks in future. With some hesitation I acceded to his request and was able to walk out of the compound.

'We were ferried to the station at Düsseldorf and saw a city devastated by bombing. The majority of the workers in the repair gangs were women and we discovered that these were Russian. They looked wretched. Armed guards surrounded the area in which they were working. Quickly we boarded the cattle trucks, which were similar to those in which we had travelled from Venlo.

'This time there were no incidents. Eventually we disembarked at a town called Memmingen in the district of Thuringia. Our home was to be in a beautiful Opera House, which had been stripped of its finery to accommodate large numbers of PoWs.

'The residents were for the most part captives from the Arnhem operation, but also there were many aircrew held in the wire compounds. Entertainment seemed to be the order of the day. Impromptu concerts seemed to take place daily, added to which was the opportunity to view a group of circus performers who were camped outside the fence. Somehow, they seemed to have dodged the call-up.

'Food was of the highest quality, or maybe we were now becoming used to taste of ersatz; ersatz that was frequently embellished with the contents of

LAMSDORF AND BEYOND

Red Cross parcels. Almost daily the number of prisoners grew and it became obvious that some would soon have to be moved on, but no one really wished to go. Despite the overcrowding, the camp was reasonably comfortable. Perhaps this was because it was classed as a rehabilitation unit. It was with some regret that we took the journey to the station, there to board compartments of an ordinary passenger train but still guarded by Home Guards.

'It was night time when we neared Frankfurt and the train was diverted into a siding as an air raid was taking place on the city. We disembarked at around ten a.m. and as we left the platform, we were attacked by German citizens who wanted revenge for the raid that had taken place the previous evening. Who could really blame them? Our guards fixed bayonets and eventually drove the angry people away. Not all were happy to leave and some followed the tramcar, which was to take us to the interrogation centre just outside the town. Bricks rattled against the coachwork. Metal bars were used to smash windows, but our guards stuck to their task and we escaped without injury.

'At the dreaded Dulag Luft, so often the subject of talks back in Britain, we could expect to be questioned on the activities of the RAF and secret equipment of the Allied Forces. We had been instructed to provide only our Service number, Rank and Name and under no circumstances to enter into any discussion.

'At once we were placed in cells which had only a bed on which was a straw palliasse and by the door a device to attract the attention of the guards when the "call of nature" came. This gadget was used frequently, so keeping the guards busy. They were not happy about this ploy to keep them on the move and the language they used to describe the prisoners was pretty choice. A childish prank but effective.

'Messages in Morse code were tapped out on the walls between cells and on pipe work, but the contents were not within my knowledge of the Morse code even though its use had been part of the navigator's course. Food was very poor. As the first day in solitary confinement drew to a close, I realised that this was the first time I had really been alone since my capture. I was on my own.

'There was no window in the room that I occupied, so I tried to get to sleep and to prepare myself for the interrogation I was to face very soon now. Would it be as testing as I had been led to believe back in England? The heat in the cell was overbearing and there was practically no ventilation, so it was no great surprise that I slept very fitfully and by morning I was not a very happy PoW.

'The introduction to Stalag Luft IXC Kraysburg[1] was so weird. Between the entrance gate and the outer fence were a number of small wooden structures that looked exactly like dog kennels and each one of us was told to creep into one of these, leaving our kit outside. There we remained for some time until ordered out again and told to retrieve the items that had been left outside. Next, we were given a number and admitted into the main compound. The number was that of the barrack room we would occupy for the time we would be at the camp.

'There was a reception committee and a barrage of questions about the progress of hostilities, but alas, there was little we could add to what they already knew for the majority had been captured much later than we had. At last there was time to look around the room. It contained four sets of bunk beds, each with a paper palliasse filled with straw, supported by a few wooden boards. A small cupboard took up the space at the side of each set of beds. Near one wall was a cast iron stove with a chimney disappearing through the ceiling. Strung between the walls were lines of string on which hung articles of clothing that had recently been washed. A shuttered window took up part of the remaining wall. It did not take long for me to be introduced to my roommates and to be advised which "mess" I would join.

'Next I was told of procedures and the daily routine of the camp. In no time at all I was asleep.

'"*Raus! Raus!*"

'Such a banging and clattering, it was time to rise, dress and present ourselves for roll call. What a motley collection! There we stood in ranks of five, lined up on three sides of the huge open square. German soldiers counted us five by five and informed the senior NCO of the total number present. On a cold, bleak day this procedure lasted for no longer than twenty minutes but when weather conditions were good all sorts of pranks were played to keep the prison staff employed for anything up to two hours.

---

1. Although its headquarters were located near Bad Sulza, between Erfurt and Leipzig in Thuringia, its sub-camps – *Arbeitskommando* – were spread over a wide area, particularly those holding prisoners working in the potassium mines, south of Mühlhausen.

LAMSDORF AND BEYOND

'Each block was allocated a time for taking a shower – cold – and once each week there was the luxury of a hot shower if you managed to get a place at the head of the queue. On odd occasions clothes could be bagged and passed through a steam plant but this procedure was not popular as clothes tended to shrink so the cold water wash was the most sought after. The food we were served was appalling but we were informed that it was the same as that served to equivalent ranks in the German Forces, this was very difficult to accept and it made us eternally thankful for the extra items we received in the Red Cross parcels now regularly provided. A British parcel would have in it basic items for providing nourishment, such as tinned bacon, tinned sausages, tinned margarine, dried milk, chocolate, prunes and a supply of cigarettes and other sundry items.

'An American parcel would contain similar articles but the sausages would be replaced by Spam and there would be a larger tin of dried milk, the prunes would be replaced by raisins and in addition there would be toilet soap, much loved by the Germans and so very useful for trading purposes. A Canadian parcel would be a mixture of the two and parcels from France and the Commonwealth would generally be in a bulk delivery and passed to the kitchen for general use. The cardboard, string and empty tins were hoarded and used for many, many purposes. It was truly amazing what could be done by tradesmen who enjoyed practising their civilian skills in the recycling of tins etc. Empty "Klim" tins were just the right size to fit the chimney of the stove and gradually the stove would be extended towards the middle or the floor, so enabling more people to benefit from the heat generated, unfortunately, just when the stove had reached the centre, the German guards would organise an SS visit and not only the stove would be dismantled but many items were confiscated and food that had been carefully stored, scattered and made quite unfit to eat. In retrospect it seems a futile pastime but at the time it was a question of trying to outwit the enemy.

'Day by day the camp became an organised society. Rules of behaviour were drawn up and strictly adhered to; this was very necessary for the well-being of all concerned.

'Educational sessions became the norm and talks and lectures provided an additional interest for those not interested in studying for examinations, the results of which would be accepted on return to the UK. Again materials and exam papers were provided by the Red Cross.

STORIES FROM THE STALAGS

'Entertainment was a must. Regular concerts were organised and again the inmates showed great prowess in making scenery and costumes from "bits and pieces".

'News of the progress of hostilities was produced from I know not where, but there was a clandestine radio in use. Bulletins were issued on a daily basis and, of course, each new batch of prisoners was questioned on initial admission to the camp.

'At the beginning of December, the weather changed for the worse. Snow fell and the temperatures dropped alarmingly. The walks which had been taken daily, now became runs but physical effort burned up energy and food supplies were not good. However, a supply of ice skates arrived and soon work started on constructing a makeshift ice rink. The Canadians among us were overjoyed as gradually the rink took shape. Promises of skating lessons were made and for a few days hunger was forgotten.

'Christmas would soon be with us and of course an entertainment to beat all previous efforts was to be produced.

'A few days before these marvellous dreams were to become reality, there was the sound of aircraft overhead, not British, not German, but on closer examination, these were found to be Russian planes. What was happening? The news bulletins had said nothing of this but it now became obvious by the behaviour of the German troops that something was amiss.

'We were ordered to leave the outdoor areas whenever an air raid siren sounded. Sadly, one airman lost his life when he reacted too slowly to this order. Perhaps the reader can imagine the tension that now built up within the camp. Few were brave enough to leave the barrack blocks and arrangements had to be made to ensure that those bringing food from the cookhouse were not made targets, should a raid occur on the journey. The number housed had been increased because places had to be found for new inmates that now included glider pilots, victims of the raid on Arnhem.

'Twelve bodies now filled the space previously used by four. It was essential that discipline was maintained and thanks to previous training, it was. A few days passed and the sound of heavy artillery was heard. There was little doubt that the Russian forces were not too far away. Were they aware that we were in the area? My mind went back to the advance on Brussels and the hope we had of being released. No promises were made this time. We received orders to gather our scant belongings together and prepare for a long trek to a camp within the German border. No transport would be available and the snow was still very deep. How would we survive? Makeshift rucksacks were made, as were sleds that would carry food and equipment during the coming days. Some acted in groups but the majority elected to be responsible for their own future.

'Christmas Day 1944. The gates of the camp were opened and we set out on our journey. The guards took up their positions either side of the column, thankful that they were not being left to face the advancing Russian forces. No longer were we the enemy, but a means of escape into the Fatherland.

'Not many hours had passed when we realised that civilians had joined the column. Old men, women and children, all striving to put as much distance as possible between themselves and the enemy. They were terrified that they would become prisoners of those who their own propaganda had warned were little better than animals. It was not long before mothers asked us to care for their children and overnight we found that we had been left with several young boys and girls, hoping that they would be safe with us. Obviously, this was not possible and at the first village we reached, we made provision for them to be transported by the German authorities. I often wondered what became of those children.

'The greatest barrier we faced was at the River Oder. There was a town on our route – Oppeln – but we would not be passing through this town, but would walk across the frozen river. Now we were in Germany proper. The next stop on our journey would be the huge camp at Lamsdorf. This camp had been used as a camp during World War I. Now it was home to thousands of prisoners of every nationality where Germans had occupied the country of origin.

'Lamsdorf filled me with foreboding. It was huge and the inmates looked so intimidating, as they took their daily exercise. Gaunt figures in clothing which had seen better days, faces deeply etched showing that they had not had quite so comfortable a time as we who had just joined them. Many had spent several years in Lamsdorf and were looking towards the final days of captivity.

'We soon learnt that although the appearances were poor there was still spirit and determination within the wire. The family atmosphere of Kraysburg was absent but the organisation necessary to provide a reasonable code of conduct was definitely in place. The quarters I was allocated were cold and damp; the only heating coming from the personnel living in the cramped space. Personal hygiene was not of a very high standard and the attitude of my companions bordered on hopelessness. My thoughts turned towards getting myself moved to some other section of the camp where life would not seem so dreary. I was not prepared for events of the next few days.

'As at Kraysburg, a makeshift open-air ice-rink had been constructed and tiered seating had been installed. Obviously not all had the same approach as my room-mates. Crowds gathered in the freezing air to watch an ice hockey game between a Canadian side and a side made up of various nationalities. It was exciting and many looked forward to further contests as well as using the rink simply for amusement.

'I was granted my move, but after only a few hours, was ordered to pack what few possessions I had and join a group of sick and lame colleagues for onward transfer. Enquiries revealed that our small group was being transferred to yet another camp where we would be medically examined to determine whether or not we were suitable for repatriation. A couple of hours' train journey took us to a camp specifically for army NCOs. The rest of the day was spent preparing ourselves for inspection when we appeared before the panel of Swiss Red Cross Medical Officers who would decide our future. Would I be repatriated?

'"No!" was the short answer but I would remain at the new camp. Here was a camp where 90% of the inmates had been captive since Dunkirk. The organisation was superb! Units in which I had been stationed back in the UK were not any better than this. I am sad to say that I cannot remember the name of this camp. Every inmate seemed to want to help the newcomer. Of course, this could not last. This had been the story of my life for almost a year. The Russians were coming. This time I was able to ready myself for the next move. We were advised to gather in groups of four and to ensure that there was not more than one "disabled" person in each group. When all was ready, we evacuated the camp and set off to face what was to be a pretty horrific experience.

'During the daylight hours we rested in pine forests or on farms on our route south. At night we walked and walked and walked. This arrangement was made so that our winding columns would not be mistaken for marching German troops and so become targets for any roving aircraft. Whenever possible we would stock up on food. Crops would be raided and farmyard animals killed to provide sustenance for hungry mouths. I was appointed quartermaster for our small group mainly because I was not ruthless enough to carry out the pilfering necessary to sustain the four of us, whereas the others had become skilled in the art during the long years of working on German farms and in factories. I was most fortunate and shall be eternally grateful to my colleagues.

'After several weeks of "marching" we arrived at a railway siding and were ordered to board cattle trucks for the next leg of the journey. Forty men and their equipment to each truck! How degrading this was cannot be imagined. Toilet facilities were non-existent and as each stretch of the journey was carried out during the hours of darkness, it was such a relief when dawn came and the doors to the truck were opened. Cold though the weather was, there was no hesitation should there be a stream nearby. The first task was to wash and prepare for the next night's journey. Now there was not a supply of Red Cross parcels and we relied upon the rations provided by our captors; these were very meagre indeed. Tempers frayed but astonishingly there was no pilfering of supplies.

'After almost three weeks travelling back and forth across the operating rail system, we came to a halt at a major railway station. Prague! Much to our surprise we received hot soup from ladies who were the equivalent of the WVS [Women's Volunteer Service] and we were allowed to draw water from the boiler of the engine to make tea (those who still possessed tea leaves), but sadly, our stomachs could not cope with the intake of potato soup and brackish water, and many PoWs were very sick indeed. Another day passed and once again we journeyed along the rail system until there was just nowhere to go by rail.

'Trucks were unloaded and prisoners and their guards set off over the countryside. At about this time the older guards were taken away to bolster the army elsewhere and their places taken by schoolboys enlisted in the Hitler Youth Movement. The situation was very delicate as the majority of these young boys were fanatical in their hatred of the enemies of the Reich. Time and time again they treated their prisoners cruelly and took little notice of the older members of the guard. On at least two occasions, prisoners were killed because of their failure to respond quickly to instructions from some youngster. When a batch of Red Cross parcels appeared, there was increased tension as these were strictly for distribution to captives and the new guards were loath to hand the parcels over. Common sense prevailed and the daily routine continued. On and on we roamed, unaware of our destination or indeed the final outcome.

'An overnight stay at a camp near Munich, too crowded to receive any other bodies, simply helped to fix our position and to receive news of the progress of the war. A few more days and our section of the column were ordered to stay in a primary school building in the Austrian village of Kirschberg. Now we were in the American battle area. We settled into our new billet under the watchful eyes of the local population and slept through the sound of gunfire and raiding aircraft. Dawn broke and there was no sign of guards of any age. Walking out of the school, I saw many inhabitants walking towards a church nearby and on enquiring whose feast day it was, I received the answer, "The war is over."

'On 7 May 1945 a troop of American soldiers appeared and gave the official news. They left sufficient food and other items to supply a small army. With great care borne out of weeks of shortage, we divided the rations and prepared to be taken to an Allied base.

'It was such a strange feeling to be free to wander where we pleased. There was an airfield at Strauben a few miles away and it was towards this that we headed, only to find that every aircraft had been destroyed and so were unfit for our use. Nothing for it but to wait for the US Army to return and arrange for us to be transferred the United Kingdom. The food we had been given was strange to us; the white, fluffy bread and real butter seemed to be so unappetising after the rough rations we had become used to.

'Almost a week passed before an army truck arrived and our journey home began. Our destination was the airfield at Rheims in France and on arrival we saw several Lancasters with crews. These were to be the means by which we would finally make the journey home. Groups of ex-prisoners were allocated to each aircraft, told to hang on to anything they could, and in a very short time we would land at an RAF base at Wing. Once again there was disappointment for my group. The navigator for the aircraft had "gone missing". Wasn't I a navigator? The pilot was quite prepared to trust my ability to map read until he could pick up radio contact. So, away we went and each occupant of the aircraft was allowed in turn to visit the flight deck and view the white cliffs of Dover as we approached England.

'After landing at Wing, we were escorted to a huge marquee where we suffered the indignity of being fumigated, given a cursory medical examination and then the luxury of a very hot shower.

'Almost three and a half stones lighter and almost unrecognisable from the person who had left on the disastrous trip to Aachen – I was home.'[2]

---

2. People's War site by Roger Marsh of the 'Action Desk – Sheffield' Team on behalf of Edward L. Humes.

Chapter 5

Behind the Wire

At Frankfurt the reception camp for all downed fliers was designated Dulag Luft. Here there was a proper interrogation ... [but] apart from the odd fag or two the meeting was not very fruitful for either side. In the end my interrogator gave up by saying that I could not tell him anything he did not already know. He knew I was from 10 Squadron based at Leeming and that I was bombing Cologne. For good measure he knew that our CO had recently changed his car and told me the make of it. He was correct of course, but I told him it was a load of codswallop, or words to that effect.

Warrant Officer Basil Craske, an RAF Whitley V pilot on 10 Squadron, shot down on 16 August 1941. He was one of fifty-two men who made a mass escape from Stalag IIIE Kirchhain on 11 May 1942 before being sent to Stalag Luft III. He discovered that the difference in approach between the IIIE army guards and the Luft III guards who collected them for their relatively comfortable journey to Sagan was very apparent – 'Cool, calm, and collected' were the latter, as opposed to the army types. Similarly, the camp at Sagan was in complete contrast to Kirchhain – quite vast by IIIE standards and there was room for sporting activities in each compound and even some equipment.

By the end of August 1943 PoW camps throughout the Reich were beginning to burst at the seams. At Stalag Luft III, Sagan [Żagań] in western Poland, downed RAF and American crews were arriving in the camp with alarming regularity. One of the luckiest men to be alive and be taken prisoner was Sergeant Nicholas S. Alkemade on 'K-King' flown by Flight Sergeant Jim

Newman of 115 Squadron at Witchford, which had dispatched eighteen Lancasters on the raid on Berlin on the night of 24–25 March 1944, the night that seventy-six men had escaped from the North Compound of Stalag Luft III. Seventy-two missing bombers was the price paid by Bomber Command for the delivery of 2,493 tons of bombs on the 'big city's' vital war factories. 'K-King', better known as *Werewolf*, was one of four missing Main Force Lancasters on 115 Squadron, hit by flak over Frankfurt before the crew got to the target. By the time they reached the German capital it was close to midnight. They were attacked by a Ju 88 shortly after dropping their bomb load. Cannon and heavy machine gun fire set the starboard wing and fuselage on fire and Sergeant Alkemade's rear gun turret received a direct hit from a cannon shell, blowing out all the Perspex and setting part of the hydraulic gear system on fire.

It was 21-year-old rear gunner's thirteenth operation. Alkemade had joined the RAF in 1940 and served in Air Sea Rescue launches before transferring to Bomber Command. Alkemade returned fire at the Ju 88 and saw its port engine burst into fire and the aircraft dive away. 'K-King' was set on fire and was losing height rapidly and Newman gave the order for the crew to bail out. Alkemade, however, was not wearing his parachute. It was still stashed away in the fuselage, apparently ready for an emergency. Alkemade went to fetch it but the wall of flame between the turret and the rest of the aircraft made it impossible. By now as the smoke filled the gun turret and the flames reached his gas mask, his clothes were already alight and he had first-, second- and third-degree burns on his face and hands, and burns on his legs. 'I had the choice of staying with the aircraft or jumping out,' Alkemade recalled later. 'If I stayed, I would be burned to death – my clothes were already well alight and my face and hands burnt, though at the time I scarcely noticed the pain owing to my high state of excitement ... I decided to jump and end it all as quick and clean as I could. I rotated the turret to starboard, and, not even bothering to take off my helmet and intercom, did a back flip out into the night. It was very quiet, the only sound being the drumming of aircraft engines in the distance, and no sensation of falling at all. I felt suspended in space. Regrets at not getting home were my chief thoughts, and I did think once that it didn't seem very strange to be going to die in a few seconds – none of the parade of my past or anything else like that.'

Having thrown himself out into the night sky at 18,000ft altitude, blissfully, he passed out and then he came to three hours later on the ground. His fall had been broken by pine trees in the Arnsbergerwald near Schmallenberg and deep snow cover and his 120mph terminal velocity had been safely cushioned by foliage and branches. He had a twisted right knee, a deep splinter wound in his thigh, a strained back and slight concussion but he was still alive! Unable to move, Alkemade blew his whistle to get attention. He was found by local members of the Volkssturm. No one believed his story that he was an airman who had landed without a parachute and on suspicion of being a spy Alkemade was placed in solitary confinement in the room where, a week earlier, the 'Great Escape' had taken place. 'Alas, they had filled in the tunnel!' he said. Eventually the harness of his parachute was examined. Rivets that held his harness snap hooks flat to his chest and would break once the ripcord was pulled were still intact and the Germans realised that his story must be true.[1] Sergeant Roy Keen, who was a flight engineer on one of four Lancasters of 166 Squadron that were shot down, met Alkemade in Luft III. 'He'd just got a bit of sticky plaster over one of his eyebrows! Falling at speeds of up to 120mph, it would have taken him about two minutes to hit the ground. He was fantastically lucky. All in all, I was very fortunate too. War teaches you a lot, especially as a prisoner; material things aren't that important. I saw gold watches exchanged for half a loaf!'[2]

As Alkemade languished in Luft III, his sweetheart, a 21-year-old Loughborough girl named Pearl Belton, was at home pining for her airman. 'Existence here is pretty humdrum,' Nicholas wrote. 'But it's quite bearable and, what with theatre shows, sports meetings, reading, swimming and occasional spells of working, time flies quickly.'[3] Alkemade left Stalag Luft III in May 1945. He returned to Leicestershire, married Pearl and worked as furniture salesman, wowing people with his amazing story until the day he died in 1991.

---

1. Sergeant Geoffrey R. Burwell the wireless operator and Sergeant Joe Cleary the navigator were the only other members of the seven-man crew to survive.
2. On 21–22 January 1944 on a raid on Magdeburg, Flight Lieutenant T.P. McGarry DFC, a Northern Irishman in 35 Squadron, bailed out of his Halifax, landed in fir trees and survived after his parachute failed to open.
3. Nicholas's diary tells of monotonous boredom, so the pictures were one way of passing the time. One such drawing shows an airman presenting a medal to a busty, long-legged service woman. The caption reads: 'The dear old groupy gets quite a kick from pinning on these medals.'

STORIES FROM THE STALAGS

The Germans could not believe their luck when on 12 August 1944 a 92nd Bomb Group B-17 piloted by Lieutenant Eugene M. Wiley, was shot down with Colonel Delmar T. Spivey on board. The 92nd had started out for the marshalling yards at Gelsenkirchen but bad weather forced them to bomb a target of opportunity at Bochum. Wiley's B-17 was hit by flak just after bombs away and they crash landed in Holland. Spivey, who was on only the second of his five scheduled missions as part of an inspection trip, recalls: 'All the crew survived although several of us, including me, were wounded. Interrogation was normal – all senior officers (and those with special knowledge) were given especially tough interrogations. It was startling how much detailed information the Germans had on us. In my case I was on secret orders. Not even the crew I was flying with had ever heard of me. Yet after sweating it out in the "snake pit" at the Dulag Luft interrogation centre I was taken out of solitary and treated like the senior Colonel I was.

'I was cleaned up and given a good room and books, food and clothes. Then the questions. After two days the interrogator became angry with nothing but "name, rank and serial number". He told me I was a fool to be in the ETO on an inspection trip instead of having my feet on my desk at Training Command headquarters. Then he told me my life history, correctly and in detail, winding up by giving me my young son's birthday and the fact that my wife should be told I was safe – which he would do if I co-operated. Many PoWs were so impressed with such information that they confirmed the interrogator's information and gave him more. Thus, they added to the great store the Germans had already acquired from previous interrogations, papers, magazines and official registers of service etc, which they could get in neutral countries and from spies and friends in Allied countries.

'I was put in the North Compound at Stalag Luft III with the SBO [Senior British Officer], Group Captain Massey.' Group Captain Herbert Massey, the SBO at Sagan had suffered severe wounds to the same leg in both wars. He had lost half of his leg and his observer was killed when their aircraft was shot down by German ace Werner Voss on 4 February 1917. Shot down again during a raid on the second Thousand bomber raid, on Essen, on 1–2 June 1942. Massey was a veteran escaper himself and had been in trouble with the Gestapo.

'All American flyers were with the British until the autumn of 1943,' Spivey said. 'There were so many of us the Germans had to build a new compound. On 1st September 1943 about 700–800 of us were moved to the Centre Compound and I was SAO (Senior American Officer). My duties were to act as representative of the all-American compound in dealing with the Germans, the Protecting Power (Swiss government), Red Cross and the YMCA. The Red Cross got all the praise and glory, whereas the YMCA did equally good work. In effect, I was the Commanding Officer of all the PoWs in the Centre Compound until our evacuation in January 1945.

'The compounds were very similar. The senior officers organized the men along military lines – forming squadrons, and arranging staff for welfare, morale, escape (the most important of all the activities), education, athletics, entertainment, religion etc. I worked very closely with Group Captain Massey. He was an excellent SBO in every respect. The German Kommandant respected him and so did we all. I liked all the SOs but Massey was the "old man" for all of us until his repatriation. He did not involve himself in escape and was thus always "clear" with the Germans.

'Although the SOs collaborated at Stalag Luft III they had different philosophies about their duties. I knew one SAO at Barth [Stalag Luft I] who stated to all concerned that it was the duty of all PoWs to taunt, aggravate, inconvenience and impede everything the Germans did regardless of the consequences to PoWs. Massey believed, and I agreed with him, that working in harmony with the Germans frequently paid off in better treatment for the PoWs. We believed it was our duty to do that which in the long term would ensure the welfare and safe return of our PoWs while at the same time not compromising in any way our duty to our countries and their efforts to defeat the enemy.

'Collaboration with the enemy was never practised or condoned when such action would aid or comfort him. We tried to live by the Geneva Convention and insisted, frequently without success, that the Germans do the same. In general, the Luftwaffe lived up to the Convention whenever they could.'

Late in September 1943 Major Jim O'Brien, in Stalag Luft III at Sagan, received the news he had been dreading. A letter informed him of the tragic news that 'Mac' Howell had been killed on the Kiel raid. More bad news was to follow. On 15 October newly shot-down crews, including some from the 44th Bomb Group, arrived in the camp. They told O'Brien that in four months beginning January that year O'Brien's squadron, the 68th, had lost nine Liberators with only four survivors from the ninety men in them. O'Brien wrote, 'No friends left it seems'.

STORIES FROM THE STALAGS

First Lieutenant Mike O'Shea, navigator in the 351st Bomb Group, was shot down twice during four months of combat. On 9 August 1944, on his fourteenth mission, his B-17, *Thunder Ball* was shot down over the North Sea after bombing Germany. All of the crew bailed out before the plane exploded. Seven crew including O'Shea were rescued by the RAF Air Sea Rescue service but two died. On his twenty-fourth mission, on 7 October 1944, O'Shea's B-17 was shot down by flak over the Pölitz synthetic oil refinery, near Stettin. Taken prisoner of war, he was imprisoned at Stalag Luft III and Stalag Luft VII-A. He received the Purple Heart when he was injured in landing by his parachute. 'A typical day would have us getting up shortly after dawn, jumping down from our high sacks and falling out for *Appell* ([roll call or "the count") taken twice a day. We usually had all our clothes on in winter because the rooms were freezing. We stood at attention in a large field at one end of the compound in set formations from all the individual blocks, about 150 men in each.

'The "goons" would then carefully count the entire compound (over 2,500 men) one block at a time and record the tally. God help us if there was even one missing Kriegie [*Kriegsgefangener* or prisoner of war] in the count. The guards would then proceed to count again and again until the problem was resolved. Any escape would trigger turmoil.

'The entire camp could be standing for hours, in snow and rain. After Appell we were free to do as we pleased. Most went back to their rooms or would walk the perimeter. We organized touch football games; if we had the energy.

'The washroom facilities were very skimpy to say the least. We did have a Saturday inspection by our own senior officers to maintain a minimum of morale and check for a clean shave and decent hair length. Truthfully, I can't remember where we got our safety razors or scissors, because the Germans would not allow any cutting instruments.

'The blocks were divided into rooms big enough for four men, into which were crowded fifteen or more, sleeping on five triple-decker bunks. Each room prepared its own food from the monotonous Red Cross parcels that were rationed to each man. One man was elected cook and usually he prepared some very tasty dishes by mixing the ingredients of the parcels with other perishables that the Germans allowed us. But we never had enough to eat, while at the same time our captors continuously cut our supplies of food. Needless to say, the cook was always the best fed in the room.

BEHIND THE WIRE

'We always kept the tin cans from the parcels. The "craftsmen" in the room made our pots and pans and dishes from the sides. It was unbelievable what they could do with such little to work with. Each room had a small iron stove and we cooked on it. We were given just enough fuel to barely warm the food – none to keep the room warm.

'A Kriegie's life, especially in the last few months of the European war, was miserable at best. As the vice closed on the Third Reich, our captors, already hungry and war-weary, were much less willing to abide by the Geneva Convention that stated enemy PoWs were to be treated as well as their own soldiers. The Germans had little regard for us who had sacked their homeland. They had a serious food shortage themselves. In addition, they had much difficulty getting any American Red Cross parcels to the PoW camps because of the bombings and strafings. As a result, we suffered much hunger.

'American Kriegies never had the slightest doubt about eventual victory. However, we all expected it sooner than it happened. I remember a fear I had while behind barbed wire in the west camp of Stalag Luft III. I worried that when the end came the enraged, brainwashed Nazi mobs from the cities would attack and kill us all before we were freed. This secret fear I kept to myself, but it was real.

'In the coldest winter on record, the Russians advanced towards our camp. To avoid falling into Soviet hands, we evacuated the Stalag and started our death march across Germany. It was then that I found out that people in the nearby cities and towns were petrified that the PoWs would ravage them when we were released. Neither happened, and I'm sure they had a lot more to fear from the Russians.'

In October the first of two famous escapes from Stalag Luft III occurred. On 29 October three men escaped from the British Compound through a tunnel which started close to the wire. This had been ingeniously achieved by placing a wooden vaulting horse in position with two tunnellers inside. During exercise periods the men had dug a tunnel and at the end of the sessions, sealed it up and covered the trap door with sand. This operation continued until the tunnel was outside the wire. Three men were then transported to the exercise area concealed in the horse and after crawling the full length of the tunnel they got clean away and made it safely to Sweden. The full story has been excellently chronicled in *The Wooden Horse*, by Eric Williams, one of the three escapers.

STORIES FROM THE STALAGS

The morning after the escape the RAF prisoners were called to parade in the usual fashion. It did not take the Germans long to discover that three men had escaped. Group Captain Massey told his men that the Germans were going to make an identity check against the identity photos to discover who were missing. Massey instructed his men to make this check as difficult as possible for the Germans. Chaos reigned with tables being knocked over and ball games in progress. The prisoners would not come to order and the guards fired shots into the air. In desperation the German Kommandant called in about 100 fully armed soldiers to restore order. In no time at all the guards dispersed through the eight huts in the compound with orders to shoot. With this the 'Kriegies' tumbled out and stepped into their parade positions.

The Kommandant started to read the riot act. Then two British prisoners stepped from the squad, sat down on the sand in front of the Kommandant and began to play chess! One of the guards brandished his rifle and rushed across, obviously with the intention of shooting both players. Oberfeldwebel Glemnitz took his life in his hands and kicked the chess game 'from here to Christmas', as one observer put it, and told his men to take the two prisoners to the cooler. Without the officer's intervention they would have been shot dead.

The Germans later made attempts to photograph the PoWs for their records. When their backs were turned for a second the camera was stolen, complete with film, and the PoWs used it to good advantage for their escape passports. The Germans were furious and demanded its return. Group Captain Massey said they could have the camera back minus the film if no further action was taken. Rather than risk reporting the incident to higher command, the offer was accepted. It was 'goon baiting' at its morale-boosting best.

'Luft III, of course, is well known for the documented escapades of "The Wooden Horse" and "The Great Escape,"' wrote Warrant Officer Basil Craske 'but there were other less serious episodes that raised our morale. For instance, every quarter or so it seemed a German general would make a tour of inspection and we would gamble upon the colour of the stripe down his breeches. On one occasion the pompous individual ignored the advice of his specialist Kriegie minders and insisted upon showing off his large Mercedes by being driven in it into the heart of the compound. It was of course immediately surrounded by hordes of admiring Kriegies, whose one thought was to filch as much of the equipment as possible. Of course, there were repercussions, but as a top-secret codebook was missing from the glove box, we compromised by keeping all the contraband other than their codebook, which, after copying, was returned to them with every page stamped "Geprift" (censored).'

Meanwhile, the Allies continued pounding German cities. On 18 November mass formations of Eighth Air Force Liberators and Fortresses were seen. Thousands of PoWs watched the four-engined bombers overfly the camp and felt the weight of their bombs when concussions and vibrations were experienced at Sagan. Four days later the Eighth Air Force returned and followed this with raids throughout November and early December. A *Luftangriff* (air raid) on 14 December was audible in the camp and spirits soared. That night singing could be heard in the blackout mingled with renderings of Lieutenant Runner's trumpet to fuel the fires of German discontent. 'Kriegies' derived great satisfaction when the Germans were under the hammer.

On Christmas Eve heavy bombing could again be heard in the distance. It proved a better Christmas present than the PoWs could have hoped for. Although the war would not be over by Christmas, they believed that the end could not be long in coming. It led to even greater enjoyment among the prisoners, who attended carol services, saw a Christmas play and enjoyed meals of banquet proportions.

On Christmas Day there was even bacon, sausage and toasted bread for breakfast and the Germans entered into the festive spirit by waiting until 11.00 hours to hold Appell. At night celebrations got into full swing. Many different nationalities used the occasion to climb the wire fences into adjoining compounds and it became so bad that gunfire was heard. Next morning counts and recounts tried to establish the imbalance between British and Polish personnel in the American compound. Many prisoners were marched away to the cooler while others rapidly consumed the last of the home-made alcohol before it was confiscated.

By the afternoon of New Year's Day, snow began to fall and added to the post-holiday gloom. Appell was held indoors and the lighting and hot water supplies were cut off. Hopes of a quick end to the war were diminishing rapidly. The Germans remained in good spirits and some guards joined in with British, American, Russian and other nationalities in a huge snowball battle. Meanwhile, the real battles continued. On the fighting fronts Germany still felt secure behind the Atlantic Wall, while in the PoW camps throughout the Reich, the other battle, for survival, went on.

At Sagan no escape attempts were made during the long winter months but plans were laid for a full-scale breakout from the North Compound in the spring. The mastermind behind this operation was Squadron Leader Roger Bushell, a South African-born ex-barrister who had outwitted the Gestapo on several occasions but whose experience had left him a marked man. 'Big X', as he was known in the camp for security reasons, intended to cause the Germans as much trouble as he possibly could. Bushell reasoned that a large-scale breakout would pin down thousands of troops and reserve forces throughout the Reich and cause maximum disruption.

Roger Joyce Bushell was born in Springs, Transvaal, South Africa, on 30 August 1910 to English parents Benjamin Daniel and Dorothy Wingate Bushell. His father, a mining engineer, had emigrated to the country from Britain and he used his wealth to ensure that Roger received a first-class education. He was first schooled in Johannesburg, then, aged 14 went to Wellington College in Berkshire, England. In 1929, Bushell then went to Pembroke College, Cambridge, to study law. Keen on pursuing non-academic interests from an early age, he excelled in athletics and skied for Cambridge in races between 1930 and 1932 – captaining the team in 1931. One of Bushell's passions and talents was skiing: in the early 1930s he was declared the fastest Briton in the male downhill category. He even had a black run named after him in St Moritz, Switzerland, in recognition of the fact that he had set the fastest time for the run. He also won the slalom event of the annual Oxford–Cambridge ski race in 1931. At an event in Canada, Bushell had an accident in which one of his skis narrowly missed his left eye, leaving him with a gash in the corner of it. Although he recovered from this accident, he still had a dark drooping in his left eye as a result of scarring from his stitches. Bushell became fluent in French and German, with a good accent, which became extremely useful during his time as a prisoner of war. Despite his sporting prospects, one of Bushell's primary wishes was to fly and in 1932 he joined 601 Squadron Auxiliary Air Force, often referred to as 'The Millionaires' Mob' because of the number of wealthy young men who paid their way solely to learn how to fly during training days at weekends. By now Bushell had become a barrister-at-law of Lincoln's Inn.

Bushell was given command of 92 Squadron in October 1939 and his promotion to squadron leader was confirmed on 1 January 1940. During the squadron's first engagement with enemy aircraft on 23 May, while on a patrol near Calais, Bushell was credited with damaging two Bf 110s of ZG 26 before being shot down himself (probably by future ace Oberleutnant Günther Specht). He crash-landed his Spitfire and was captured before he had a chance to hide. On arrival at Dulag Luft he was made part of the permanent British staff under 'Wings' Day, the senior British officer, who placed Fleet Air Arm pilot Jimmy Buckley, RN in charge of escape operations with Bushell as his deputy. Day had previously set up an escape organisation at Dulag Luft, headed by Buckley, by which all escape attempts, intelligence gathering and escape preparations were controlled. This organisation became the model used at all other Allied PoW camps for the remainder of the war.

Several escape tunnels, one of which was completed in May 1941, were started. On the day of the escape Bushell wanted an earlier getaway so that he could catch a particular train, so he cut through the wire surrounding a small park in the camp grounds. He was recaptured on the Swiss border, only a few hundred yards from freedom, by a German border guard. He was treated well and returned to Dulag Luft, before being transferred to Stalag Luft I with all the seventeen others who had tried to escape in the tunnel (including 'Wings' Day and Jimmy Buckley).

After a short period, he was transferred to Oflag XC at Lübeck, where he participated in the construction of another tunnel. This was abandoned unfinished on 8 October 1941 when all British and Commonwealth officer PoWs were removed from the camp and were entrained for transfer to Oflag VIB at Warburg. During the night of 8–9 October the train stopped briefly in Hannover, where Bushell and Pilot Officer Jaroslav Zafouk, a Czech navigator on a 311 Squadron Wellington who was shot down on 16–17 July 1941, jumped from the train and escaped unnoticed by the German guards. They made their way to Prague in occupied Czechoslovakia and made contact with the Czech underground movement, staying in 'safe houses' while arrangements for their onward journey was being made. However, following the assassination of Reinhard Heydrich in May 1942 the Germans launched a massive manhunt for the assassins; during the round-up Bushell and Zafouk were arrested. Both were interrogated by the Gestapo and were very roughly treated. Bushell was eventually sent to Stalag Luft III at Sagan, arriving there in October 1942. Zafouk was sent to Oflag IVC at Colditz.

Bushell, who took over control of the escape organisation from Jimmy Buckley, who was being transferred to another camp, became known as

'Big X' of the Escape Committee and was the mastermind behind the mass escapes that occurred from the camp. He had developed an intense hatred for the Nazis and his plan was to strike back at them as best he could – by organising mass break-outs from the PoW camps he was in. In spring 1943 he masterminded a plot for a major escape from the North Compound from three tunnels: 'Tom', 'Dick' and 'Harry' dug simultaneously. Falling back on his legal background to represent his scheme, Bushell not only shocked those present with its scope, but injected into every man a passionate determination to put their every energy into the escape. 'Tom' began in a darkened corner of a hall in one of the buildings. 'Dick's' entrance was carefully hidden in a drain sump in one of the washrooms. The entrance to 'Harry' was hidden under a stove. More than 600 prisoners were involved in their construction.

By the spring of 1944 all three were well under way. The tunnels were remarkable engineering feats created by men working with only meagre tools. The biggest job was disposing of the sand. Because of its colour it was easily recognisable but was camouflaged or hidden upon excavation. Usually, it was carried from the tunnel entrance in small bags hidden under the prisoners' clothes. They could only carry limited amounts but there was a great amount of manpower available.

Jim O'Brien recalls: 'A favourite trick was to fold the sand into a blanket for sunbathing, slowly mixing the sand with the dirty surface soil under the blanket as you sat in the sun. I remember doing this on cold, cloudy days when nobody with any sense would be sunbathing. But the Germans never seemed to understand the actions of the Americans and British. Once we loaded sand in an attic in a building used as a cookhouse until the ceiling collapsed. We mixed sand and ashes from fires used for cooking. At one time so much sand was mixed with the ashes (much lighter than sand) that a horse-drawn truck attempting to move the ashes could not budge it!'

The tunnels were very deep – about 30ft below the surface – but very small, only 2ft square, although larger chambers were dug to house the air pump, a workshop and staging posts along each. The sandy walls of the tunnels were shored up with pieces of wood scavenged from all over the camp. One main source of wood was the prisoners' beds. At the beginning, each had about twenty boards supporting the mattress. By the time of the escape, only about eight were left on each bed. A number of other pieces of wooden furniture were also scavenged. A variety of other materials was also scavenged. The metal in the 'Klim' tin cans could be fashioned into a variety of different tools and items such as scoops and candle holders. Candles were fashioned by skimming the fat off the top of soup served at the camp and putting it in tiny tin vessels. Wicks were made from old and worn clothing. The main use of the 'Klim' tins, however, was in the construction of the extensive ventilation ducting in all three tunnels. As the tunnels grew longer, a number of technical innovations made the job easier and safer.

All this work could not go on unnoticed forever. On 11 March 'Tom' was discovered by German ferrets. Work stopped on 'Dick' and the prisoners concentrated their efforts on 'Harry'. This was finally ready in March 1944, but the American prisoners, some of whom had worked on the tunnel 'Tom,' had been moved to another compound seven months earlier. No American prisoners of war actually participated in the 'Great Escape'. Previously, this escape attempt had been planned for the summer as good weather was a large factor of success. However, in early 1944 the Gestapo had visited the camp and ordered increased efforts in detecting possible escape attempts. Bushell ordered the attempt be made as soon as the tunnel was ready.

The prisoners had to wait about a week for a moonless night so that they could leave under the cover of complete darkness. Finally, on Friday, 24 March, the escape attempt began and as night fell those allocated a place in the tunnel moved to Hut 104. Unfortunately for the prisoners, the exit trap door of 'Harry' was found to be frozen solid and freeing the door delayed the escape for an hour and a half. An even larger setback was when it was discovered that the tunnel had come up short. It had been planned that the tunnel would reach into a nearby forest but at 22.30 hours the first man out emerged just short of the tree line and close to a guard tower. As the temperature was below freezing and snow still lay on the ground, any escapee would leave a dark trail while crawling to cover. Because of the need to now avoid sentries, instead of the planned one man every minute, the escape was reduced to little more than ten per hour. Word was eventually sent back that no prisoner issued with a number higher than one hundred would be able to escape before daylight. As they would be shot if caught trying to return to their barracks these men changed into their own uniforms and got some sleep. An air raid then caused the camp's (and the tunnel's) electric lighting to be shut down, slowing the escape even more. At around 00.01 hours the tunnel collapsed and had to be repaired. Despite these problems, seventy-six men crawled through the tunnel to initial freedom.

STORIES FROM THE STALAGS

Finally, at 04.55 hours on 25 March, the seventy-seventh man was seen emerging from the tunnel by one of the guards. Those already in the trees began running while New Zealand Squadron Leader Leonard Henry Trent, who had just reached the tree line, stood up and surrendered. (Trent had been a Ventura pilot on 487 Squadron RNZAF and he was awarded the Victoria Cross for his action on 3 May 1943 when he was the only survivor from the fateful raid on the Amsterdam power station.) The guards had no idea where the tunnel entrance was, so they began searching the huts, giving the men time to burn their fake papers. Hut 104 was one of the last huts searched and despite using dogs the guards were unable to find the entrance. Finally, German guard 'Charlie' Pilz crawled the length of the tunnel but found himself trapped at the other end. Pilz began calling for help and the prisoners opened the entrance to let him out, finally revealing the location.

An early problem for the escapees was that most of them were unable to find the entrance to the railway station until daylight revealed it was in a recess in the side wall of an underground pedestrian tunnel. Consequently, many of them missed their night-time trains and either decided to walk across country or wait on the platform in daylight. Another unanticipated problem was that March 1944 was the coldest recorded in thirty years and snow lay up to 5ft deep, so the escapees had no option but to leave the cover of woods and fields and use roads.

Of seventy-six escapees, seventy-three were captured. Only three escapers made home runs; Per Bergsland, a Norwegian pilot on 332 Squadron, RAF; Jens Müller, a Norwegian pilot on 331 Squadron, RAF; and Bram van der Stok, a Dutch pilot on 41 Squadron, RAF. Bergsland and Müller made it to neutral Sweden first, by boat, while van der Stok travelled through France before finding safety at a British consulate in Spain.

The day after the mass escape Hitler gave personal orders that every recaptured officer as well as Commandant von Lindeiner, the architect who designed the camp, the camp's security officer and the guards on duty at the time were to be shot. Reichsmarschall Hermann Göring, head of the Luftwaffe, Field Marshal Wilhelm Keitel, head of the German High Command, who had ultimate control over prisoners of war, Major General Westhoff and Major General von Graevenitz, who was head of the department in charge of prisoners of war, all argued against any executions as a violation of the Geneva Conventions. Göring pointed out to Hitler that a massacre might bring about reprisals to German pilots in Allied hands.

Hitler agreed, but insisted 'more than half' were to be shot. Reichsführer Heinrich Himmler, chief of state security, fixed the total at fifty and passed the selection on to SS Gruppenführer Arthur Nebe. The general orders were that recaptured officers would be turned over to the criminal police and fifty would be handed to the Gestapo to be killed. Nebe was later executed for his involvement in the 20 July plot to kill Hitler.

As the prisoners were captured, they were interrogated for any useful information and taken out by motor car, usually in small parties of two at a time, on the pretext of returning them to their prison camp. Their Gestapo escorts would stop them in the country and invite the officers to relieve themselves. The prisoners were then executed singly or in pairs at close range from behind by pistol or machine pistol fire. Roger Bushell and his partner, 22-year-old Souse Lieutenant Bernard W.M. Scheidhauer, were among the first few to leave the tunnel. Scheidhauer was a Spitfire Vb pilot on 131 Squadron who on 18 November 1942 had run low on fuel and landed by mistake on German-occupied Jersey.

Under the guise of Frenchmen who had been working in Germany and were going home on leave the two escapers successfully boarded a train at Żagań railway station. A day or so later they reached Saarbrücken and were waiting on the platform for a train to Alsace when two Kriminalpolizei questioned them. They answered every question without raising suspicion and their passes were given back to them but one of the policemen turned around and shot a sudden question at Scheidhauer, who involuntarily answered in English. The policemen drew their pistols in a thrice and took them away to Lerchesflur prison. They had no alternative but to confess that they had escaped from Stalag Luft III. Three days later they were driven to a remote spot just outside Saarbrücken, where they were shot in the back by Dr Leopold Spann, a local Gestapo official. Scheidhauer died instantly but Bushell was only injured and lay writhing on the ground. Spann ordered his driver, Emil Schulz, to 'finish him off'. Field Marshal Keitel gave orders that the murdered officers were to be left for retrieval, after which they were cremated and returned to Stalag Luft III as a deterrent to further escapes. Roger Bushell is buried at the Poznan Old Garrison Cemetery in Poznań, Poland. On 13 June 1946 he was posthumously Mentioned in Despatches for his services as a PoW.

The 'Great Escape' marked the end of Colonel von Lindeiner's career as camp Kommandant. He was removed for court martial and replaced by

Oberstleutnant Erich Cordes. He served as acting Kommandant for a few weeks until Oberst Werner Braune assumed full-time command of Stalag Luft III. Braune was a tall man, born on 9 December 1897 in Schweidnitz. He had a lined, sad and patient face and thinning fair hair. He wore the Iron Cross First Class on his left breast pocket. Although strict, he behaved reasonably well at all times towards the prisoners.

Other far-reaching effects of the 'Great Escape' included the introduction of three appells a day and lock up was brought forward to 21.00 hours. The arrival of 120 new prisoners from Dulag Luft placed an even greater burden upon the camp and soon all ten-man rooms were full and six-man rooms overloaded. It was not until the end of March that fresh rations and some bulk issues of Red Cross parcels were received. The arrival of 1,400 letters from home was also a big boost to morale.

On 6 April a memorial service was held for the fifty PoWs murdered by the Gestapo. Afterwards, prison life returned to its normal uneventful existence. Prisoners continued their slow walks around the perimeter wire, looking across the countryside and glancing now and again towards the sky as the drone of aircraft could be heard in the skies. On 11 April the entire camp watched the Eighth Air Force fly over on one of their mass daylight raids.

Soon overcrowding in the West Compound prompted the Germans to introduce three-decker bunks. Each bunk started life with nine slats but these were soon reduced as they were burned for fuel or used in the construction of tunnels. The mattresses were made of burlap and filled with uncomfortable wood shavings. Two lightweight German blankets were provided, together with an American issue but the prisoners still had to sleep with their clothes on to keep warm.

The Vorlager, or Front Camp, consisted of several administrative buildings and storehouses. The Red Cross parcel building was situated among them and a group of prisoners were permanently assigned to prepare and distribute the parcels. Red Cross food parcels saved the life of many a prisoner. The Germans made certain that all cans were pierced to prevent them being stored for escape purposes. Two holes were punched in the tops of all cans except fish, which received a single hole. The prisoners sealed all the holes with margarine to stop the contents going bad.

All the food was brought into the camp on horse-drawn wagons or ingenious wood-burning trucks. 'Food Acco', the camp trading post, had its headquarters in the cookhouses, although the camp library, also located there, was eventually moved to the theatre building.

The cookhouses were situated near the centre of the camp, adjacent to the fire pool. German rations were issued from this building. Black bread was the usual issue. Reputedly made of sawdust and other ersatz ingredients, it tasted sour but when toasted it was bearable. Potatoes, kohlrube (similar to turnip), margarine, jam, sugar, occasional blood sausage (really congealed blood with a few slices of onion added) and a few green vegetables in season, were also given out by the Germans. Issues of pea and barley soup, usually wormy, were made every other day at noon. Occasionally there was cooked millet. Each prisoner was given an eating bowl and cup engraved with swastikas.

The Germans also made available a small quantity of seeds and these were planted more in hope than anything else by the prisoners. The pine needle-saturated soil tended to produce poor vegetables and disappointed gardeners produced ears of corn only 4 inches long at the most!

The cookhouse issued cooked potatoes nearly every day, although on occasions they were distributed uncooked. The cookhouse boilers made hot water for use in individual rooms where the stoves were inadequate. The cooks experimented with new dishes but generally the 'Kriegie' diet was monotonous. Improvisation took many forms. Tooth powders were used in cake baking, although it sometimes affected the flavour, and indigestion tablets were used successfully as a leavening agent. Crackers ground to a fine powder were used as flour. Even ice cream was made with fresh snow and powdered milk and sugar. It was whipped up with jam. Pancakes were made from Canadian biscuits soaked in water for three hours inside 'Klim' tins and then dipped in milk and fried.

Despite the poor diet and shortage of kit and equipment (shorts were made from overcoat linings), various sports like volleyball and softball were played in the compound and inter-barrack competitions were held, with the winners receiving accumulated cigarettes and candy bars as prizes. Swimming was held in the camp fire pool until it became stagnant and infested with vermin. Boxing and gymnastics were held on special occasions like 4th July and Labour Day. Kite flying gained in popularity but it was soon stopped by the Germans to prevent messages being passed between compounds.

BBC news broadcasts were relayed between each barracks by a newsman, whose arrival in a prearranged room was greeted with 'Soup's On!' This signal was changed from time to time to allay suspicion. Each group would send its own representative to listen to the news and he then repeated it to his roommates. Not surprisingly, the 'Kriegies' went to great lengths to hide their radios. A crystal set was even concealed inside a cigarette packet. The Vorlager also passed on its own version of the war news. Each day a radio broadcast was delivered over the loudspeaker system to the cookhouse. The news was written down and read to the assembled groups at roll call in the afternoon.

Another source of excitement was the unpredictable but constant searches made in the compound. The Germans would gut a whole block looking for concealed radios, escape items and other illegal items. Even ceilings were pulled down but the searches often proved fruitless. 'Ferrets', German guards clad in blue overalls, clambered underneath the prisoners' huts probing with steel rods for possible tunnels.

This was a further opportunity for 'goon baiting', as Second Lieutenant Franklynn V. (Frank) Cotner, a B-24 Liberator pilot in the 466th Bomb Group at Attlebridge, England, recalls. 'After the "Great Escape" the Germans dug tunnels under our barracks for the "ferrets" to lie in and overhear our conversations to glean valuable information. However, we had already established a system whereby when one of the "ferrets" entered the compound the whole camp knew about it in advance. The minute he went under one of the barracks the men in the hut would get an overwhelming desire to scrub the floor! The floors of course had many cracks in them and when we heard a "goon" underneath we would throw hot water onto the floor and start scrubbing and singing. Many times the angry "ferrets" would jump up and hit their heads on the beams!'

Cotner and his *Play Boy* crew had been shot down on 29 April 1944 on only their eleventh mission, to Berlin. At the initial point (IP) *Play Boy* received a direct hit from a Ju 88, which knocked out the number three engine. Despite this Cotner continued his bomb run before heading for England. But *Play Boy* could not maintain speed and had to drop back out of formation. Cotner tried to tag onto the end of a Fortress formation but he could not get sufficient speed from his ailing bomber. Out on a limb and alone, *Play Boy* came under attack from about twenty Focke Wulf Fw 190s. A handful made their attack from six o'clock, pumping 20mm shells into the stricken B-24. Tech Sergeant Robert F. Pipes, the engineer, and Staff Sergeant Edward Mount, the tail gunner, hit back with .5 calibre ball, tracer and armour-piercing rounds. Two, perhaps three, fighters fell away on fire but the German pilots had found their mark. The tail turret received several direct hits and caught fire. Mount was hit, suffering burns while Staff Sergeant Robert Falk, flying his first mission with the crew as right waist gunner, was killed instantly by a shot through the head.

Other German fighters knocked out the number two engine before they were forced to retire by escorting P-47 Thunderbolts. The damage to *Play Boy* was considerable. Cotner asked Pipes to check out the fuel supply. Pipes told him there was only enough for another thirty–forty minutes' flying time – not enough to reach England. The bomber lost height rapidly but Cotner decided to fly on the two good engines for as long as his fuel supply held out. He would not risk ditching in the Channel.

When the fuel supply finally ran out *Play Boy* was down to only 9,000ft. Cotner gave the bail-out order and gripped the stick while the co-pilot, navigator, bombardier and radio operator jumped. Pipes was sent to the rear of the ship to make sure everyone had left. Two of the crew were standing on the catwalk at the rear of the bomb bay and one could not bring himself to bail out. He was helped out by Pipes and Staff Sergeant H.L. Heafner, the right waist gunner. Heafner followed him out while Pipes went forward to check on Cotner. He was already on his way from the flight deck after trimming the aircraft. Pipes bailed out, linked up with Heafner and the two of them evaded capture for the rest of the war.

Cotner followed Pipes out of the bomb bay. 'When I bailed out, I could see that there was a hole approximately 3 ft in diameter between our number three and four engines. There was a similar hole through the bomb bay doors which might have had some effect on my ability to control the bomber in level flight. I could see that the fuselage had sustained thousands of holes and the right stabilizer was almost destroyed. The left was severed near the middle. This damage was a result of the attacks by the Luftwaffe.' [*Play Boy* made a soft belly landing at Daarle in Holland with the body of Falk still aboard].

'I landed in a little farming community in Holland and was almost instantly surrounded by very friendly Dutch civilians. I had injured my left side in the landing and this made walking very difficult. Some farmers brought a door and laid me on it and carried me into a large house. I was there only a few minutes when one of them spoke to me in English. He said, "We could help you to escape except that you are so badly hurt." Another fellow arrived and came to the centre of the group. He looked down at me and said, "Hi buddy, where are you from?" I told him I was from the United States, to which he replied, "Well I'm from Chicago myself!" Apparently, like a lot of Americans, he had got caught in Holland when war was declared.

'The villagers took me to a small hospital at Almelo. I was put into a hospital bed and I had a typical Dutch grandmother with white hair and rosy cheeks take care of me. During my short stay she told me that if my leg had been broken the Germans would probably have allowed me to stay in hospital until it mended. However, since it was only severely strained, she thought they would take me away almost immediately. She then made me a strange proposition. With my permission she would take a sledgehammer and break my leg so that they would have some excuse to keep me in hospital!

'Before anything like that could be done the Germans arrived and took me into custody in Amsterdam. The prison looked like it was about two blocks square. I was placed in solitary confinement and served warm tea and some sort of soup twice a day. I was only there for a short while before being transferred to Frankfurt and placed in solitary confinement once more.

'Prior to my interrogation a German major brought out a book showing photographs of the commanding officers and many of the pilots in the 466th Bomb Group. The major said, "Lieutenant, we know just about everything we want to know about your mission, except how many bombs you carried." I told him I had no idea because I wasn't the bombardier. I was sent back to solitary confinement. Again and again, I was called in, asked the same question and I always gave the same answer.

'This went on for over a week and a half until one day I looked out of my window and saw the Germans working on what I believed to be an RAF blockbuster bomb. It had a delayed action fuse and was only about 30ft from my cell. Next time I was called in I said we had been carrying fifty 100 lb bombs (we had in fact been carrying 75 anti-personnel bombs). The Major said that was all he needed to know and I could join my comrades.'

Another arrival at Stalag Luft III during May 1944 was 21-year-old Second Lieutenant Rueben 'Ruby' Fier, a B-17 navigator in the 94th Bomb Group at Bury St Edmunds, Suffolk. Fier was shot down on his tenth mission, on 31 December 1943 over Cognac in *Pacific's Dream*. His pilot, Second Lieutenant Edward J. Sullivan, co-pilot 2nd Lieutenant Cliff Robinson and Tech Sergeant Elmer Shue, the flight engineer, were captured on landing by parachute. The remainder of the crew evaded capture, escaped over the Pyrenees into Spain and were subsequently returned to England. Fier evaded capture for two months by living in various parts of France with Maquis groups and others who risked their lives to hide him. He was captured on 15 March in Ariège. He was handed over to the Gestapo in Carcassonne before being transferred to Fresnes and a German camp.

Like Frank Cotner, Fier's account is another in a series of 'horror stories' told to fellow prisoners at Żagań. 'Many times, I was moved elsewhere as the Germans approached to conduct a search for downed fliers reported hiding in the area. When travelling with the Maquis, I carried a Sten-gun because I was informed it was every man for himself if we engaged in a fire-fight with the enemy. Fortunately, it did not happen in my case, though I recall the night a French gendarme "eye-balled" several of us sitting in a car on a dark street. We all had guns pointing at him if he decided to challenge us. Apparently, he thought better of it and continued on his way.

'Many times, while commuting from one location to another by bus or train, I would be rubbing shoulders with German military personnel – if they only knew! Once, I had just disembarked from a train in Carcassonne and left the station as a convoy of Vichy police pulled up to the station and threw a cordon along the street, checking everyone as they entered or left. I was across the street from the station and took it all in. A week before my capture, I managed to send a disguised Red Cross telegram to an uncle in the States letting him know I was still alive.

'Unfortunately, after an unsuccessful attempt to cross the Pyrenees, in which I developed frost-bitten toes, three of us were apprehended by French gendarmes on a road between Axat and La Pradelle. Staff Sergeant Levi Collins, ball turret gunner on *Iron Ass* in the 351st Bomb Group; Flying Officer Clifford Tucker, an Australian Hawker Hurricane pilot; and I, were transported by taxi to the local jail in Axat and given a warm meal in the office of the Chief of Police. For a while we hoped they would assist us in making our way to Spain but one of the three gendarmes who apprehended us was apparently a Nazi collaborator who intimidated the others.

'We were locked up for the night and early the following morning the other two arresting officers visited us in our cell and with what appeared to be genuine tears running down their cheeks, begged our forgiveness and put the blame for our present predicament on the Adjutant, who insisted we be turned over to the Germans. They also informed us that several members of the Gestapo would arrive soon to take us away. (The Adjutant of the Police Department in Axat who was allegedly responsible for turning me, Collins and Tucker, over to the Gestapo, was executed by the Maquis in the evening of 16 March 1944 as he left the Police station.)

'Four Gestapo men arrived and put the three of us in handcuffs. They transported us to Gestapo headquarters in Carcassonne in a canvas-covered truck with the rear flap drawn down to obscure our view of the outside and anyone else's view of us. After questioning, being threatened and being smacked a couple of times because of my responses, I was taken to Paris by train and then by bus to Fresnes Prison on the outskirts of the city.

'During my stay at Fresnes Prison, Levi Collins, a Dutch Sergeant and I, were caught trying to cut our way out of our fifth-floor cell. The Dutch Sergeant was taken from our cell and I never saw him again. Levi Collins and I were removed to individual cells on the first floor of our section of the prison. I was put in a darkened cell with all bedding removed and my hands were handcuffed behind my back.

'After four days' confinement Collins and I were taken to the Kommandant's office and after a "royal chewing" through an interpreter, were told that we would be confined to solitary on half rations for a week as punishment for our attempted escape. Though we were told our punishment would be in solitary, Collins and I were put in a corner cell in the condemned row, without bedding and with a damp, cobblestone floor. After many attempts to obtain bedding by banging on the door and yelling in general, the door opened and the guard threw four blankets into our cell. Two were spread on the damp floor and the other two were used to cover us when we lay down, which is what we did most of the time.

'What really concerned me was that the food was better in the condemned prisoner's cell, in comparison to the rations we received in our fifth-floor prison. Our meals consisted of "coffee" for breakfast and supper, while we were given soup or a piece of bread on alternate days for lunch. Our commode in the corner of our cell also served as a sink with a water-spicket about 18 inches above the commode. Writings and scratchings on the walls of the cell indicated others condemned to death by German tribunals had been occupants of the cell prior to our incarceration there.

'After one week, Collins and I were taken out of our punishment cell and placed in different cells but still on the fifth floor of the prison. During my stay in Fresnes Prison I was interrogated two or three more times as the Gestapo attempted to learn where I had been for the two and a half months I was on the loose and who had aided me. Needless to say, they obtained no information from me and I got a few clouts across the face. After spending five weeks in Fresnes Prison I and eighteen other Allied fliers who were captured after a period of evading, were removed to Frankfurt am Main by train.

'En route, while waiting to change trains at Darmstadt station, a group of civilians on the platform looked us over. We were in civilian clothes, surrounded by armed guards and handcuffed. When they found out we were downed fliers their invectives came our way. If the guards hadn't kept the growing crowd back, I believe we would have been lynched. Bombing results were evident everywhere.

'At the Frankfurt am Main jail we were placed in individual top-floor cells for 21 days. During air raids we were left in our cells while other prisoners were removed to shelters. Viewing the raids was exciting but knowing you were in the middle of a raid by your own people was very frightening. Fortunately, the jail was not hit while we were there. I underwent my last two interrogations by the Gestapo and was removed to Dulag Luft at Oberursel, 13km north-west of Frankfurt am Main.

'After one week at Dulag Luft, without being interrogated, I was sent to Stalag Luft III, arriving there on 14 May 1944; four months and fourteen days after being shot down. The feeling of security which came over me on entering Luft III and joining thousands of other Allied fliers, was tantamount to being home free after the interrogations, getting cuffed about and threatened with execution as a spy and saboteur.'

Among the new intake of prisoners at Luft III on 29 May 1944 was Major Ronald V. Kramer of New Paris, Indiana, in the 713th Bomb Squadron, 448th Bomb Group. On 9 May Kramer had been flying in the co-pilot's seat with Captain Richard T. Lambertson on a mission to the railway marshalling yards at Liège, Belgium. The Liberator was hit by flak and burst into flames just as the bombs were released. All attempts to control the fire proved futile and the crew were ordered to bail out. Nine men made it and were captured. Staff Sergeant Andre Long, the right waist gunner, was KIA.

'We were at 18,000ft,' Kramer wrote. 'It looked a long way to the ground but I did not hesitate. I jumped and dropped several thousand feet on my back. There was a terrific jerk after pulling the ripcord. Everything seemed very quiet after the terrific noise a few minutes before. I saw the burning pieces of our aircraft falling and tremendous palls of fire and smoke coming from the target. It was a lonely feeling to see our bombers disappearing in the west when in another hour I knew they would be back at Seething.

'I guided the 'chute to an open field. Several Belgian farmers came running and helped me to my feet. I told them I was an American and they shook my hand and kissed me. They took me into a nearby wood immediately because German soldiers were scouring the countryside. A civilian suit was brought for me and we started walking through the fields in the direction of France. The Belgian who accompanied me was presumably an underground agent to be returned to England. At about 1230 [hours] we were intercepted by two German soldiers. They examined the Belgian's papers but they did not hold up and he was later shot.'

Kramer was arrested, searched and taken to Luftwaffe headquarters in Brussels. He was questioned repeatedly and threatened with execution if he did not give them information. Kramer was incarcerated in an old stone jail. When he was taken through the Belgian capital for further interrogation he was winked at by the Belgian people, who seemed very anti-Nazi. The air raid sirens sounded repeatedly during his stay as American bomber formations headed for the railway yards. The German soldiers were either very young or very old and Kramer's opinion of the 'master race' took a big drop.

On 13 May Kramer was moved by train to Frankfurt interrogation camp with a number of other American airmen from Brussels. The journey through Holland and along the River Rhine was pleasant with old castles and vineyards nestling along the river. Thoughts of war were far from their minds until they reached the war-torn cities of Cologne and Frankfurt. At Frankfurt Kramer started ten days' solitary confinement in a dirty cell with only a daily diet of four slices of bread and a bowl of watery soup to eat. He was often questioned but still he refused to give his captors any information. As a reprisal he was refused washing and shaving facilities. The many lonely hours were silently passed with prayers and thoughts of home.

On 24 May he was finally released and taken to Wetzlar distribution camp with 100 other American flying officers, where they were able to make contact with the American Red Cross and receive food and clothing. After Frankfurt it seemed 'better than Christmas' but on 29 May when Ron Kramer arrived at Stalag Luft III, it seemed like 'a life sentence'. The only consolation seemed to be meeting several old friends from the 448th Bomb Group and catching up on their news.

Kramer discovered many fellow Liberator crewmen at Stalag Luft III. Most had been shot down, captured and then processed, prior to being sent to Luft III, where they came under Luftwaffe supervision. However, airmen who were caught in civilian clothes were passed to the Gestapo to prove their military identity or be shot as spies. The Gestapo was not subject to the Geneva Convention.

One airman at Żagań in June 1944 who endured this treatment was Colonel Joseph A. Miller, CO of the 453rd Bomb Group at Old Buckenham, which flew B-24 Liberators. On 18 March 1944 he was in *Little Bryan*, the lead ship at the forefront of the Second Combat Wing, aiming for Friedrichshafen. It was only his fourth mission. After bombing, *Little Bryan* got into difficulties and dropped out of formation. The crew bailed out, Colonel Miller landing in a French field. He was soon in the hands of the French Resistance and, disguised as a priest, made his way across France to Perpignan. He was captured by a German border patrol as he waited to cross into Spain. Because he was in civilian clothing, Miller was handed over to the Gestapo.

He was sent to Fresnes Prison, where the Gestapo treated him harshly, certain that a man of his rank would have information invaluable to them. Colonel Miller stuck to 'name, rank and serial number' and his captors' patience began to run out. While in his cell Miller thought back to 1938 when three German officers were attempting to set a new record flying from Berlin to Tokyo. Everything had gone well until over the South China Sea on the return flight their Focke Wulf Fw 200 Condor developed engine trouble and they were forced to ditch in the Philippines. Their distress calls had already been picked up by the American Army Air Corps in Manila and a rescue mission was launched. It was Colonel Miller who found them and who arranged for their eventual return home. Miller told his Gestapo interrogators of the incident.

Because of the Luftwaffe's insistence that the Gestapo release downed airmen to Dulag Luft with the minimum of delay, the Gestapo chief of the Paris region, T.T. Schmidt, drove to Oberursel to discuss the matter. The Chief of Interrogation at Oberursel was Major Heinz Junge, who on 28 November 1938 was the Condor's *verkaufsdirecktor* (sales director) who had been the single passenger on the flight from Berlin to Tokyo to demonstrate the long-distance capabilities of the new civil airliner. After the meeting Schmidt asked Junge to tell him about it. Junge recounted the rescue and Schmidt casually remarked that he was holding an American colonel in Paris by the name of Joe Miller. Junge was convinced it was the same man who had rescued him in 1938. Schmidt arranged for Miller to be taken to Dulag Luft and Junge made a positive identification. Miller was put under house arrest at a nearby hotel before being sent to Żagań. (After the war Junge was sentenced to prison for war crimes. However, before the war ended, he had managed to get his family to Switzerland and on to Ecuador. Shortly after the war ended, Miller, who was head of the American military mission to Ecuador, learned that Junge's family were in need of money and he assisted them to return the favour!)

June 1944 at Luft III began with sunny days and thunderstorms in the evening but by far the biggest noise seemed to be on the morning of 6 June. Prisoners seemed to be running in all directions and gradually word spread that the Allies had established a bridgehead in Normandy. Every prisoner in the Reich had waited for this day. Celebrations followed and soon almost everyone was laying bets that the war would be over by Christmas. Morale received another boost when, on 21 June, almost 300 Eighth Air Force bombers flew overhead, their silver wings glinting in the sunlight. It only increased everyone's hopes of victory.

A newsroom situated in the West Compound theatre, which was completed by Russian prisoners in June 1944, displayed maps of the war fronts taken from German propaganda handouts. The camp also enjoyed hand-printed weekly newspapers called the *Kriegie Klarion* and the *Stalag Stump*. Both contributed greatly to morale. The Germans also provided two Berlin newspapers, the *Deutsche Allgemeine* and the *Volkischer Berbachter*. The only publication printed in English allowed on the camp was the *OK* (*Overseas Kid*), which was a German propaganda newspaper with selected news from America. All the German publications succeeded in doing was to keep out rain when wedged in various parts of the huts! Prisoners were also allowed to watch some American-made films such as *Orchestra Wives*. They were such a welcome change; no one seemed to mind the continual malfunctions of the camp projector. The 'Sagan Players' also presented three one-act plays and drew attentive audiences for a Shakespearian production and a minstrel show.

News of the capitulation of the German garrison at Cherbourg and the capture of 73,000 German troops 3 miles south of Caen reached the camp. In the east Russian forces were rolling ever westward on a 400km front. It all sounded very encouraging to success-starved ears. Further bulletins announced that American fighters and bombers based in Russia had bombed an oil refinery in Poland and in Italy there was an uprising.

FOOD PARCELS

ONE PER WEEK PER MAN

RED  CROSS

BRITISH

Condensed Milk	1 can
Meat Roll	1 can
Meat & Vegetable	1 can
Vegetable or Bacon	1 can
Sardines	1 can
Cheese-4 oz.	1 can
Margarine or Butter 1 8oz.	
Biscuits	1 pkg.
Eggs-Dry	1 can
Oatmeal	1 can
Cocoa	1 can
Tea-2 oz.	1 box
Dried Fruit or Pudding	1 can
Sugar-4 oz.	1 box
Chocolate	1 bar
Soap	1 bar

AMERICAN

Powdered Milk-16oz.	1 can
Spam	1 can
Corned Beef	1 can
Liver Paste	1 can
Salmon	1 can
Cheese	1 can
Margarine-16 oz.	1 can
Biscuits--K-Ration	
Nescafe Coffee-4 oz.	1 can
Jam or Orange Pres.	1 can
Prunes or Raisins	1 can
Sugar-8oz.	1 box
Chocolate-4oz.	2 bars
Soap	2 bars
Cigarettes	5 pks.

CANADIAN

Powdered Milk	1 can
Spam	1 can
Corned Beef	1 can
Salmon	1 can
Cheese-8 Oz.	1 can
Butter-16 oz.	1 can
Biscuits-soda	1 box
Coffee-ground-8 oz.	1 bag
Jam	1 can
Prunes-8 oz.	1 box
Raisins-8 oz.	1 box
Sugar-8 oz.	1 bag
Chocolate-5 oz.	1 bar
Soap	1 bar

REICH ISSUE

WEEKLY RATION

Army Bread-1 loaf	2100 grams	Soup-Oatmeal, Barley or Pea	3 times
Vegetables-Potatoes	400 grams	Cheese	46 grams
Other Seasonal	?	Sugar	175 grams
Jam	175 grams	Mare	215 grams
Meat		Salt	
Flour---on occasion			

Red Cross food parcel contents.

Left: Winston Churchill Parker and Geoff Parker, and their older sister Jessie.

Below left: Sergeant Churchill Parker, RCAF.

Below right: Harold 'Harry' D. Church who was shot down on the night of 3-4 November 1943.

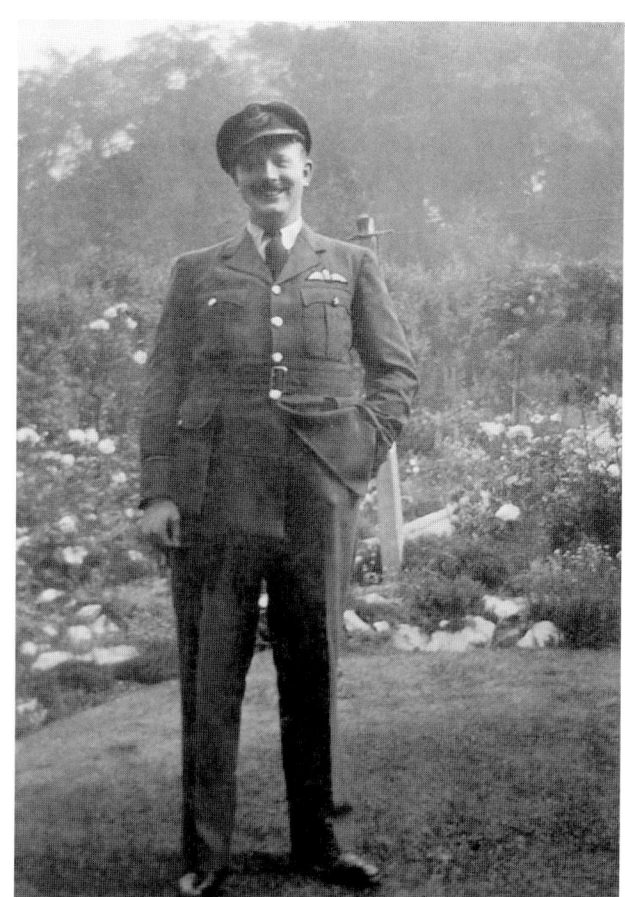

Right: Harold D. Church's pilot Flight Lieutenant Norman Henry Carfoot on 49 Squadron at Fiskerton.

Below: Harold Church's German PoW record card.

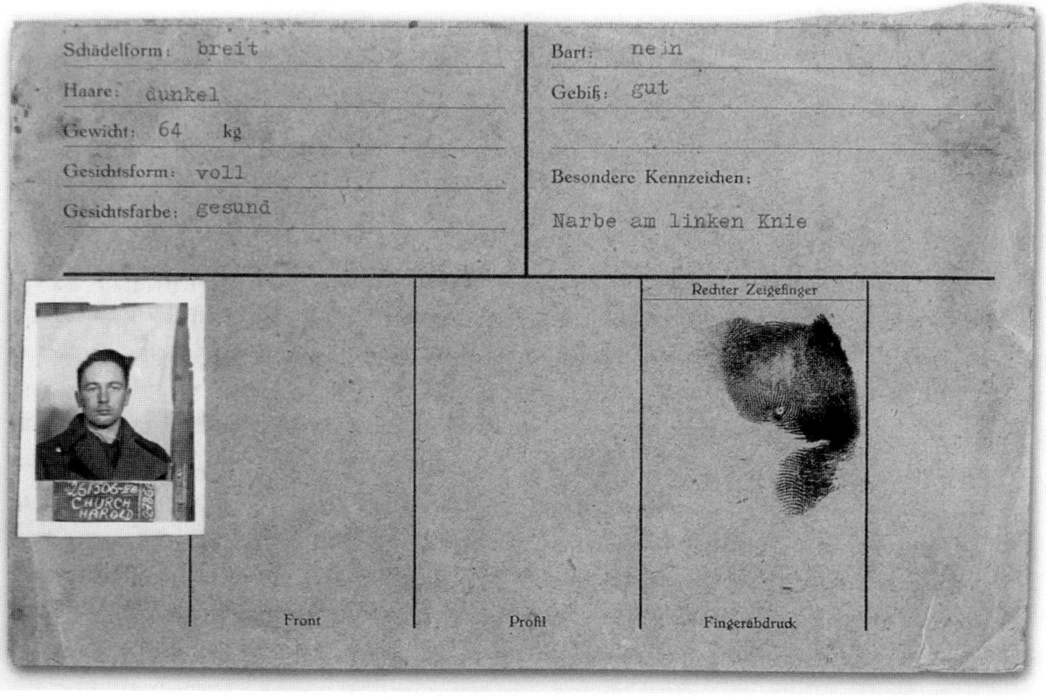

Schädelform: breit
Haare: dunkel
Gewicht: 64 kg
Gesichtsform: voll
Gesichtsfarbe: gesund

Bart: nein
Gebiß: gut

Besondere Kennzeichen:
Narbe am linken Knie

Rechter Zeigefinger

CHURCH
HAROLD

Front
Profil
Fingerabdruck

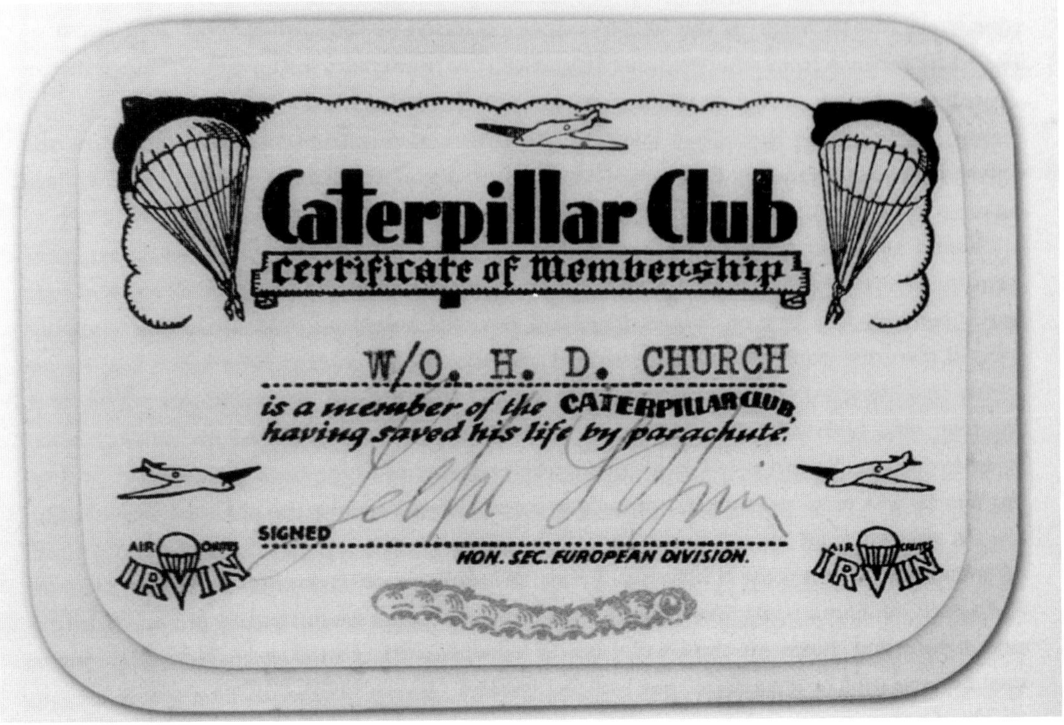

Harold Church's Caterpillar Club Membership card.

Lamsdorf carnival day, August 1944.

Stalag VIII-B located in the village of Lamsdorf, Ober Silesia.

"A" Lager - the backs of Barracks #1, 2 & 3, taken from a guard tower.

Stalag Luft IV at Gross Tychow, Pomerania.

Left: Navigator Sgt Edward Eddy Leo Humes, the only survivor of a Lancaster shot down on 11/12 April 1944.

Below left: Colonel Delmar Spivey who was shot down on 12 August 1944 during an inspection trip in England. He became SAO (Senior American Officer) at Stalag Luft III.

Below right: Colonel Joseph A. Miller, CO of the 453rd Bomb Group at Old Buckenham, which flew B-24 Liberators, who on 18 March 1944 was shot down and taken prisoner of war.

Jim O'Brien and crew in the 44th 'Flying Eightballs' Bomb Group at RAF Shipdham in 1943.

Jim O'Brien's Liberator, the *Rugged Buggy*.

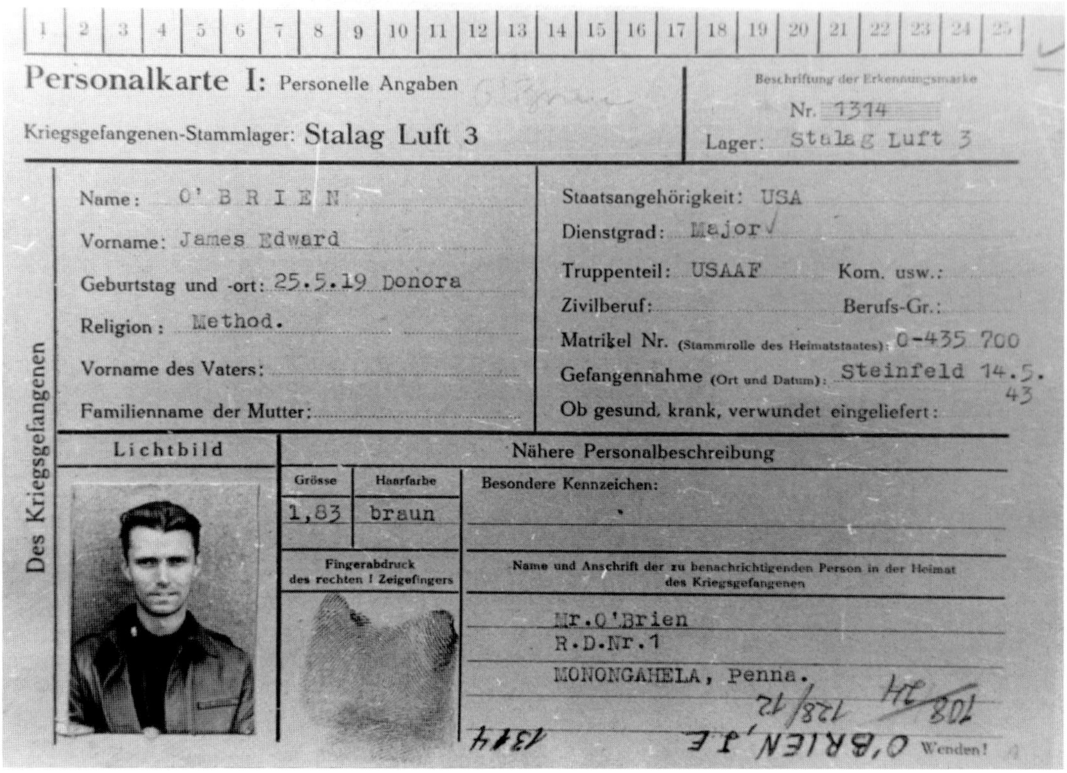

1 2 3 4 5 6 7 8 9 10 11 12 13 14 15 16 17 18 19 20 21 22 23 24 25

Personalkarte I: Personelle Angaben

Kriegsgefangenen-Stammlager: Stalag Luft 3

Beschriftung der Erkennungsmarke
Nr. 1314
Lager: Stalag Luft 3

Des Kriegsgefangenen

Name: O'BRIEN
Vorname: James Edward
Geburtstag und -ort: 25.5.19 Donora
Religion: Method.
Vorname des Vaters:
Familienname der Mutter:

Staatsangehörigkeit: USA
Dienstgrad: Major
Truppenteil: USAAF Kom. usw.:
Zivilberuf: Berufs-Gr.:
Matrikel Nr. (Stammrolle des Heimatstaates): 0-435 700
Gefangennahme (Ort und Datum): Steinfeld 14.5.43
Ob gesund, krank, verwundet eingeliefert:

Lichtbild

Nähere Personalbeschreibung

Grösse	Haarfarbe
1,83	braun

Besondere Kennzeichen:

Fingerabdruck des rechten ! Zeigefingers

Name und Anschrift der zu benachrichtigenden Person in der Heimat des Kriegsgefangenen

Mr. O'Brien
R.D.Nr.1
MONONGAHELA, Penna.

108/24 128/12

1314 O'BRIEN, J.E. Wenden!

Major Jim O'Brien's German PoW record card.

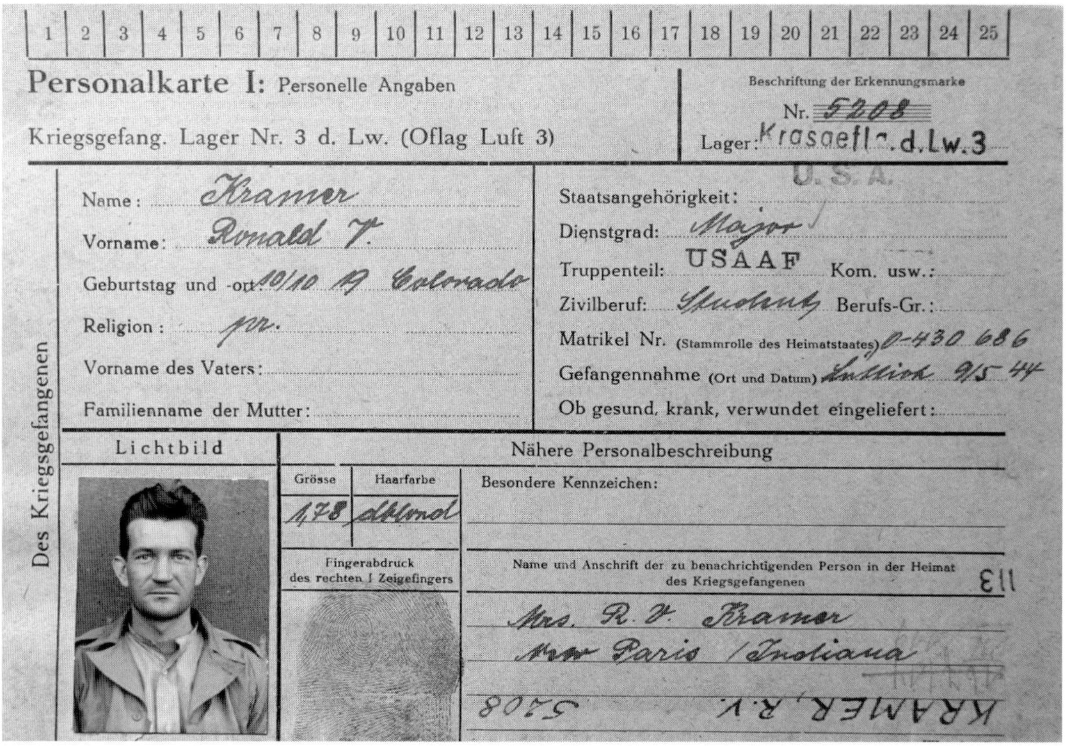

1 2 3 4 5 6 7 8 9 10 11 12 13 14 15 16 17 18 19 20 21 22 23 24 25

Personalkarte I: Personelle Angaben

Kriegsgefang. Lager Nr. 3 d. Lw. (Oflag Luft 3)

Beschriftung der Erkennungsmarke
Nr. 5208
Lager: Krgsgefl. d. Lw. 3

Des Kriegsgefangenen

Name: Kramer
Vorname: Ronald V.
Geburtstag und -ort: 10/10 19 Colorado
Religion: pr.
Vorname des Vaters:
Familienname der Mutter:

Staatsangehörigkeit: U.S.A.
Dienstgrad: Major
Truppenteil: USAAF Kom. usw.:
Zivilberuf: Student Berufs-Gr.:
Matrikel Nr. (Stammrolle des Heimatstaates) 0-430 686
Gefangennahme (Ort und Datum) Lüttich 9/5 44
Ob gesund, krank, verwundet eingeliefert:

Lichtbild

Nähere Personalbeschreibung

Grösse	Haarfarbe
1,78	dblond

Besondere Kennzeichen:

Fingerabdruck des rechten ! Zeigefingers

Name und Anschrift der zu benachrichtigenden Person in der Heimat des Kriegsgefangenen

113

Mrs. R. V. Kramer
New Paris / Indiana

5208 KRAMER, R.V.

Major Ron Kramer's German PoW record card.

Stalag Luft I.

The *Play Boy* crew in the 784th Bomb Squadron, 466th Bomb Group, Eighth Air Force shot down on 29 April 1944 on only the crew's eleventh mission, to Berlin.

B-24 *Play Boy* in the 466th Bomb Group at Attlebridge, Norfolk.

Consolidated-B-24 Liberators of the 44th Bomb Group 'Flying Eightballs' taxiing out at Shipdham for takeoff.

Flying Officer Patrick Graham Agur, RCAF pilot of Halifax II MZ302 on 429 'Bison' Squadron shot down on the raid on Metz close to the Franco-German border on 28-29 June 1944.

Hub Zemke's photograph for the German PoW record card.

Gerfangenen – prisoner of war gazette, September 1944.

John C. Morgan's B-17 which was shot down on 6 March 1944 on the mission to Berlin.

Above: John Cary 'Red' Morgan MoH lending a hand at Stalag Luft I.

Right: Lieutenant Colonel Charles Ross Greening who was imprisoned at Barth in January 1944.

Above: Telegram to Second Lieutenant Bernal Loraine 'Rusty' Lewis's wife, Helen, informing her that her husband had been reported missing in action, 19 December 1944.

Left: 'Rusty' Lewis of the 379th Bomb Group who was shot down on 30 November 1944.

Above: A convoy of Red Cross trucks carrying supplies for prisoners of war in Germany in January 1945.

Right: Sergeant Douglas S. Cady of 170 Squadron at Hemswell who was shot down on 16 March 1945.

PoWs from Oflag IX-A/Z walk away from village of Dachrieden in central Germany on their way east to Wimmelburg where PoWs were liberated early in April 1945.

An Avro Lancaster and repatraited PoWs during Operation Exodus at Lubeck in May 1945.

BEHIND THE WIRE

It all called for a celebration and it was fortunate that most prisoners had saved their food and cigarette rations so that on 4 July they could celebrate American Independence Day. Jim O'Brien recalls, 'We made liquor from potato peelings and sugar from our Red Cross parcels to mark our celebrations. We distilled it through a trombone supplied by the Red Cross but the first batch was undrinkable. It was so strong it took the plating off the instrument! A German guard was not so smart and wanted to drink our first, strong batch. It nearly killed him. We took his gun and credentials, knowing full well he would not tell his superiors.

'One hears of blind drunks and our home brew tasted so good, after a few drinks on empty stomachs the liquor caused temporary blindness! Drunks lying around the camp were thrown into the fire pool and the habit soon spread. Everyone, including all the senior officers, was thrown in. The Yankee Doodle Spirit of '76 band played Dixie jazz as they marched through the barracks. At first other nationalities thought we were crazy but soon they were in it more than we were.

'The most evocative moment of all came when we were allowed to sing the "Star Spangled Banner" at the end of the programme. A lump came to many a throat.'

Chapter 6

Gefangenennummer 331

Sergeant Jack Warrington was the flight engineer on Halifax II MZ302 AL-E on 429 'Bison' Squadron RCAF piloted by Flying Officer Patrick Graham Agur RCAF, which was shot down on the raid on Metz close to the Franco–German border on 28–29 June 1944. A total of 202 Halifaxes of 4 and 6 Groups with twenty-eight Pathfinder Lancasters hit the railway yards at Blainville and Metz for the loss of eighteen Halifaxes and two Lancasters. The combined loss rate was 8.7 per cent. Thirteen 'Tame Boar' crews were credited with twenty-one Viermots (four-engined bombers) destroyed.[1] 'Pat' Agur, Pilot Officer J. F. Kennedy; Flying Officer Donald F. Hay RCAF and Sergeant Keith K. Lyle RCAF on the crew evaded capture and, supported by the Resistance, reached the evaders' camp in the Forêt de Fréteval, where they could avoid being trapped behind the front lines safely away from the direct battle areas while they awaited liberation. MI9, together with Comète and local Resistance groups, hid 152 aircrew evaders in three perfectly organised camps in the forest between May and September 1944 under the very noses of German troops. Warrington and the two gunners, Sergeants G. E. Dunham and 'Ed' O. Clinton RCAF, were captured and taken into captivity.

'Unfortunately,' wrote Sergeant Jack Warrington, 'I can only start from the date of my unhappy last "op", which wastes 4½ years of rather unusual adventure.'

---

1. The Luftwaffe converted a number of Fw 190s into night fighters, using the 'Wilde Sau' (Tame Boar) tactic, which meant that they would fly over cities during air raids, without ground control, to attack Allied bombers illuminated by ground fires.

GEFANGENENNUMMER 331

I have read books about people who had some sort of premonition of any eventful happenings, but until we were shot down, I had no warning or feelings at all out of the ordinary. Briefing was quite normal, though the trip was further than the last few the squadron had done. My first night op I was rather excited – at last I was down to brass tacks. The daylight ops I did had been very easy, hardly more than a cross-country. We all went out to the kite, joking as usual – corny jokes without much point, but getting a laugh just the same. I talked the fuel system and all-up weights over with Pat and ate half my ration and loafed around, making last-minute checks, till Pat said "Figure we'd better start up, eh?"

'All the engines went OK; in fact, everything was wizard.

'Keith on the intercom: "Hullo, rear gunner. Intercom, OK?"

'"All OK here," came back from "Ed".

'Keith [Sergeant Keith K. Lyle, RCAF] checked everyone else. Jamie giving out the time check; the usual argument about half a second. "Don" [Flying Officer Don F. Hay, RCAF] saying the usual "Well I don't rightly know" in his attractive Western drawl. James's well-educated cultured voice coming back with the usual "Aw, you're full of prunes", sounding so incongruous from him. As usual, not a sound from Don, he could keep quieter longer than anyone I ever knew.

'We taxied out, behind the other kites, came the green, Pat's OK for take-off, Jack. Quick check, gills half open, temps and pressures OK.

'"Yes, Pat, she'll do."

'Pat's "off we go" and we were belting down the runway. I could see the ground crew watching us, sweating the take-off out, just as much as we were – "2,400+2". The crew going to their positions and everything settled down nicely.

'Darkness soon came down. I got the all-up weight at target worked out for Don and wondered for the hundredth time what it was all going to be like. I soon found out. The minute we crossed the French coast we were ringed by fighter flares, big yellow lights that made one feel twice as big as usual. Ed came on: "There's a fighter out there about 1,000 yards."

'Pat – "Well watch it. I saw a kite way out on the front beam."

'"A fighter on the port beam, skip. No! Sorry it's a Hally corkscrewing."

'Then it happened. A hell of a banging on the starboard wing and a fire at the trailing edge, inboard. I didn't feel a bit excited. It was entirely different than I had expected. I said, "We're on fire, skip. It looks like No.1 tank's bad. I'll turn the petrol off."

'"OK," said Pat. "Put on parachutes." He said it like he would say "have a cigarette" or "it's a nice day".

'I knew it was pretty useless, the fire was getting bigger, it was like a gigantic blowlamp; already the flames were as far back as the rear turret.

'Pat said, "Well, boys, it looks like an emergency."

'I acknowledged along with the rest of the crew. I looked at "Pat". He was sat there just like he was driving a bus. He said, "Jump, jump."

'I wanted to do something, but there was nothing, it was useless. I checked my chute and discarded my intercom and oxygen. I nipped smartly down the fuselage. The door was open. Don had gone. The kite was going pretty fast. I thought, "Well here goes" and dived out. I don't remember pulling the cord; the chute was swaying me about gently. My feet were cold and I suddenly realised that I had lost my boots. My left leg was aching at the knee. I felt awfully lonely, but glad to be alive. The sky was full of flares and I could see five more chutes. There was no dropping sensation. I began to wonder if I was going down at all. I could see a forest below me and suddenly I seemed to be dropping at a hell of a rate. I thought "Christ! I'm not ready" and I was down very gently with the chute on top of me. I felt like staying there, I was dazed and couldn't think coherently. I got up. The woods were silent.

'I walked away and could feel my leg stiff and hurting like hell. I went about 200 yards and thought "I'd better get rid of my Mae West". I dropped it near a tree. I wondered where the Jerries were. My leg was getting stiffer and when I came to a road I stopped and rested under a tree. I was lost and wondered where the crew were. I heard shots but I was too dazed to worry. The morning seemed ages coming. I wished like hell I could see one of the crew. I got up when it became light and walked down the road. My map was useless as I didn't know where I was. My feet were getting cut by the gravel on the road and my leg was giving me hell. I could neither straighten it nor bend it. My face was burned by the chute as it opened, I must have looked a sorry mess. I went down a bend in the road and found myself in the middle of a village. Some soldiers were sat on a wall. I walked on and had got past the Jerries when one came to ask me what the matter was. If I could have spoken French I would have got way; they didn't know I was English.

'The Jerry took me and fixed my leg. It was bruised across the knee. I must have hit the kite on the way out. I was given coffee. It was ersatz and I didn't like. He asked me for an English cigarette. I had none, so he gave me a

GEFANGENENNUMMER 331

German one. I realised then why he wanted an English one, it was like straw. He asked me what was going to happen to Germany after the war. He knew they couldn't win. He was in the last war and wasn't very interested in this one. Unlike the young Germans I was to meet he didn't believe in the "master race" propaganda. They put me in a small room and I found out that I was in a small village 10km south of Paris. Looking out of the window all I saw was the French people all looking at me. They gave me the V-sign and some of the women kissed their hands and waved. It heartened me considerably and I wished that I had been able to get in touch with them before the Jerry packed me up. I was given a receipt for my money and they put me in a lorry to go to Paris. I noticed that all the lorries and cars ran on producer gas and that the apparatus was neater than the ones I had seen in England.

'The trip to Paris was quite uneventful, I nearly choked on a piece of bread they gave me, it was black and sour tasting. In Paris everyone seemed to be cycling. The girls were the smartest I had seen for some time, very chic, in silk stockings and bright summer dresses. The weather was beautiful and I felt miserable being a prisoner. I still had no shoes and I had to walk along in my stockings. I was put in a cell, my first taste of solitary. They had left a pencil in my pockets so I made a calendar. The food was good, but I still didn't like the bread or the coffee. I used to try and make the guard jealous by telling him of the white bread and real coffee, but it also made me homesick so I stopped. I tried hundreds of ways to pass the time, the window was high up but I could see out by standing my bed on end and clambering up. I was opposite a park and could see the people walking about. I realised what freedom meant. The third day I was taken to an interrogator. We walked in the park; it was Sunday. The people made the V-sign when the guard wasn't looking. I enjoyed myself. The officer wasn't bad, when I refused to tell him anything we talked of England, and he gave me two American magazines. I read them the same night and the next day I read them again and the adverts backwards.

'They sent for me on the afternoon of the fourth day and we entrained at the Gare de l'Est for Frankfurt. The journey seemed interminable. The train kept stopping for air raids and I saw some bad damage in some of the railway yards. After 26 hours we arrived in Frankfurt. The bomb damage was terrific, I saw no undamaged buildings. I was told later that Berlin was worse still, it seemed very stupid and rather unnecessary to me. After another two or three hours. we arrived at Dulag Luft at Oberursel. I was put in a very small cell and really knew what solitary was then. We were only allowed to the toilet singly and I never saw another soul. We were not allowed to wash or shave. I was filthy and could smell myself. The windows in the cell were opaque so on the second day I forced them open. I tried everything to pass the time, but it was impossible. I recited poems; sang songs, cursed and considered. I took every fitting apart in the cell and longed for a smoke. I was hungry too, four pieces of bread and a bowl of soup a day. After three days I was told I would be moving. I couldn't stop laughing. I felt slightly drunk and the cigarette I scrounged was wonderful, but it made me dizzy.

'The next morning, we got two pieces of bread at 0530 and we entrained for Wetzlar, still unwashed, but happy just to have someone to talk to. There were several Americans. We were all filthy and dressed in the funniest clothing. We had two fags each for the trip, but I had been given a packet by a flight lieutenant who had pinched them. I gave so many away though that I had none left by afternoon. We were very hungry but got no food. We got to Wetzlar about 1500 hours and had to walk to camp, about an hour in blazing sunshine. We were all lathered in sweat, which made us smell all the more and three men flaked out. In the camp we were issued with a vest, pants, shirt, boots, three bars of toilet soap, one of common. We were unlucky as they had no razors or toothbrushes left, one towel and a kit bag. They gave us a shower bath, the water lasted for three minutes. It was the best shower I ever had.

'We lived in tents and had our first experience of Red Cross parcels, the only thing which makes life worth living as PoW. Food was good and we all felt happy. After two days we were sent to a permanent camp at Gefangenennummer 331, Stalag Luft VII Bankau. The journey took four days and nights in a sort of cattle truck, again no wash. For rations we had half a Red Cross parcel, half a loaf and a piece of sausage which stank of garlic so much that I couldn't eat it. I was never so browned off on a train before, the journey was ghastly. We saw bags of evidence of RAF and American bombing.

'Upon arrival we found a fairly new camp and soon got settled, six in a billet with a parcel per man per week, which makes very good food. I wish I could let mother know, as I know she will be worried. I am very happy though under the circumstances, especially as I picked "Ed" up at Wetzlar. I wish I knew where the rest of the boys were. There is a nice library here, I have a book of Russia short stories and there are several games to play. The best thing that has happened so far is the issue of this book, the best news that

Stalin is in East Prussia. The best bet, that we are home for Christmas. We are eight miles from Poland, about 25 from Czechoslovakia.

'As I became more settled in this camp I realised my colossal luck; so many men had lost members of their crew – killed, maimed etc. that I was very fortunate in being whole. A previous experience in Malta helped me to bear this life; the boredom was the only snag. I had a very good crowd of companions in the billet, three Canadians, one of whom was "Ed" my rear gunner, an Aussie and another Englishman who is an engineer also. Fortunately, "Ed" doesn't smoke, so I get his gags and cope just nicely. I have had a few books from the library, some good; the majority however rather indifferent. The camp has just acquired a few more sports' articles, softball, badminton, boxing, football, all are practised daily. We have a band too. Quite a happy camp.'

Two months after Jack Warrington was shot down, on the night of 18–19 August when the target was Bremen, Sergeant Richard Gerald 'Shorty' Enfield RAFVR, a Lancaster flight engineer on 428 'Ghost' Squadron, RCAF at Middleton St George, was captured after his aircraft was shot down by flak on the raid on Bremen. Arriving at Stalag Luft VII, 'Shorty' considered that he was lucky after jumping from his Lancaster, which was piloted by 25-year-old Canadian Flying Officer Cyril Mansford Corbet from Owen Sound, Ontario. He and his fellow Canadian navigator, 29-year-old Flying Officer Stuart Francis Bryans from Blyth, Ontario, were captured and sent to Stalag Luft III. The 27-year-old air bomber, Flying Officer Greville Llewellyn Jones, RCAF, was also captured and he was sent to Stalag Luft IX-C at Mulhausen. In Canada his wife Berna and seven children waited desperately for news that he was alive. Flight Sergeant Ralph Edward Good, RCAF, the 20-year-old rear gunner, was killed. Twenty-year-old Sergeant Thomas Davidson, RCAF and Sergeant Alan Rae Richard McNaught, the 23-year-old Canadian wireless operator, joined 'Shorty' Enfield in Stalag Luft VII.

'We were at about 18,000ft when I bailed out near Bremen,' "Shorty" wrote. 'All I could see were fires burning, the searchlights and flak over the city, but where I floated down it was completely dark. There was quite a strong southerly wind and as I weighed less than ten stones my descent took about twenty minutes. I could distinguish nothing below and had no idea when or what I was going to hit until "splash", I was underwater. As I was quite unprepared and didn't even have my feet together it was fortunate that I had gone into water. I came up under the canopy but as I was a good swimmer

I was able to detach myself and swim free. The water was salt so I knew I was in the sea or the estuary of the Weser. There was nothing to see but the fires and searchlights so I kicked off my boots and swam in that direction. After about a half-mile I found myself in saltings. Staggering up banks and falling down into more saltings, I finally decided to wait until light. Taking off my Mae West, I lay down and went to sleep.

'On waking I walked along the shore and finally found a little lane leading inland. Just as I reached a bend in the lane, round the corner came a German policeman on a bike and carrying a fishing rod. He must have had a shock because I was covered from head to foot in mud and orange sea-marker dye from the tablet attached to the Mae West. But he just rode past and said "*Morgen*," to which I replied, "*Morgen*" and kept on walking. A few seconds later I heard his bike go down and a voice said "Halt!" Turning round I saw he had a revolver pointed at me so the sensible thing to do was raise my hands. He took me along until we came to a small cafe on the main road. The people there must have been slightly sorry for this enemy because of the mess I was in. They made me a cup of ersatz coffee and treated me well, until I was collected by Luftwaffe people.

'Before being sent to prison camp I went through the interrogation centre at Oberursel. For about ten days I was kept in solitary and brought out each day or so for an hour and asked questions. They knew more about the squadron than I did! When I walked into the interrogation room there was a book laid on a table in front of me with the heading 428 Squadron. The questions ranged over all sorts of subjects, but aware they might try and trick me I stuck to the usual name, rank and number and nothing else. Many of the questions about the squadron I would not have been able to answer anyway. They asked the name of the CO and while I wouldn't have told them I honestly didn't know. They tried vague threats, but chiefly seemed to be trying to wear one down. They used to shut the windows and put the heat on during the day and at night open the windows and shut the heat off. This and the most atrocious food – black bread and weak soup – must have been all part of the treatment to break your morale. There was no contact with any other Allied airmen, but one day when I was being escorted to the toilet, I found the fellow from the next cell was also being taken there. He was a Wing Commander who complained bitterly that somebody in passing had whipped his good shoes – which had to be placed outside the cell each night – and left a battered old pair in their place.'

GEFANGENENNUMMER 331

'At Stalag Luft VII the guards in the sentry-boxes were changed at the same time every day,' wrote Jack Warrington. 'The relief guards always marched up along the other side of the wire singing marching songs. A whole bunch of our people would form up in threes and when the guards arrived, they would march along beside them inside the wire singing "Roll Out the Barrel" and other ditties at the top of their voices. Each group tried to out-sing the other, although we probably drowned them out because of greater numbers.'

'Well we have now been liberated for fourteen days,' wrote Warrington, 'and nothing has been done to get us out. There has been a wizard battle round the camp and 120,000 Germans were captured. The area is pretty clear now and tomorrow I am breaking out to make my way to the "Yank" lines about thirty miles away. I have come to the conclusion that it will be the quickest way home.'

After making his break for freedom from the camp, Warrington wrote: 'Today is Thursday, 10 May. Since last Friday four of us have been on the road to proper freedom. We have had the time of our lives. Friday, we stayed in a house that was evacuated, had mushrooms, spam, potatoes, beans, asparagus, pancakes and gooseberries. Saturday walked to Zahna, tapped a "Russkie" for beds. He barged into a house and told the people to feed us and give us beds – or else. The Germans get rough treatment from the Russkies. The people were good though and had a very interesting talk with them. They burst into tears when you tell them that the Yanks aren't coming there. Sunday arrived at Wittenberg and found that the "Yanks" were not there, but at Bitterfeld, about 50km further. Pushed on the Entzsch. A woman asked if we were French, but seemed even more pleased when we said no, but English. Decided to stay in Entzsch.

'We found a flat which formerly belonged to one Baron von Schele. Running water, electric kettle, toaster, bath, shower and oceans of clothing. Next door lived three women, who were only too pleased to have us about for protection from the Russians, who rape the women wholesale. We were so comfortable that we stayed until Wednesday. We pressed on to Gossa, where we had a good experience. Feeling hungry we asked a Russkie for some food – we picked the right one as well. He had been a prisoner for two years, so couldn't do enough for us. We got white bread, a cake, bacon, sausage and eggs, so we asked him for a bed. He dived into a farm and told the people to feed us tonight and in the morning and give us a bed. If they didn't, he would shoot them. Then he went away and came back later with white bread preserved plums and cherries (about 20lb), 5lb of bacon and two big German sausages. When he went away again, we had another good meal and this morning had bacon omelette for breakfast. We were in a good position. The Russians would do anything for us and the Germans were all very friendly because having an Englishman in the house was protection for the women; we couldn't go wrong. This morning we crossed the Mulde River and are now safe and happy with the Yanks. We had a marvellous holiday. Just now we are waiting for transport to take us for a bath and clean clothing etc.

'All is good!'

After his return to the UK, Warrington wrote: '... I was sent home on leave and then received orders to report to Wittering, where I expected I would soon be demobbed. Instead, I was told I had to undergo a Rehabilitation Course to turn us from obstructionists into complying with discipline again! There would be no demob until my age and service group number came up – in my case two years later.'[2]

---

2. Jack Warrington died in November 1987.

Chapter 7

Wheeler's War

Potato peelings are saved and boiled up again as soup for an evening meal. From the two slices of black bread, which, with half-a-dozen rotting potatoes and a mug of turnip or millet soup, is your ration each for 24 hours of sub-zero cold, you cut the crusts and shred them into crumbs ... Mixed with water and a hoarded spoonful of ersatz German jam made from turnips, the crumb pudding is a weekly treat. Generally, we have it on Sunday night. It's very important that the pudding should be eaten at night, for its becoming increasingly difficult to sleep at nights ... There are of course, fleas, bed bugs and lice, but then they have always been with us. Bouts of dysentery on a diet of rotting potatoes also disturb the night with hasty visits to the stinking, frozen latrine pit inside the barrack door.

Geoffrey ('Sqizzy') Taylor, RAAF, from his book *Piece of Cake* (George Mann, 1956). Born in 1920 in England, he arrived in Adelaide at the age of 3. By the age of 14 he had won a cadetship and became the shipping reporter on the *Adelaide News*. He joined the RAAF in 1939 and became a Lancaster pilot with Bomber Command. After being shot down by Friedrich-Karl Müller in 1943, Taylor spent the rest of the war as a PoW in Stalag Luft IVb, Mühlberg on the Elbe.

On the night of 23–24 September 1944 RAF Bomber Command attacked three targets in the Reich; 549 aircraft raiding Neuss, 136 Lancasters of 5 Group attacking the Dortmund-Ems Canal near Ladbergen, just north of Münster and 107 Lancasters bombing the German night-fighter airfield at Münster-Handorf. From 923 sorties, 22 aircraft were lost. One of the fourteen Lancasters that failed to return from the Dortmund–Ems Canal raid was

STORIES FROM THE STALAGS

LM718 QR-K on 61 Squadron at Skellingthorpe flown by Squadron Leader Hugh Wilkinson Horsley AFC. It was shot down by Hauptmann Ernst-Wilhelm Modrow and Feldwebel Schneider of 1/NJG1 flying an He 219A-2 'Owl'. Two of the crew were killed. Horsley, Pilot Officer C.A. Cawthorne DFM and Sergeant R.T. Hoskisson managed to evade capture and return to England. Flying Officers J.C. Webber and Johnny Wheeler were taken prisoner. (Horsley re-joined 61 Squadron and resumed operational flying, as did Hoskisson. On 1 February 1945, both were briefed for a raid on Siegen but their Lancaster crashed on take-off, killing Horsley. Hoskisson survived.)

'The night fighter attack on "K-King" on the night of 23–24 September 1944 and the following defensive corkscrew tactic was a terrifying experience,' wrote John Wheeler. 'And when the skipper finally gave the order "get out" I quickly ejected the escape hatch in my bomb aimer's compartment. In front of me was a black hole through which the slipstream whistled and an occasional flash of light could be seen far below. Time seemed to stand still as the emergency drill ran quickly through my mind: Don't bale out feet first as the slipstream from the aircraft could force the lower part of your body backwards and you could decapitate yourself as you left. Check that your parachute is securely attached to the harness. Head between legs, kneel at the side of the exit and roll out. If sufficient height left, a quick count to ten and deploy the parachute.

'After clearing the aircraft, the first sign that I might survive the night's traumatic events was the jerk on the parachute harness that indicated the canopy had deployed and I was floating serenely down to earth. Shortly afterwards I experienced an intense feeling of relief that I had managed to get out of the aircraft alive but at the same time wondered how the rest of the crew had fared. In the distance the sky was lit by searchlights and apart from sporadic flak the only noise I heard on the way down was the drone of Lancaster engines high above as the heavily laden bombers continued their way to the target. One advantage of bailing out in the dark is that all your muscles are relaxed as you hit the ground and therefore you minimize the chance of injury to your ankles. I landed quite safely in a field full of cabbages.

'The main points of the aircrew Escape and Evasion lecture continued to run through my mind. We were told, "Once on the ground get rid of any evidence as to your whereabouts." I quickly rolled up my parachute and harness and looked for somewhere to hide them. Close by I discovered a small pond, so without further delay I hid the gear amongst the reeds and then weighted it all down under the water with large stones. I then moved away from my landing area as quickly as I could and hid behind a boundary wall and took stock of my situation.

'Fortunately, I had managed to get down without losing my flying boots. This was a bonus because I was wearing the older type of suede boot with a zip fastener which were notorious for coming adrift under such circumstances. In order to help me formulate a plan of escape I took out the escape kit from my pocket. Amongst the things in front of me were:

'Small silk maps of the area we were flying over.

'Currency – Dutch Guilders, German Marks, French and Belgian Francs.

'Concentrated chocolate bars and Horlicks tablets.

'Water purifying tablets.

'Also, one of my battledress buttons could be converted into a magnetic compass. The top portion of the button unscrewed and when turned over became free moving on its base. In order to evade enemy forces, we were advised to walk by night and sleep by day.

'As we were flying over Holland when we abandoned the aircraft, I decided to try to join up with some of our Airborne forces still fighting in the Arnhem/Nijmegen region. I did not know that the decision to withdraw the Allied troops from Oosterbeek and Nijmegen sector had already been taken and the area was full of German troops.

'I remembered we were flying over the city of Eindhoven when our aircraft was attacked by the night fighter, so I estimated my present position to be about 20 miles south of Nijmegen. Feeling confident, I set off north and hoped to get my bearings from the next village I came across. Unfortunately, it was not to be because as I made my way down a narrow country road, I was suddenly accosted by a German soldier who was on guard duty outside a small village. Although I did try to make a break for it without too many histrionics, I was surrounded by German soldiers within a few minutes.

'After being searched and relieved of a packet of cigarettes by the guards, I was taken to a forward command post where I was interviewed by a young German officer. He asked me if I had anything to say, to which I pointed out that my cigarettes had been removed. The guard who had them was still with me and he received quite a rollicking from his superior and the cigarettes were returned to me. Thank goodness I had been taken by front-line troops. My school language lessons were becoming very useful, enabling me to reply to all questions in German with my name, rank and service number. I also quoted the Geneva Convention of 1926 as to what I was allowed to say as a prisoner of war.

'After a short while I was taken under escort to German Headquarters in a large staff car. When we arrived, the place seemed to be in complete chaos and I began to think and hope that it wouldn't be too long before the Allied troops overran this sector. Unfortunately, it was not to be and after further questions I was bundled into another staff car, which took me at great speed from Arnhem to a civilian jail in Nijmegen. Artillery and small arms fire could still be heard in the vicinity of the Nijmegen Bridge and again my hopes were that I would soon be released by Allied forces. The Dutch prison officers were very kind and there was a great feeling of optimism among them and the local Dutch population. Regrettably it was premature. Two days later I was taken from the jail under armed escort for the journey to the German Luftwaffe interrogation centre at Oberursel near Frankfurt am Main. We joined a column of captured airborne forces from the Arnhem area. Amongst the British and American paratroopers and glider pilots were a few more RAF types and we were all herded into the infamous enclosed rail wagons. Lieutenant Colonel McCardie of the South Staffordshire Regiment was the senior British officer present and we helped him look after the walking wounded until they could be sent to a German hospital. Most of this group had survived ten days of intense fighting around Oosterbeek and I had the utmost admiration for their courage, tenacity and humour.[1]

'Upon arrival at the Oberursel interrogation centre we were each allocated a sweat box. Originally designed for solitary confinement, the sweatbox was a small cell the temperature of which was controlled from outside and used to soften up prisoners prior to interrogation. There were, however, so many prisoners from Arnhem that these solitary cells were holding up to eight PoWs at a time.

---

1. Lieutenant Colonel W. Derek H. McCardie had served in the Territorial Army before the war and was given command of the 2nd South Staffords on 7 April 1943, shortly before the battalion left for North Africa. Upon his release from captivity, McCardie joined the Parachute Regiment and was given command of the 17th Parachute Battalion in Palestine. He died on 3 April 1977. See *Air War Market Garden: Shrinking the Perimeter* by Martin W. Bowman (Pen & Sword, 2013).

'The usual methods of interrogation were applied, but fortunately we had been forewarned of these German methods by our Squadron Intelligence Officer and were prepared. I think the German authorities were embarrassed by the number of prisoners at the centre and after seven days we were on the way to our permanent Kriegsgefangenlager (prisoner of war camp).

'The following rail journey showed us just how much the Allied bombing campaign had affected the transport system throughout Germany. On our way north we passed through Rheydt/Mönchengladbach, a large rail communications centre, which we had bombed a week before, and there were still only a couple of lines intact taking any form of traffic.

'Later the same day we were attacked by American fighter aircraft. The train suddenly stopped with a jerk and all the German guards jumped off the train and disappeared into the ditches that ran alongside the track. Fortunately, the strafing attack was not too accurate as we were left locked inside the cattle trucks.

'The camp was located near the town of Barth on the Baltic coast some 30 miles west of Stettin. From the camp we could see the test firing of V2 rockets from the area of Peenemünde. It was a typical PoW camp with its posten [sentry] boxes, barbed and electrical wire, guards, dogs, machine gun posts and huts raised above the ground so that tunnels could be located more easily. The guard dogs, let loose in the compounds at night, were often lured under the huts, where they were dosed with a sprinkling of pepper in order to control their ability to pick up scents. Tunnels in the camp went up to 52 with no success. Over the last tunnel attempted in the camp a notice was erected by the German Kommandant with the following words:

R. I. P.
Roses are Red, Violets are blue.
This goddam tunnel makes fifty-two.

'Routine for the day started with the emptying of the barrack blocks by the guards followed by the Appel (roll call). This was in the form of an outdoor parade inside the compound. Depending on how we felt, this could take up to two hours since there were many ways of putting doubt into the mind of the Oberfeldwebel (Regimental Sergeant Major) who was responsible for giving the number of prisoners present to the officer in charge of the parade.

STORIES FROM THE STALAGS

'Subject to availability, breakfast consisted of one or two slices of German ersatz black bread. This was a strange concoction. When mixed with water on the fire stove in the room it would cement bricks together! Lunch and dinner were usually a helping of very watery soup supplied by the Germans from their cook-house, with one slice of bread. Sometimes sauerkraut, turnips and other vegetables were supplied by the Germans but these became very scarce towards the end. Apart from the soup collected from the German kitchen, all our cooking had to be done by ourselves on a coal-fired field stove within the room.

'If Red Cross parcels were available, they supplemented the diet. The contents of a typical British Red Cross Parcel were as follows:

1 tin of Nestle's condensed milk
1 packet of prunes or apricots
½lb of margarine
1 tin of bacon, salmon or pilchards
4 oz of cocoa (Terry's or Rowntree's)
12oz tin of corned beef or Gallantine
1 cake of soap
4oz slab of chocolate
1 slab of Tate and Lyle sugar
1 tin of cheese, ½lb of biscuits
1lb tin of jam
Creamed rice or fruit pudding
2oz of tea
1 tin of curried beef
50 cigarettes or 2oz Tobacco
1 tin of Tate & Lyle syrup

'These Red Cross parcels were excellent, but I cannot remember at any stage anyone receiving one parcel per person per week. It was always a shared ration and we received no parcels for three months in the autumn/winter of 1944 and none for the last two months of the war.

'Life inside a prisoner of war camp presents an ideal situation in which to study factors affecting morale. Factors such as the weather, quality and quantity of food, lack of home news and a continuous diet of censored news influenced our day-to-day outlook on life. However, by using various clandestine methods we did manage to receive the BBC news reports at least once a day, so by comparing the BBC broadcast with the German news service it was possible to keep track of the Allied army's progress during the last six months of the war.

'Mail from home became almost non-existent. From my arrival in the camp, in late September 1944, I received no mail until two letters on 25 December and three more in February 1945, one letter in March and one in April. A letter posted in Dover on 28 December 1944 had a stamp on it saying "This letter formed part of undelivered mail which fell into the hands of the Allied Forces in Germany. It is undeliverable as addressed and is therefore returned to you". This was returned to its sender at the end of hostilities in Europe.

'Home mail was naturally a great boost to morale, except in some cases where "Dear John" letters were received. Some letters were humorous and others very sad. A few excerpts are given below:

> *If you need any money let me know* – to Lieutenant H.B. – from his mother.
>
> *I have been living with an army private since you were shot down, but please do not stop my allowance as he does not make as much money as you* – to an RAF Sergeant from his wife.
>
> *I knew I should have kept you here and joined the Air Corps myself. Even when you were a kid I knew you would end up in prison* – to Lieutenant D.M. from his father.
>
> *When and if you return, I'd like a divorce. I am living with a cadet and wish to marry him. He's wonderful and I know you'll like him* – to Lieutenant V.R. from his wife.
>
> *Do you get to town often where you are?* – to Lieutenant M.L. from his wife.

'The German camp guards were kept busy all day with roll calls and searches for possible escape activity. To the prisoners these unfortunate guards were known as Goons (two pounds of shit in a one-pound bag) and were baited constantly by the prisoners from the time they opened up the barrack blocks in the morning until the night shift left. They were also taunted with threats of being posted to the Russian front. One particularly successful time-wasting raid was carried out by the prisoners on the German Administrative Block situated in the Vorlager. Many documents were stolen and destroyed. This resulted in our being locked outside our huts for about eight hours whilst the Goons carried out a massive search. Nothing was ever found. Occasionally the Germans complained to the British and American senior officers about the use of the word Goon by the prisoners. The following notice was displayed in the camp during July 1944:

> Kriegsgefangenlager No. I, Barth den 2.7.1944
> de Luftwaffe. Gruppe II
> To Senior American Officer North Compound
> Senior American Officer South Compound
> Senior British Officer South Compound
> Re Use of the word GOON
> The use of the word Goon was granted to prisoners of war by the Kommandant under the condition that this word would not have any dubious meaning.
>
> It has, however, been reported to me that prisoners have been using the phrase "rocking goon up", the meaning of which is beyond any doubt. Consequently, the use of the word Goon or Goon up is prohibited, severest punishment being inflicted in future disobedience against this order.
> Shroder leiter gez
> V Gruppen.
> Major

'Fuel became very scarce during the winter months. Our bed bunks consisted of straw mattresses on top of wooden slats. These slats of wood provided excellent fuel and by the end of our time in the camp we were sleeping on an average of two slats per bunk.

'During a lifetime one meets certain characters who are outstanding and their qualities remain in your memory. Such a character was Captain the Reverend H.A.M. Mitchell from Dunedin in New Zealand. He was our camp padre. For a time, before and after Christmas, food was very short and roll calls were eventually taken inside the barrack blocks as many of us were suffering with a degree of malnutrition and quite literally passing out during any form of exertion. It was well known that Captain the Reverend Mitchell had passed on his very meagre rations to those he thought were in greater need, until one Sunday morning during his sermon he became a victim of these privations and passed out! The effect of his work, his cheery disposition and simple, very practical faith had a great influence on keeping up the morale of the camp. At Christmas 1944 he conducted the camp Carol Service. His meticulous organisation down to the printing of the service sheets with the facilities available within the camp had to be experienced to appreciate his untiring energy. The Remembrance Service in November, held on the parade area, was also an example of his indomitable spirit in difficult circumstances. After Christmas 1944 German rations became scarce and Red Cross parcels non-existent and it was not until late March 1945 that there was a slight improvement. The end of the war was now in sight with the Allies as very obvious victors. Our typical menu for the first four months of 1945 based on German rations, no Red Cross parcels being available, was as follows:

Breakfast	2 slices of toast from German ersatz bread with turnip jam. 1 cup German ersatz coffee.
Lunch	1 slice toast with turnip jam. 2 slices toast with mashed turnips.
Dinner	Stew (?) consisting of German-issue soup, potatoes and turnips.

'Note: by saving bread it was possible to make one cake with no fruit.'[2]

---

2. *Thundering Through the Clear Air: No. 61 (Lincoln Imp) Squadron at War* by Derek Brammer (Toucann Books, 1997)

Chapter 8

Life as a PoW

Flight Sergeant Denis Innell Humphrey[1]

After a few days' break from operations, 3 Group sent 150 Lancasters back to the Gremberg railway yards at Cologne on Sunday, 28 January 1945 when two of the twenty 218 Squadron aircraft failed to return. Crews began arriving over the target at around 20,000ft shortly after 1400 hours to face accurate heavy flak. Wing Commander William John Smith's Lancaster was hit repeatedly, sustaining in the process damage to the front turret and the airscrew lever quadrant and the trim control next to the pilot's seat was also smashed. Undeterred, Smith, operating in the role of deputy base leader, continued on his bomb run. The operation was led by 35-year-old Warrant Officer Gilbert Davey Evers piloting Lancaster PD296 'E-Edward' on his 30th and last trip of his tour. Evers had a reputation within the squadron of being an exceptional pilot, having been a pre-war regular, who left the RAF to join Imperial Airways. When war was declared he re-joined the RAF with something like four thousand hours in his log book. Apparently, he had refused a commission, but there was absolutely no doubt that he was a very senior pilot on the squadron and was known in the mess as 'Pop' Evers. Operating as group leader for the squadrons of 31 Base, the crew contained an additional navigator, Flying Officer F. Norton. 'Edward' was hit by flak over the target. Evers managed to regain some control, but the Lancaster was hit again by flak and went into a dive, crashing near Bergisch-Gladbach about 14 miles from the target, killing all except Norton, who was badly

---

1. *Memories of a Lancaster Navigator*, WW2 People's War.

LIFE AS A POW

injured. LM281 flown by Flight Lieutenant V. M. Hodnett was hit by flak just before bombing and the Lancaster was observed by other crews to be losing height with both port engines feathered. All seven men successfully abandoned the aircraft to its fate, to spend the rest of the war as PoWs. It had been the crew's seventh operation and Hodnett's tenth.

'After five, ten, fifteen minutes maybe,' recalled Flight Sergeant Denis Humphrey, the navigator on Flight Lieutenant Hodnett's crew, 'I'm walking through this forest and suddenly there's a figure ahead, coming towards me. Now I can see as he gets closer that this is a kid in uniform, he's somewhere between fourteen and fifteen, so the question is "what do we do now?" So I thought well, I'll walk past him, I'll say "good day" and hopefully he will ignore me. But before I could get close enough to him to say "good day" he said to me "*et zu Englander?*" Well, I knew what that was and when I saw the little Luger pistol strapped to his belt, I thought "oh blimey, yes I am". So I admitted the offence and put myself in his little hands and I really think the bugger wanted to shoot me. The first thing he said was "pistol".

'In all my time in the services I think I fired every sort of gun, from a Lee Enfield .303 rifle to a Browning machine gun through to a Sten gun and all the rest of them – and the only thing I never fired was a handgun. So, in the wisdom of the bureaucracy of the RAF they issued all aircrew each with their own .45 Colt. What a ridiculous thing to do. This pistol was enormous and it must have weighed two pounds, at least that's what it felt like. And the ammunition was so large: .45 is damn near half an inch, so you've got a bullet that's the best part of half an inch wide. All of us in the RAF agreed that the best place for these bally weapons was left in the billet. And that's what we did with them – mine was locked up in the locker and there it stayed.

'Well, this bloke's asking for a pistol I haven't got, so I opened the front of my blouse and I show him all around the top of my trousers and he eventually twigged and says "*nix pistol?*" Well, I know what he's talking about then, so I nod and say "*nix pistol*" and he says "*kommen zei mit*", which I gathered meant "come with me you wretched man". So, away I went with him.

'He led me to a farm house somewhere outside the south-west side of Bonn, I suppose it must have been, and I was taken in front of three German officers. There was a bit of a misunderstanding first of all because I made it plain to them that I didn't speak German and they said "no, but you speak in English and so do we", so that was that. And then it's a question – it's drilled into you all through your service – if you're captured all you give is your rank, name and number. So, it was a question of repetition. Rank, name and number. Rank, name and number. And they got a bit tired of this, so they sent me outside to the – I suppose the farmyard. And two youngsters – two infantrymen – were behind me and they prodded me up on top of a load of farmhouse muck. Now, this farmhouse muck was stacked up in the corner of a pair of wooden gates and a wall, so there am I like an idiot, up to my ankles in what's-his-name with my hands held up and two blokes behind me playing with the – I think they were tapping the clip of their rifle sling against the barrel. There's a clip there and if you move it properly you can make it click and this click-click-clicking was going on behind me. And after the first five minutes – or rather during the first five minutes you're afraid you're going to be shot. And during the next five minutes you're afraid you're not going to be shot because every time your arms drop down, they come along and they bump you at the bottom of the elbows so up go your arms again – it gets a bit fatiguing after a time.

'After I suppose about fifteen minutes, they brought me in from this and they stuck me in a room, sat me on a sort of settle and put two young SS men who were about 19-21 to guard me. One of them said "For you the war is over". I sort of said "Yeah, I know all about that mate but you are SS". And they said "yes". I twisted my fingers together and I said "*SS-Gestapo ist ein*" ("are one"). And oh, my word that didn't half put the cat among the pigeons; that really upset them. They were nothing to do with the Gestapo; they didn't want to know anything about them. The Gestapo was "this, that and the other". After that they quietened down a bit, once they'd convinced me that they were not Gestapo, because one of the things the intelligence officer had said to us – they knew most things that went on in Germany – but one of the things he said to us was, "Recently the prisoners have been taken over by the Gestapo and if that happens to you, I'm sorry, I can't help you." He walked out of the briefing room and we thought, "Oh blimey, well that's nice." And here am I, in with a crack German regiment, the SS, whom I believe are closely associated with the Gestapo.

'We settled down for a while and then I was taken to meet the rest of my crew, who had all been rounded up with the exception of the bomb aimer and the rear gunner. So that left five of us together. They took us outside, marched us and formed us up in line and they marched us away. About ten in the morning, a bright day, not a cloud in the sky and suddenly there appeared five Flying Fortresses going to bomb Bonn, about six miles down the hill. As they approached the town, Jerry threw up four or five anti-aircraft shells and they popped up with their usual lump of black smoke and all those Flying Fortresses turned right and flew away and they dropped their bombs on open ground. We bloody nearly wept.

'Now where they marched us to, I've no idea but it was something that looked like the bottom of a windmill, it was probably the bottom of a hayloft or something there was plenty of straw about and they indicated that we should make ourselves a bed with this straw, which we did.

'And then time started to pass. I'd eaten about half past five on the Sunday morning, so we bedded down in Germany on the Sunday night. Came the Monday morning, it wasn't warm. In fact, it was damn cold. There was still snow on the ground so we were doing exercises to try and warm ourselves up. There was no mention of food and all we could do was chat amongst ourselves and lay on this bundle of straw. And so Monday passed. Tuesday dawned and was a repetition of Monday – nothing to do, plenty of time to do it, nothing absolutely happening. The German army administration must have been just about as good as ours, because we were still there on the Wednesday.

'On the Wednesday afternoon about 4 o'clock somebody brought along a billycan thing with some soup in it and they indicated that we should try and find something to drink this soup from. So, we all started looking around and we found odd tins. Some of them had rusted right through, but we plunged them into the old soup and we drank the soup from them and it tasted absolutely vile. It was a filthy dirty grey colour and the taste was really obnoxious, but it was something to eat and it more or less warmed us up a little bit. But when I looked at the tin, I'd used I realised why it had tasted so foul – it was an old DDT tin! Now DDT was the old wartime flea powder, they used it for everything. Anything that crawled, flew or moved DDT would knock it off. But needs must when the Devil drives.

'On that particular Wednesday they moved us to a French prison camp nearby. In one corner there were a couple of dozen American infantrymen. God knows how long they'd been there or how long they were going to be there, but us five were shoved up there with them. We kept very much to ourselves because the old American infantryman's a bit of a lout – a bit of a rogue, and we weren't very impressed with them at all. (I don't think they were very impressed with us!)

'We were housed then in breeze block huts, I think the roofs were corrugated iron, but all the walls were 18ft × 12ft breezeblocks, 4½ft thick and it was still damn cold; there was still snow on the ground. The only thing we had to sleep in was some bits of old sacking that we'd found, Hessian. The only way we could keep warm was to huddle up to one another, lying on the concrete floor. We weren't on ration strength so once again we went a bit short of grub. They only catered for Frenchmen but they did manage to squeeze out for us half a cup of soup each day and half a cup of water. We had nothing to wash in, we just had half a cup each day for drinking and I think this must have gone on for about seven or eight days.

'During this time, we were all sent to an office in the HQ and the swine stole our flying boots. They were basically a wool-lined shoe with a fur-lined piece attached to it. It was stitched in such a way that if you managed to get away you could cut the stitches, dump the leg part and you had an ordinary looking pair of shoes. They were most comfortable. They were taken from us and in their place, we were given snow overshoes. Terrible things, but beggars could not be choosers and we had to put up with it.

'We settled down one night, we'd dropped off, I was asleep, when I got a dig in the ribs and my flight engineer said, "Hey look at this "Den", we're going to be in the middle of this lot." Looking out of the windows we saw two green flares descending and the old briefing came back, "Always bomb the green, always bomb on the green." Pathfinders put these flares down right over the target, you see and the ordinary bombers come along and they bomb on the green lights; that is their target. Now pathfinders do this because they're so bloody clever at navigation that they are never wrong, but in this case, they were about five or six miles out because Bonn, which was their target, was five or six miles down the hill.

'Everybody was woken up and we were out of that cement hut like long dogs. Dotted around the place were trenches, six-foot deep, 18 inches wide, about six-foot long and, of course, we made for those straight away. We got well down into them and it was a good job we did, because all hell broke loose. I won't say it was a thousand-bomber raid, it was probably five, six hundred of the lads up there, but they sent down tons of it and all so quickly it was unbelievable, it was all over in about eight minutes. When we returned to our huts there were about four lumps of concrete about four foot long six inches thick and about a foot wide, right where our heads had been. If we'd been there, we'd have got crushed to a pulp.

LIFE AS A POW

'We started to gather our stuff from under all this rubble – the bits of Hessian we slept in, our boots and that sort of thing and gathered them all together. The wire fence had been blown down and the lights had been put out, obviously, but before you could say "jack-knife", in all the gaps in the fence there was a German guard with a dog. Once that was all over and we left that camp we walked in as column down the road, only about eight or nine miles to another camp. As we marched through the gates somebody spotted our uniforms and they separated us. The five of us were put on a truck and taken to a railway station. We had no idea where we were going, but it turned out to be an interrogation centre at Frankfurt. We'd been together for a couple of weeks or so and we had been boosted by each other's company, so we were quite chipper. We arrived at Frankfurt station and again had to march, with a platoon of guards and an officer, towards the interrogation centre. At one time we halted and we hung about and then the English-speaking German officer said to us: "You will notice that your guards have been doubled. This [is] not to stop you escaping, this is to keep you from the German civilians. You are going to walk through Frankfurt. Do not laugh, whistle, talk or look up," and we continued the march. The inference was that we could escape if we wanted to but we'd do better to stay where we were because we were being protected. Needless to say, we all stayed where we were.

'You could march with your head down and quietly turn your head to one side and look up and see what was going on but quite honestly there was not, relatively speaking, two bricks one on top of the other. The only movement was people trying to sort the rubble, get it tidied up in some sort of manner, but other than that there was absolutely no life in the city at all. And so we finished up in our interrogation centre at Dulag Luft. We were one each to a cell and as a crew we were well separated, one from the other. This started quite a quiet, slow, lonely existence. To draw attention to yourself alongside the door you had a flat key set into the wall, which turned. As it turned, it lowered a chunk of steel, which dropped down outside the cell door and went "clang, clang, clang" and the guard then knew that you wanted something. You used this to go to toilet but they were very careful that you were on your own in the toilet. You never saw another soul and you never spoke to anybody; the guards wouldn't speak to you and you were quite frankly in solitary confinement.

'About ten days later I was thinking it was about time I saw an interrogation officer. I woke one morning and my left eye was closed up with my face swollen and the left side of my neck was absolute agony. I dropped the flag to call the guard and he came and opened the door and I made signs and he twigged that I was sick. I was put on the sick parade. This involved going to see the doctor. It was still very, very cold, there was still plenty of snow on the ground and the doctor was very busy – patients were queuing up in a long line all around the corner of this room that was his surgery. His desk was in the corner and next to that the length of the room was a bally great big radiator and it was pounding out heat like a furnace. It was really battling on and it felt wonderful to stand by this. He didn't know what was wrong with me but he stuck a thermometer under my arm and then turned away to attend to the next patient. Well, that was wonderful for me so I leant on the radiator and it was red hot! God knows what temperature that thermometer went up to but by the time he turned around to look at me I was standing up straight again and he took the thermometer from under my arm. The next thing I knew, I'm in a motor car being taken to a hospital run by nuns and it was a very pleasant place to be. There was an orderly, destined to look after me, who I called "Adolf". He was a nice enough bloke and he put me into bed. This bed was immaculate, the sheets were absolutely spotless, as were the pillowcases and I hadn't seen sheets in weeks. This was going to be a bit of all right. And then he told me to undress. My golly Moses, I was filthy!

'In Stalag Luft I'd been sleeping on the normal Geneva Convention of, I think it's five boards four inches or so wide. You had to have one under your ankles, one under your knees, one under your hips, one under your shoulders and one under your head. If you can get more than that you're more comfortable, but that is minimum that the Geneva Convention says you are to have. Whilst I was there all I was sleeping on was a sack affair, filled up with wood shavings. In the French prison camp to which we were attached we'd had no washing water. And in the two weeks or so that I was in the interrogation centre I'd had no washing water. I had had nothing and I was in a right state. I must have stunk like the back of a sewage works. Old "Adolf" held up his hands in shock-horror and I said *"nix Wasser"* and he understood, so he put me into bed and it was gorgeous and I think I slept for about three days. I was awakened by a Luftwaffe officer standing by the bed and he said, "Well sergeant I have got no questions for you. I know all I want to know about you and your lot." I said, "Oh do you sir?" He said, "I've learnt all I want to know." I thought, "That's good; that lets me off the hook." What he did tell me was that we were supposed to follow our "Gee-Leaders" on the daylight raid because he was an expert on "Gee". He'd been shot down on his thirty-first flight and they'd all got lost.

'He went and then "Adolf" came in and he put me in front of a sink with some hot water in it and he gave me a razor and a bit of soap and I had my first wash since I didn't know when. He stood over me all the time to make sure I didn't cut my throat with the razor, although it was a safety razor, and then I had to try to get this growth of beard off my face. All I had was a bit of toilet soap of a sort and one razor blade. I lathered it up as best I could and wetted it as well as I could and "tore it off".

'Once I was fairly presentable, I was sent back to the interrogation centre and on the way out, lo and behold they gave me twenty cigarettes. By golly what a gift that was! Why they did it I've no idea but they did. We were put into a room to await transport to Frankfurt railway station and prison camp. We didn't know where we were going but we were going to Nuremburg but because of air raids, train schedules were all up the creek and we had to wait about twelve hours at Frankfurt station. We were in a sort of waiting room and we got our heads down. I was well dozed off when all of a sudden, I got such a hammering on my legs I woke up and realised that some swine of a bloody guard, escorting a single prisoner, had hammered me across the ankles with his rifle. It woke me up pretty sharply and he did this because he wanted one of the chairs my legs were on. The prisoner that this fellow was transporting was quite a pleasant bloke and of all the wonderful things he had, he had some bread and jam and he gave me a couple of slices and by golly it was good. Unfortunately, somebody else woke up and they all wanted bread and jam but by that time it was too late; the poor blighter only had a couple of bits.

'Eventually we were loaded on the train and put into cattle trucks with doors that slid down the side. We lay on beds of quite generous amounts of straw. It wasn't uncomfortable. When, suddenly, the engine stopped, there was a deadly hush and we heard that an American Mustang was about. They took a great delight in strafing railway trains because apparently when you hit a steam engine with a cannon shell it blows up in quite a spectacular fashion and they loved it. The German guards locked us in and went and laid on their bellies alongside the railway line! We had a Mustang pilot in the truck with us and he was damn near going berserk. You didn't know whether to lay down the length of the truck, in the hope that the shells and the machine gun bullets would go each side of you, or lay across the truck in the hope that they would go the other way each side of you; it was quite a dilemma. We weren't attacked, fortunately, but the officer in charge of prisoners and the officer in charge of Germans had a right "up and downer" by the side of the railway. The former told the latter that if anything like this ever happened again on this journey, he would make very certain he was up for war crimes. The Germans had it at the back of their minds by then that they were losing the war and so it was agreed that whatever happened we wouldn't again be locked into the cattle trucks.

'When we left the trucks, we were walked some miles to a most strange place. It was a prison camp and I suppose there were German guards somewhere but I never saw one. We were met by Americans and the officer told us we would not be there long and then he asked us if we had lice would we please move "over there". So, with others we were marched into a store room and given American uniforms. We were told to take off all of our clothing but to keep our battledress jackets, which showed our rank and brevets. After that we had our head hair cut off and our heads were shaved, so we looked a peculiar lot. Then we were guided into some hot showers and had a good cleansing wash (oh bliss) and scrub to get rid of the lice. After getting dry we changed into the gear with which we had been issued; and what an issue. There were two high-necked long-sleeved vests and two sets of long johns (long-legged underpants), a pair of khaki-coloured trousers, two pair of socks and a pair of American infantry boots and a woollen scarf. I must say we looked a bit strange in all the khaki and a blue jacket, but the jacket was essential for identification purposes. We were then taken back on a parade and told that all the Red Cross parcels were pooled and we would eat in the mess. We were also told that because we had been lice infested, we were being got rid of the next day.

'Eventually we arrived at our camp at Nuremburg. It was an Oflag, or officers' prison camp. Of course, one of the reasons that air crew were all given rank – we were all made sergeant – was so that under the Geneva Convention, the Germans couldn't make us work, because anybody below the rank of sergeant could be made to work and a lot of privates and the rest had to work down coal mines and in cattle stations and God knows what else. They were used very nearly as slave labour but fortunately having the rank we had that didn't happen to us and once we got settled down in the camp all we had to do was pass the time. We had plenty of packs of cards from the Red Cross parcels and I taught one or two of them to play crib and by the time we finished everybody played crib. We held cribbage drives and that used to pass an evening quite happily.

'I'd made up my mind when I first got shot down that under no circumstances were [sic] I going to try to be a bloody hero and try and escape. I realised by then along with everybody else that the war was fast coming to an end. British and American troops were on the Meuse and it wasn't going to be long before they were on the Rhine and all we had to do was wait for them, which was basically what we did. Another way of spending our time was to walk round and round the wire.

'When we'd been in this camp a while, we were all gathered together and the officer i/c [in charge] told us that we were on the move and we were going to make a march. And we were instructed on what to do with certain contents of the Red Cross parcels. To make iron rations we mixed oats up with condensed milk and let it dry and put cocoa with it and all that kind of flaming rubbish, because they told us it was going to be a longish walk. Well, it turned out to be a walk from Nuremburg to Munich; about 180–200 miles. With something like 12–15,000 prisoners, this was quite a march to organise, but the one thing the Germans were good at was organisation. And we had with us guards well into their sixties and I suppose given the chance we might have got away, but it really wasn't worthwhile even trying and the whole column when it was spread out seemed to be about a mile and a half, which was fortunate for me because I was about two thirds of the way down from the front of the column. We were on our first day's march when all of a sudden, we were strafed by a bloody Spitfire. It only hit the front of the march and I don't think anybody was killed, but I saw the most amazing thing the next day because the blighter returned. We took shelter, but our part of the column was up a hill and as we looked towards the front of the column down in the valley at the side of the road in a field there were the three letters 'PoW' which must have been something like eight foot – ten foot long, made with food tins. The sun was shining on them and they were reflected in a silver brilliance. Fighters came over again, daily and they seemed to be checking our position on the road and I think this observation must have lasted for the next five or six days.

'At night we slept where we could, when we could, but fortunately for us in the main the weather was quite good and we used to nestle down in ditches and in fields. Before we left the prison camp, we'd each been issued with one blanket and that was a very useful thing to have, because you could roll yourself up into it and get yourself lost and it was very comforting. We paired up and if we came to a village, we had our Red Cross parcels and if there was anything in it that was improved by cooking or we wanted to put some potatoes with it which we'd knocked off from the fields we got to the stage of such confidence that we would knock on the doors of the village houses and go in and cook our meal. Where we got the impertinence from, I don't know but we did. We were the conquerors; they knew we were the conquerors, it wasn't finished yet and while they didn't exactly welcome us in, they let us and we went in and we did what we wished in their kitchen – never took anything, never hurt anything. We used their pots and pans and left them to wash it up.

'One day, walking along these roads in between these forests in the area of the Bavarian Alps we came across some wooden huts. Along with my flight engineer we went into these wooden huts and it was the first night's sleep we'd had under a roof for days and days and days. Being a nosy sort of Scot – he was on the top bunk – and he went rooting around among the rafters of this wooden hut and he came out with a packet of tea wrapped in a bit of old brown paper. We looked at each other and I said, "Do we smoke it or do we drink it?" He said, "Let's smoke it." Now that was a silly decision really because we should have drunk the bally stuff first, dried it out and then smoked it afterwards, but we weren't bright enough to think of that then. The only thing we had to roll it in was bits of German toilet roll, which was alright for what it was intended but wasn't a lot of good as cigarette paper because it was so porous and as you sucked in air the cigarette was going out so the answer was to keep on licking it. It was quite pleasant, thank you very much.

'The march became quite routine. The Red Cross met us on the road every other day with half a parcel each and they really saved our lives. As the march went on, the poor old German guards got more and more shattered. Early one morning I woke, it was daylight and it was hammering down with rain. I was lying in a pool of water; my blanket and all my clothes were absolutely saturated, but 20, 30ft from me in this pouring rain the South Africans built a blooming great big fire. This fire must have been going up 20ft; it was enormous. Where they got the wood from, how they did it, I've no idea, but I woke and there was this wonderful warm air coming from this fire and it was great. It was so big and it was so hot that we actually managed to dry everything off. The Germans came along and said "put the fire out" but nobody took a lot of notice because it was daylight and it dried everything off. It was a real Godsend. Eventually we got to our final camp at Munich. We didn't know it at that time, but the German plan was that we were to be held as hostages for certain conditions that they wanted to lay down at the end of the war.

'Count Bernadotte, the great peace-maker, was at this camp and we got a whiff that something was up. At about this time we heard heavy gunfire in the distance as the troops got closer. Then one glorious morning an American tank drew up outside the wire. They were surprised to see us and had no idea we were there. We yelled and screamed and called at them to come and knock the wire down and bring their tank in, but they wouldn't. It turned out that it was General Patton's mob – General "Pearl Handle Revolver" Patton. From then on we knew that it was all over and we were going home.'

Chapter 9

Raid on Nuremburg

The RAF seemed to have a calling for me and when a local branch of the ATC (Air Training Corps) was formed at Halesworth in June 1941, I quickly became one of its first members with the then Headmaster of St. Lawrence School Mr. E. Wurr becoming the commanding officer of 1486 Halesworth Suffolk Flight. It turned out to be a wonderful preparation for the RAF. The year I most vividly recall was 1943 when I, at just eighteen years old, was called to the colours in so much that I was recruited into the ranks of the Royal Air Force. On 6 September I left behind all those who I knew and indeed loved and travelled to the still great city of London to report to the Royal Air Force recruiting centre at the Lord's cricket ground. As I left Halesworth railway station in the old steam train waving farewell to the local vicar, the Reverend Tong who had kindly transported me from Chediston to the station, little could I imagine what the next four years held in store for me. I don't think I have ever felt so lonely as I did on that day because outwardly, I was surrounded by thousands of people each going their separate ways and yet inwardly I sensed a real true feeling of loneliness.

Doug Cady

'On 22 May 1944 I attained my greatest ambition in so much that I gained my flying badge and from now on, or so I hoped, flight engineer was to be my full-time occupation. I was soon "crewed up" with a crew of a Lancaster bomber and we started our flying training. Everything went along fine until I fell sick and had to go in hospital for six weeks involving an operation and my place in my crew was soon taken by another engineer. My greatest blow was yet to come; on leaving hospital I was informed that I was being grounded for three months. The weeks that followed seemed to drag wearily by until I had another medical and was pronounced fit for flying again. I soon met another crew skippered by Pilot Officer Arthur Steainstreet. Born in Rotherham in 1920, he was the first child of six children. In 1942 Steainstreet married in the town and a daughter was born early in 1945. The other members of the crew – all sergeants – were 23-year-old Robert Surtees, navigator from Haverton Hill, County Durham; J. Burns, bomb aimer; S. W. Kirk, wireless operator; Ronald Charles Rayment, air gunner, aged 24 from Grays, Essex and Cyril Edwards, rear gunner, aged 23 and married, to Margaret Eluned Edwards, of Llandiloes, Montgomeryshire.

'Once again started my training with them and we soon had completed our flying training when, in early March, we were posted to 170 Squadron at Hemswell in Lincolnshire flying Lancasters. More extensive flying training followed and we began to wonder when we were going to start our operational training.

'Ron Rayment and I were special pals and our cycle rides through the lanes of Lincolnshire on our government-issue cycles were memorable; like the time when we returned from leave 24 hours before the eventful night, when on Friday, 16 March 1945 we were told that we were on "ops". Ron recalled how he thought his case seemed rather heavy when he went on leave and he found two bricks in it when he got home and, although I was blamed, I was in fact entirely innocent! Ron was also so proud of the fact that he had become engaged to his girlfriend on the previous six days' leave, the future was so full of expectation but was to be so short of jubilation. As we met at our pre-arranged rendezvous at one of the "watering holes" of Lincoln and travelled back to Hemswell, little did we suspect that life fuelled by the cruelty of war was to claim four lives from our party of seven and in less than 24 hours they would be lying in the tangled wreckage of Lancaster "K-King".

'A tense feeling of excitement seemed to creep over us and when we finally learned that our target was Nuremburg, we began to wonder what we should feel like at the end of the eight to eight-and-a-half-hour trip. We were carefully briefed and then made our way to our respective aircraft ("K-King"). The usual procedure followed, the checking of the aircraft, the warming up and checking of the engines, until at 1730 hours approximately we taxied to the runway to await the final signal for take-off. It finally came and I carried my hand behind the throttles as the pilot pushed them gradually forward to full throttle. Slowly we increased speed until we eventually became airborne and a quick glance to my left as we sped down the runway revealed to my eyes that we were being cheered on our way by those gallant ground crews. This was really it!

'Having become airborne, we had to make our way over Reading, this being the forming up point, so to speak, of the entire force. It did not seem to matter which way we looked as there were aircraft in every direction and finally, we set our course to Nuremburg. The hour or so that followed turned out to be quite uneventful until about 2115 hours when our navigator said we were nearing our target and we were also flying at a predetermined height of 16,000ft. Suddenly, as if from nowhere, the whole plane lit up as though it were daylight and then there was darkness again. I very quickly checked my instruments which seemed OK and then the voice of the mid-upper gunner broke the deadly silence over the intercom reporting a fire in the rear gun turret. The pilot repeatedly tried to contact the rear gunner over the radio but with no avail, so, he instructed the wireless operator to go to his aid. Almost simultaneously I noticed that our entire port wing had caught fire, the pilot must have noticed this also, because the next words he uttered were "abandon aircraft". I could not seem to realise what this really meant, my heart missed a beat yet I knew it was either jump and take my chance or remain in that fiery furnace which, at any moment, might explode as our bomb bays were full of our quota of bombs which were intended to rain death and destruction on Nuremburg yet which might, at any moment, mean death to the seven persons that were in the plane.

'I fitted my parachute to my harness and took my place behind the bomb aimer, being placed second to jump from the aircraft. The seconds that followed seemed like hours and I soon realised that the bomb aimer was having difficulty in opening the hatch. He struggled with it for several seconds, then suddenly the plane went into a terrific dive. What happened next, I do not remember until I "came to" in mid-air and found myself falling at a fast speed through space. I looked down at my parachute through the mist which seemed to hang over my eyes and discovered I had in my excitement put it on upside down, the release handle was now on the left instead of the right. Nevertheless, I pulled it and my descent was halted somewhat abruptly! I floated the rest of the way at a more moderate speed not knowing where I was going to land, the night being very dark, so I had to hope for the best. Suddenly I hit the ground with a terrific bump and, having fear of my parachute taking me along the ground, I quickly released my harness complete with parachute. I then tried to recover myself and take bearings of my surroundings. I discovered the mist which seemed to hang over my eyes came from blood, which was gushing from a cut in my head and running down my face. Also the forefinger on my left hand was broken, my clothes were torn to ribbons and my boots appeared to have fallen off in the descent. Apart from this and numerous bruises I was intact, so I gathered.

'I tried to think but my thoughts seemed miles away with the other aircraft which continued on their course powerless to help us who were not so lucky. As I sat there, of one thing I was certain: any decisions to be made I had to make myself and the people I was near were not of a friendly nature. As I sat under that tree, I was conscious of a light flashing near me with every move I made of my body. This I found to be was a signal lamp attached to my "Mae West" which I was still wearing and became ignited with each movement of my body. The thought which flashed through my mind then was had this light betrayed my presence to the enemy? My eyes by this time were becoming somewhat familiar with the surroundings and I could see in the distance an outline of a farm house. Having decided that escape was rather out of the picture with no boots I decided to try the building.

'Picking up my parachute, I made my way very slowly because I was stiffening up from my fall. My presence was betrayed by the barking of a dog. As I approached my parachute became entangled in some bushes so I left this and knocked loudly on the door, the sound echoing through the quietness of the night. I became aware of someone behind me and as I turned, I was confronted with an elderly man, standing there with his hands raised high above his head. I quickly did the same so we both stood there as if we were about to commence some native war dance. The door of the house was soon opened and I was taken inside. The welcome was not exactly overwhelming although the house seemed to be full of people of both sexes. I had not been there long before a member of the German army appeared, who quickly searched me and then neatly took a seat beside me.

'While we sat there a woman seemed to resent my presence. She shook her fist at me angrily and pointed towards in the direction of the raid. She was firmly rebuked by the soldier. The time dragged wearily by. As I sat there, I tried countless ways to make my captors understand I should like a mirror to view my face and to survey the damage done to my head. After several attempts at this I was provided with one and what I saw rather shocked me and it could only be explained, no more or less, as a bloody mess! Having still got my first aid kit, I produced a bandage from it and put it around my head. When we had sat there for what seemed like hours the door opened and two members of the Volkssturm (Home Guard) arrived. We left the house and made our way along a rough cart track. I found the going very difficult as I was now starting to feel the effects of my landing and also the track was very rough to my stockinged feet. After quite a distance we arrived at a public house. To my great surprise and greatest joy, sitting there with his hands tied firmly around his back was the bomb aimer. The look on his face showed a great deal of surprise at my appearance but at the same time he was overjoyed to see someone he knew. We knew it was useless to try to talk. The other people in the room viewed us with a great deal of suspicion and did a great deal of talking but we did not understand what they were saying. Then presently, their eyes fell upon my stockinged feet and after some discussion a pair of boots was produced for me to put on. I donned these with some difficulty and pointed out to a lady the state of my trouser leg and she promptly gave me a monstrous-looking hat pin for me to keep one side together.

'After a while we were taken out into the cold night air accompanied by a member of the German Army who had a bicycle. While we were walking slowly along the cart tracks another soldier caught up with us and said something to our guard. He then turned, pointed to us and said "comrade". This gave us new hope of a member of our crew being alive. We continued our journey until we came to another house. We were viewed in the same way as before. We sat there thinking, while my frequent requests for water were ignored, until it seemed someone understood what I wanted and bought a glass of what tasted like ginger beer. Suddenly the door opened and a rather pathetic figure entered. To our joy we saw that it was my wireless operator. He too had lost his boots and had cut his parachute harness up and tied it to his feet with cords from his parachute. As we sat there my captors viewed my "newly won" boots and these were taken away from me. The bomb aimer was forced to give me his flying socks as he still had his boots and socks.

'Having sat there for about an hour we had to be on the move again, a horse and cart being provided for our transport. As we travelled silently over the rough cart tracks my mind went back to my base and, knowing that my comrades in other aircraft had now returned, our presence would now be missed. My thoughts went back to those at home who, with the dawning of a fresh day, would receive a telegram with those dreaded words "We regret to inform you" and I realised for the first time that for me at any rate the war was over or, at least, the fighting part of it was.

RAID ON NUREMBURG

'We travelled slowly along, the silence of the night being our only companion, until we finally came to a fairly long hill, whereupon the members of our company, with the exception of myself, were made to get out of the cart and help push it up the hill. At long last we reached a small town and we were taken to the house of what seemed like the local chief of police or something, and then taken to an upstairs room where our identification cards were taken from us and anything else in the way of papers we happened to be carrying. Presently a tall bald man entered the room and came towards me and, on removing the bandage which covered my wound on my head, proceeded to dress and rebandage it. He, I supposed, was the local doctor as his appearance seemed typically German.

'After much consultation between various people in the room, two us were taken to a room with a single bed its only piece of furniture and given to understand by means of a watch that we had until 0615 hours to get some sleep, the time now being 0315 hours! The other member of the crew was taken to a separate room. Sleep didn't come very easily that night as I felt too stiff and sore to rest much at all. The next three hours seemed to drag wearily by until almost on the dot at 0615 hours we heard the key turning in the door and we were on the move again. When we came out into the cobbled streets again it was getting quite light and we began another walk, which when we arrived at the end of it we found we were at the local railway station. We went into the waiting room, which was almost deserted, but we had not been there many minutes when it became full to overflowing, with the three of us being eyed with a great deal of suspicion by the local population.

'When our train finally arrived, I discovered only about a dozen people in the waiting room were actually waiting for the train, the rest being there from morbid curiosity! We boarded this rather ancient-looking "express" and, much to the annoyance of the other passengers on the train we were, all three of us, found seating accommodation and some very harsh words were exchanged between our guards and the members of our rather crowded compartment.

'After making several stops at various stations, we finally came to what appeared to be our destination and were told in German to get out. We were bundled into a rather queer-looking lorry and taken on a short journey by road. On alighting from this we found ourselves in what we took to be a fairly large army camp and were ushered into a large office where members of the female sex were busy typing away on noisy typewriters. They all seemed to stop automatically when we entered the room and viewed us with a great deal of curiosity. We then passed through this large airy room into a smaller room, which appeared to be the office of the camp commandant. He asked us various and numerous questions, which were answered with the usual words "I'm afraid I can't answer that", much to his apparent annoyance. When he finally appeared to run out of questions, we were taken to a small room on the other side of the building, which turned out to be the bunk of a German NCO and we were closely guarded by an armed soldier. Time seemed to stand still; we were being allowed to smoke any cigarettes we possessed but definitely forbidden to talk. During the afternoon a junior officer brought photographs to our room to show us and much to our delight these turned out to be snaps of the other four members of our crew, these being found on them. We tried to learn from our captors of the fate of our other four comrades but from what we could gather it seemed apparent that they were dead.

'As we were sitting near a window, we had a good view of what was happening outside and it was from this window that I saw my first jet aircraft, it being of the German type! The day dragged wearily on and life outside went on much the same as usual, giving us a grandstand view of its continued activities. Food was brought to us during the latter part of the afternoon, consisting of a water-like soup and quite tasteless to our appetites, not having eaten since about 1600 hours the previous day. As darkness fell, we were taken from our quarters for the day and bustled into another queer-looking lorry. We were taken for some miles until we arrived at what appeared to be a German air force camp. Having been taken into the guard room we were confronted by a room full of typical German Nazi-type youths. From the grins on their faces and their conversations it seemed apparent they were really making fun of us.

'Our clothing was searched and we were relieved of the burden of our braces, nobody caring if our trousers slipped from around our empty stomachs to our ankles. A German officer entered the room, the NCO in charge calling the whole company to attention; we were then addressed in fairly good English by a man of roughly 35 with a badly scarred face (this we later learned he received during air operations, he being a pilot). Amongst other things he said there would be no talking and the three of us were then taken to the guard room cells which, to our amazement, we found to be full and standing in the passage outside were three RAF prisoners showing signs of surprise at our entrance but we were unable to say anything. "Our" officer, before he left, told us we would stand up for four hours and sit down for twenty minutes. He then left us guarded by a young German, whom we later learned could speak good English. He was very fair and allowed us to sit down all the time but at the slightest sign of a noise outside we had to fly to our feet and stand to attention; this I found very difficult as I was now very stiff from my parachute landing.

'During our wait in the passage I heard a noise coming from inside one of the cells and later I learned that this contained an Australian who was the pilot of the other three RAF chaps who were with us. He had been very badly burned and during the night I came for the first-time face to face with death. The shock having proved too much for him, he surrendered his life for the fight which we were all engaged, freedom. I knew that one more telegram would arrive, in due course, at some anxious loved one's home, "We regret to inform you", and one more name would be added to the monuments which are throughout the length and breadth of the world to reminds us that their sacrifice must not be in vain.

'In the morning I was taken for so called "medical treatment" and it was then that the Germans discovered my watch, which they took from me but to my surprise gave it back to me before I left an hour later. Before our departure for an unknown destination a guard entered the cells carrying a number of flying boots picked from the surrounding countryside. To my utter amazement I found amongst them one of my own, which I paired up with another unclaimed one and so now at least I could move with a little more comfort.

'The time finally came for us to be on the move again and we were issued with a newspaper parcel containing a portion of "black bread" and tasteless margarine. We finally boarded a train, where there were six of us now including also two guards, and as the train moved slowly from an unmanned station, we all of us, I am sure, wondered where our destination was to be. We travelled steadily along until the train came suddenly to a halt in a sort of valley with trees growing on either side and all the passengers began to pile out of the train and head for the shelter of the trees ... we remained on the train. We gathered from our guards that an air raid was in progress nearby and everybody was afraid that the train would be attacked by supporting fighters. Eventually the train moved on again as the alarm proved uneventful and we finally arrived at another unnamed station and our stay here proved to be a long one as the railway line ahead had been bombed, which made it impossible for our train to proceed to its destination. While we were here a further air raid alarm sounded and along with the guards we were afforded the comparative safety of the station air raid shelter. After what seemed like hours it was finally decided that we could not go on, so we had no alternative but to go back and take a different route. So it was that the journey started again and we travelled along, until darkness overtook, us when our train stopped at a fairly large railway station and out we had to get.

'We were taken into a dimly lit but rather overcrowded waiting room, where its occupants seemed little interested in our arrival as most of our company were service personnel who we assumed were either going on or returning from leave. We sat squatted on the floor of this waiting room for a while until suddenly the stillness of the night was broken by the wailing of an air raid siren, which caused much confusion as our company hurriedly disappeared to the air raid shelter and we were left with our guards in the now empty waiting room. Time passed slowly until we heard in the distance the dull drone of aircraft, which we assumed to be our own and did not feel too happy about it either! Apparently, our guards felt the same because after some consultation amongst themselves they signalled for us to go and we were taken to an air raid shelter, which we discovered was reserved for station officials as we assumed that the guards were too afraid to take us to the general shelter because of the inevitable reaction of the occupants on seeing our Royal Air Force uniforms.

'Luckily for us our particular town was not the "target for tonight" and in due course the all clear was sounded and we went out again into the cool night air to await the arrival of morning and a train to start our journey again. The next day passed wearily on and we had to walk from one part of a town to the another as the railway connecting the two had been bombed and put out of action. This had happened at several places and we really got a first-hand view of what devastation and destruction the RAF had really caused.

'Finally, we came to a station the name of which I vividly remember seeing marked with the one word "MUNCHEN", which I took to meaning Munich, and here we were told to get out. Once out in the street we started to walk until we saw a tram-car approaching, which stopped and onto it we were loaded by the guards and off we went. As we went along the miles of devastation, we saw a party of British PoWs working in the streets, they recognised us as being captives and they waved as we went by. After travelling for quite a while, out we had to get and our guards took us to sit under the shade of a group of trees, the spring sun being very kind to us, where one of the guards took a photograph of the group apparently for the "family" album!

'Presently, a smartly dressed man came over to us and to our surprise spoke to us in a broad Yorkshire accent! We being uncertain if this was a kind of trap to make us talk, we treated his presence with the utmost caution. Finally, our guards stopped a passing lorry and we were all loaded on to it and our journey started again. Eventually we arrived at what appeared to be a kind of military camp, where our lorry stopped and we were ordered to get out and made a grand entry through the main entrance gates.

'Once inside we were all ushered into a rather large but empty cell and the iron gate was firmly locked behind us. This did not remain locked for long because very shortly afterwards another member of the German army arrived and, having taken a good look at all of us, pointed one finger very firmly at me. My heart missed a beat for I knew I was to be the first to face what we all knew was in store for us, "interrogation". Why he selected me first I do not know. No doubt I was the youngest one there, perhaps I looked it and he thought I might be the first to talk. I was taken to an oblong-shaped office and given a form to complete, which I was told was to be sent to the "International Red Cross" so I completed the part relating to my 'name, rank and number' and I told him I could not answer the other questions, much to his apparent annoyance. Finally, one of my two "dog tags" bearing my "name, rank and number" and religion was taken from me and I was taken into a rather bare-looking room, "bare", because it contained little more than a table, two chairs, a telephone as well as some maps. I was seated on one of the chairs on one side of the table and opposite me on the other chair was a rather superior-looking, yet stern, officer of the German Army. I think I sat rather tense waiting for the questions to be fired at me and I was surprised when he spoke, in a rather friendly sort of voice; friendly, no doubt, to try and trick me into giving more than my service number, rank and name. He asked me some routine questions, mostly of military importance. I gave him little or no information to my knowledge and once he reminded me that the SS had ways and means of extracting information. Then at length he came to the questions of the markings on my aircraft and I told him I was sorry but I could not tell him and his angry reply was "Jesus Christ man, that's not a secret" he told me everybody could see them and yet I knew if I told him of them, he would know from what squadron I had taken off with. Having come to the conclusion that it was fruitless to keep asking me, he escorted me to a building away from the main one and I had a clear picture of what was in store for me, solitary confinement.

'I was not far wrong and was handed over to the guard in charge and taken to an empty cell amongst the long line of them, which were placed on either side of the long corridor. Inside was not a pretty sight, a slanting wooden bed with three blankets and a slot in the wall at the top with bars wiping out any hope of escape. I laid on the bed using the blankets to form a sort of mattress and, gazing up at the ceiling, I wondered for how long this was going to be my home. I had hardly time to think before the door was unlocked and I was beckoned to go outside and there waiting for me was my interrogator. He asked me if I had changed my mind and would I like to tell him what he wanted to know, offering me all forms of bribes to change my mind. When I told him I could not answer that question he said something to the guard in German and I was ushered back to the "comforts" of my cell but to my dismay my blankets had now gone and only the comfort of the bare bed awaited me. I slept very little that night and when the first light of dawn came peeping through the bars, I was already awake and wondering what the coming day had in store for me. This proved uneventful, our only meal being a few potatoes cooked in their skins and a mug of water. The two following days went in almost the same way, speaking to no one except the guard, who could not speak a word of English.

'On the fourth day my cell was unlocked during the morning and I was taken back to the same small room for further interrogation by the same interrogator and to my surprise he now knew almost as much about myself and from where I had come from as I did (so to speak)! After a while I was taken for further medical treatment but, while I was waiting there, the lone "wail" of a siren sounded alerting us to an air-raid warning and all the occupants of the sick-quarters, where I was, were taken down into the air raid shelter. I remember being ushered down into the shelter feeling very uncomfortable as the other people present were Germans who did not seem happy about my presence.

'After what seemed like hours the "all clear" sounded and up into the daylight we went again. My medical treatment seemed to have been forgotten. I was taken to a large room, which was full of other PoWs, mostly American, who had been interrogated and were awaiting to be "shipped" to prisoner of war camps. This I presumed to be my fate and I sat myself down on the floor to await further developments. Various persons joined us during the course of the day until by night fall the room was well and truly full, it being almost impossible to find enough floor space on which to try and obtain sleep as everybody had to lie on their sides in order to lie down at all. The following day our numbers increased and we were allowed outside for a while, this treat proving very helpful after being cooped up in the foul air of that greatly overcrowded room. Later in the day we discovered we were to be on the move again, this time we presumed to be a prison camp. We finally moved off, which included a large number of us but not the two surviving members of my crew. I wondered what had become of them.

'After walking for a considerable distance, the strain began to tell due to the lack of food and one or two of us almost fell out by the wayside; but for the constant help of our other friends, I have no doubt that is exactly what would have happened. Having arrived at long last to the railway station we were all loaded into a cattle truck and once again our journey began to another unknown destination. We travelled for hours until we came to a halt. We had to get out and await a further train to continue on our way. This finally came and at long last we found ourselves back at Nuremburg, this apparently being our destination, where we were taken to a side room to await transport (those who were unable to walk). We knew we would soon get our first glimpse of what the view really was from behind those ugly compounds of barbed wire.

'Our wait proved a long one; in fact we had to stop there the night and, in the morning, the odd half a dozen of us had to board a rather primitive-looking lorry and once again we continued. Eventually we came to a halt and were taken to a wooden building inside a barbed wire compound, which was the prison hospital. It felt really great to talk to someone who could speak English and before long a cup of drink had been brewed for us and with it we were given a slice of bread with Red Cross jam placed before us to help satisfy our hunger. After a while an officer of the British Army appeared and he turned out to be a doctor (obviously of the Royal Army Medical Corps). He viewed my wounds, including my broken finger, and joined in general conversation advising me how best to rest my legs, which were very badly swollen, and he did what he could to my finger, which was now past setting to any degree of accuracy. Feeling much refreshed, we eventually left the hospital and were taken to another compound, which was vastly overcrowded. Here we were taken to a hutment of one of the senior British officers in the compound. He turned out to be an RAF Wing Commander and having joined in conversation with him I learned that he knew several of my pals who were stationed at other units. He gave me the general layout of the camp and said that all Red Cross parcels which came into that particular compound were pooled along with the small amount of food supplied by the Germans. All the food was put together and cooked by voluntary people who supplied us with two good meals per day. Meal times were staggered because of the inability of the small cook house to accommodate us all at the same time.

'The cigarettes which were in the parcels were allocated out at meal times and these were the main form of purchase for those wishing to exchange something. I was issued with a towel, a small piece of soap and two blankets, and was taken to my billet. This turned out to be a massive-sized tent containing some one hundred and fifty to two hundred people who were sleeping very much overcrowded. I took up one of the vacant spots and decided it was high time I had a wash and shave, the first in nearly a fortnight. I managed to borrow a razor. While I was inquiring into the possibility of borrowing this, I learned that the other survivors of my crew had arrived at this compound and luckily for me were put in the same tent as myself. Everybody turned out to be very friendly and kind without exception. One American gave me a pair of braces, another stitched my trousers for me and my two crew pals assisted me in shaving with cold water, which was not an easy task!

'In the days that followed the weather was very kind to us but my general health seemed to be suffering. My nose had violent fits of bleeding, blood simply pouring out, until one day it became impossible to check it and a doctor was called. After a period of time he succeeded and decided it would be better if I moved to a small hut within the compound which was used for medical treatment. This I did and for the first time I became the occupant of a double-tier bed. The supplies which the medical staff had were limited but nevertheless our American team of three doctors and their medical core assistants did a first-rate job.

'Not many days after my move we learned that the front line was getting near and the entire camp was to be moved back to another camp. It was decided I was to travel with the hospital group. Transport was provided for us to the station and the others had to march. We were the last to leave and we almost wondered if we were to be left to be overrun by our advancing armies. At the railway station the main were loaded into cattle trucks and we of the hospital group were afforded the comparative comfort of a third-class railway carriage. It was night when we started and before we left we were given a Red

RAID ON NUREMBURG

Cross parcel. We were now responsible for our own feeding, not knowing when we were going to receive another parcel. Finally, the journey started and we all settled down wondering where our destination was this time. Our particular carriage was not overcrowded and we managed to lay ourselves out fairly well to get some sleep.

'Morning came and with it the dawning of a fresh day of unforeseen adventures. We prepared ourselves a form of meal from our parcels and we were able to view the beauty of the surrounding countryside as we travelled. Eventually our train came to a standstill. This, we discovered, was due to an air raid in the vicinity. Our train driver and fireman seemed more concerned about this than we did and it gave us a chance to light fires by the rail side to brew tea and coffee. Suddenly someone shouted and I looked to one side of the rail track. There I saw coming towards us at treetop height were a number of American Mustangs (P-51 fighter aircraft). I ran down the embankment and threw myself flat on the ground and as I did this machine guns of the aircraft opened fire, the ground was being turfed up like a miniature sandstorm in the desert. I really felt the end had come. As if they had suddenly realised we were prisoners of war, they ceased fire and the noses of the planes went upwards and they flew away to join the bomber force for which they were affording fighter protection. I always thought they must have seen the letters "POW", which had been chalked on the side of the cattle trucks by a group of prisoners of war themselves. A survey was made after the raid and the only casualty proved to be a member of the German Army, who quickly received treatment from an army doctor PoW who was on the train with us. At last, our journey started and once again darkness overcame us and once more we settled down for the night. When once again the rays of another dawn began to break through our train had stopped and we were standing at an unnamed station. As it became light, we found we were in a railway siding and this we discovered was the end of our journey and eventually we unloaded and reloaded into horse and carts.

'The next part of our journey proved a short one and we found ourselves at another prison camp which, this time, seemed much larger than the last and much more laid out, so to speak. We all entered the large gates, which were closed behind us, and confronting us were a number of wooden huts and one or two small tents. As we had travelled with the hospital group, we were taken into a hut, which was bare apart from a table, a few forms and also one gigantic stove in the middle of the floor. We all arranged ourselves around the sides of the hut and what few medical supplies we had with us were piled onto the one table. Having got settled in, we decided to make a quick "tour" of the compound to get an idea of the layout. In two corners were built high towers, which besides holding a sentry also carried a searchlight and machine gun. On my tour around I found to my delight that the other two members of my crew had arrived and had taken up "residence" in another hut on the other side of the compound.

'The next day was one of procedure as the Germans came with forms for us to fill in that contained numerous questions in addition to the normal "Name, Rank and Number", which were ignored and apparently they expected this as nothing more was said about them. Then came the job of taking our fingerprints and the issue of a metal tag to each of us bearing a number, which was to be our PoW number, and also the writing "Stalag 7A', which was the camp we were presently in. The days that followed were uneventful apart from more and more prisoners arriving at the camp, which was already vastly overcrowded; so full in fact, that prisoners were having to crawl underneath the huts to find cover in which to sleep! Life in general was quiet and a consignment of Red Cross parcels arrived weekly and the allocation was one per person per week. It was really surprising how much food was packed inside these cardboard containers.

'Sanitation was primitive and the only baths were a wash down in a bowl in the open air. Having occupied that hut for several days, it was decided we were to move to another compound, so we gathered up our small collection of belongings and we were on the move again. It was then decided we should be given the privilege of a shower, with our clothes being fumigated at the same time. This we welcomed and having undressed we hung our belongings on a kind of hanger and these were then taken and put into a sort of oven and we proceeded to the showers. Having enjoyed the luxury of a warm bath, we proceeded into another room to dry, having no towels, to await the return of our clothes. By the time these were returned the hut was really crowded and the temperatures had risen considerably. Having got dressed, we were taken to other compounds and the hospital. We were taken into one compound which turned out to be one containing Officers of several nationalities. We did not stay here for long and in a day or two we were on the move again, back to the compound from which we had come from a day or so previous. The hut we had occupied was now full – in fact no room seemed to be had anywhere – so there seemed no alternative but to lie out in the open night. Along with another fellow we made our bed together on the stony ground and settled down for the night but this did not prove too peaceful as the searchlights from the sentry boxes swept across our faces at regular intervals. The rain which fell from the wide-open heavens above glistened upon us as the dew forming on the grass back home in England, which was now but a memory. I missed home. The night seemed long and as dawn broke, we were soon up and about and managed to get a supply of water without a half-hour queue. We decided we must try and find indoor accommodation before another night.

'The next day proved very lucky for us in so much that one of the huts was emptied and we were able to move in, however, several other people had the same idea and the hut was soon vastly overcrowded but nevertheless we were under cover and that really did mean a lot. The days that followed seemed long and uneventful. News was scarce and any we did hear was given to us by the Germans, which were always in their favour.

'The day's routine was always the same each day. The Germans would come and call us in the morning and shortly afterwards everybody would have to parade outside for the day's count to see that no prisoners had escaped. The cooking of breakfast followed, which usually consisted of porridge made from hard biscuits which had been well soaked and tea or coffee, which we brewed ourselves. Most of the cooking was done on a contraption called a "blower". This was a round or square tin with struts going across about one third of the way up, leaving an empty space at the bottom. From this led a tunnel affair which was connected to a cylinder, which had mounted inside it a series of pieces of tin on a rod to form a fan, which, when the rod was rotated by the means of a handle, it caused a flow of wind and in turn went along the tunnel. This resulted in a constant draught inside the first tin and any pieces of wood or stick were thus kept alight. By this means cooking was done over the fire. The Germans supplied one meal a day, usually midday, which was usually a watery kind of soup or something, with potatoes cooked in their skins. We found these more appetising if the skins were removed and the potatoes fried in a shallow tin or a frying pan, which some were lucky enough to possess. Mostly when the Red Cross parcels were received, we found that they had been opened and the air-tight tins had been opened. This was to prevent any prisoner from saving a quantity of food with a view to escape.

STORIES FROM THE STALAGS

'On Sundays a service was held in one of the huts if wet and outside, if weather permitted. People of all denominations joined together in their humble prayers and singing. The services were conducted by padres who themselves were prisoners but were afforded more freedom than the average in order to get around to the different compounds to conduct services at various times of the day. On one occasion an air raid took place nearby and one of the attacking aircraft had the misfortune of getting shot down and we saw the crew of this "Flying Fortress" bomber jump to safety. One day I had the good luck to be issued with an army overcoat and a pair of American boots to replace my flying boots. I also had a pair of khaki trousers given to me, which I found useful to wear in place of my badly torn pants. As the time went by, we discovered one day that a number of tents were being erected outside our compound and we did not have to wait long to find out who they were for because shortly afterwards a number of, what we took to be Indians, occupied them and they were all wearing turbans and most of them had long black beards. Apparently, the Red Cross parcels which they received contained different food to ours as there was an exchange of goods between us whenever it was possible. That was when the Germans were not looking!

'One prisoner of war hit upon the bright idea of setting up a table to which other prisoners could bring things which they did not want and they could state a price which they wanted for a particular item, either a number of cigarettes or some item of food which they may be short of. When this deal was completed, a cigarette was paid to the table operator for his services. So it was that life in the camp went on and in time we grew to know every inch of that compound and every piece of barbed wire that surrounded us. On certain days small parties were allowed out under escort into the surrounding woods to collect sticks for our fires. Towards the end of April snow fell and this proved to be a very unwelcome "visitor". With it came cold weather, which made our huts very bleak with no form of heating. Nevertheless, we survived and warmer weather followed and with it the rumble of guns in the distance; we sincerely hoped the chances of freedom would come with it. Then it happened. It was a Sunday; as the dawn broke bright and clear for us it was going to be just another Sunday, the usual parade and the cooking of break-fast [sic], but then we heard the whistle of shells as they passed over the top of us and the report as they hit their target. We realised then that we were between two front lines, no-man's-land, the Germans on one side and the advancing allies on the other. At any moment a shell might fall short of its target and land in the camp and we were so near freedom.

'I felt (and I think everybody else did) very uncomfortable and I stayed in the hut thinking maybe its four walls and roof afforded me some protection from falling shells. Suddenly someone shouted and we all ran from the hut to see what all the shouting was about and there with its tracks resting on part of the barbed wire compound was a huge American tank manned by Americans of the late General Patton's Army.

'The scene there was one I shall never forget, to see the men who had been prisoners of war for five long years with tears streaming down their faces, overcome with emotion, almost wondering if they could believe their eyes. The driver of the tank had intended coming right over the barbed wire but had been stopped because although we had been freed it was the intention of the authorities to keep us within the wire strands, probably because of the fear of snipers should we get out and roam the countryside. Shortly afterwards somebody of the American Army climbed on to the top of one of the huts and said, "In a few hours you will be on your way home." This was greeted with cheers, little knowing how wrong he proved to be!

'The rest of the day was quite uneventful. From our wire compound where we still remained we had a first-class view of the battle action, which resulted in the "mopping up" operation of the pockets of the German military. We saw the German Army being marched by the score to their captivity, some bearing a look of pleasure on their faces, to think it was all over at last.

'The roaring guns continued throughout the day and well into the night, growing fainter as the time passed by. By the time night came we were still prisoners from the point of view that we were still fenced in but our rations had been increased and sleep that night seemed to come with a deeper sense of restfulness, knowing at last we were free.

'The days that followed brought with them no news of going home. Holes were made in the barbed wire that surrounded us and in ones and twos prisoners got out to look around the surrounding countryside. I got out with another fellow, the sight outside was one of utter destruction; the Germans in their flight had destroyed bridges, railways and all means of transportation. To cross one river, we had to clamber across a twisted heavily damaged structure of what was once a bridge. In spite of the scars of war, through it all the countryside was beautiful and as we gazed around we wondered if wars were all really worthwhile. We went into a small town nearby where the streets were deserted and the thoughts uppermost in our minds was "Were there any snipers still lurking behind those closed doors just waiting to get a shot at us?" We knew that beyond those walls within that town there lived Germans who for six long years had been our enemies and could not change their hate towards us in a night.

'We were able to see from the outside what once we had seen from the inside. That little house, which had once been but a mark on the landscape, could now be seen close up, and from the other way those two church towers, so close together, could now be seen in one churchyard. Our outings to the outside world were soon stopped and guards were posted outside the holes in the wire to keep us in. The week moved slowly on and we began to wonder when the promise of a quick return home would be fulfilled and one or two prisoners, or rather ex-prisoners, who became grossly impatient managed to get outside and made their own way home! What they hoped to achieve by this effort I never really knew because home was many hundreds of miles away and also that stretch of water called the English Channel would have been a very hard task indeed. One building which we had seen outside and wondered what it was turned out to be a cheese factory and so we were supplied with an ample ration of very tasty cheese! Apparently, some members of our "flock" thought our diet was not varied enough because one party (a butcher amongst them) managed to get out and killed a cow, so it was a delicious smell of cooking steaks hovered around the camp! Towards the end of the week the Americans were moved out for the start of their journey home, probably moving first because they had undoubtedly the greater distance to cover before arriving home. This left our hut with an air of emptiness and ample room to sleep. Hung all around the hut were massive pieces of beef waiting to be cooked and eaten.

'The arrangements for our move progressed slowly and one day we were taken outside the compound for de-lousing. We were all lined up and a white powder was pumped inside our clothing. Sunday came around again and it was now a week since we had been liberated and promised a swift return home.

'In the hut now was a wireless which somebody had looted and we heard the once familiar sound of the BBC announcer reading the nine o'clock news. Sometime after this we were all settling down for the night when someone burst into the hut and said, "You must all be ready to move out first thing in the morning!" This caused great excitement in the camp and seemed to be a cue for the starting of fires and cooking beef steaks. It must have been well past midnight when the excitement died down and the silence of sleep crept in over the hut. Everybody was up and about the next morning with their small belongings and we were split up into parties for the great move. How the time of waiting seemed to dawdle! Then, finally, we were on the move to a position outside the camp where scores of American lorries were lined up to take us to an unknown destination.

'Finally, we all piled aboard. How many there were to a truck I do not remember, but we were packed in like sardines having to stand all the while as there was no chance of getting a seat. With a jolt, the lorry started and we were off. The journey was interesting and the ride rough; we travelled along rough cart tracks and sometimes arterial roads, having to make a detour when we came to a bridge which had been destroyed. The scene along the way was not a pretty one. There were miles of destruction and houses which were once some people's home were now a pile of rubble. All along the way the roadside was littered with burnt-out tanks and abandoned lorries. Some houses had white flags hanging outside them, no doubt as a sign that the occupants had surrendered. Having travelled for a considerable while we finally came to what had once been a German airfield. Sitting around the airfield were groups of ex-PoWs undoubtedly waiting for transport home. It never came that day, and by the time night began to fall there came the problem of finding accommodation for the night for hundreds of personnel. At length we all climbed into the lorries and once more the journey started with the ride being shorter this time as we soon found ourselves, without doubt, inside an old German garrison and the place was practically in ruins. We were told to find ourselves shelter for the night; the task not being made an easy one as it was almost dark and we had no form of lights. Someone lit a heap of old papers in a tin, but with us so unsure as to whether hostilities had really ceased, we decided we were making ourselves too much of a sitting target.

'At last, amongst the ruins we came upon what looked as if it had once been the sick quarters and there amongst the broken bottles and what remained of the doctor's surgery we laid down for the night. And although the bed was rough, we were soon all asleep. The first rays of light were breaking through when we awoke and we were able to see for ourselves what the place really looked like. The scene was one of almost total destruction and amongst the rubble I found a tape measure marked off in inches, much to my amazement.

'A further survey of our "quarters" revealed so much. There were the stores still containing rifles and other parts of equipment and the hurriedly evacuated living quarters with personal equipment and effects still lying around. There was the odd photograph of somebody's girlfriend, wife or mother and also a photograph of the great Adolf himself!

'It was not very long before we were loaded aboard the lorries and once again our journey started back to the airfield. It was a glorious day and once again we took up our position on the airfield to await transport home. Aircraft came and went, each time it did not seem as if our turn would come. As the sun began to set in the west it once again became apparent that we were to stay yet another night in Germany. No provision was made to find us accommodation for the night so we had to find what shelter we could. I chose an open shed at the side of the airfield and felt really glad the month was May and not January. As the rising sun bade us awake, we were all soon milling about and once again wondered what the coming day had in store for us. Food was not in short supply and we were able to eat a fairly hearty breakfast. Soon afterwards the Dakota aircraft started their arrivals and once more there was the signal to stand by and wait. The number of parties in front of us seemed countless and we began to wonder if our turn would come that day.

'A further consignment of Red Cross parcels arrived and were distributed and the day, very wearily, dragged by. Someone rumoured that the war was over but, to us sitting there with no form of news, it was just another rumour. Night came and still our turn had not come and once more began the job of settling down for the night. With another fellow I pooled my blankets with his and we made a form of tent with two of them and underneath we made the others into a double bed and had a good night's sleep.

'The next morning was the first light of the fourth day of our wait and we had now become quite accustomed to the airfield and its surroundings. We hardly dared to leave in case our turn came for transport. The day again hot and humid I, along with another fellow, decided a bath or a bathe would be very refreshing, but dare we leave the airfield to try and find somewhere? We decided to risk it and armed with towel and soap we set off. We had not gone far when we heard the noise of an aircraft approaching and as it neared the airfield a battery of guns opened fire. On spotting the plane we discovered it was a Junkers 87 and as it dipped its wings the gunfire stopped. The pilot made a perfect landing and surrendered, so we turned to continue our search for a bathing area, which we found in the form of a river and decided to take the plunge. The water was warm and as we dried ourselves in the hot sun we felt really refreshed and began to wonder how much nearer our group had come to the front of the queue. As we made our way back, we were met by a panting friend who informed us that our group was nearly ready to embark for home and so all three of us ran back to the airfield not wanting to miss our turn in the queue. We were just in time, however, and shortly afterwards we were aboard the aircraft bound for home, we hoped!

'There was about 27 of us in the aircraft as she taxied to the runway for take-off and as her engines roared into life and our speed increased, I hoped I should not have to leave it in the same way as I had left the Lancaster. As we flew over Germany the green fields and villages revealed to us little signs of war and yet, if one could have taken a closer look, much would have been seen of what the pangs of war could leave in its path. Finally, we landed and as we taxied to a standstill, I wondered what was in store for us and where we were. We were met by Americans with lorries and as each lorry received its quota, we started on what proved to be a short ride to a group of small tents which were to be our billets for the night. We received every attention and had a good meal, a good wash and a really good night's sleep.

'Morning came quickly and we were soon into lorries and on the move again. The journey was much longer this time and took us through a large town, which we discovered was Reims. On our arrival at our destination, which once again was a large airfield, we saw rows of Lancasters lined up ready to fly us back to England. Refreshments were served on the airfield and finally we were allocated to a plane and what little luggage we had was loaded into the giant bomb bays ready for home. After much waiting, our aircraft suddenly roared into life, however, it was discovered on testing the engines that one magneto was faulty and so our aircraft was unable to take off. Our luggage was unloaded from the aircraft and reloaded into another and then finally we were airborne.

'One could see little from the Lancaster but after what seemed like ages, we were told from those at the front of the aircraft that we were about to land. Once down we soon taxied to our unloading point and as we jumped from the aircraft the green grass of Tangmere seemed like a velvet cushion under our feet and the fields of England looked greener than ever before.

'The welcome awaiting us was overwhelming and we were soon on our way to Cosford for re-equipping and leave. The first duty on arrival at Cosford was to send a telegram, "Arrived in England today, be home soon." I knew then that home was not so many miles away.'

Postscript

All these words were written almost sixty years ago and for many years Doug wondered where his Lancaster crashed and how was it that his friends did not make it. In 1998 he met up with Richard Pymar of Harleston, Suffolk, who produced details of the fate of the crew that night and they became good friends. Richard had a good friend in Keith Ottywill from Ipswich, who also became very interested in the venture. Keith was also in the fortunate position of having friends in Germany. One of these was a 26-year-old German police officer, Olaf Weddern. He found contacts in the Nuremburg area, persevered with the project and eventually plans began to mature nearly two years after the project was first talked about.

On 11 April 2001 Richard Pymar, Keith Ottywill and his wife Hillary and Doug Cady visited Germany and were met by Keith and Hillary's friends, Hans and Erna Otto, who lived near Neumunster and were to prove the 'hosts of hosts'! At Dürnbach war cemetery, the air was cold; Doug soon found 'his crew'. They lay side by side, their positions marked by the now familiar headstones, set out in their regimental pattern, all recording someone's loved one and the ages starting at 18, 19, 20 and 21. The inscriptions were moving with a popular one being, 'To the world you are one, to us you are the world'. Later, the party visited the exact spot where the crash had occurred.

Chapter 10

Barth – The Final Days

We had just dropped our bombs and made a turn off the target. We received several hits by flak, then a direct hit in No.3 gas tank. The plane caught fire immediately and Lieutenant Fred Veal called, 'Bail Out!' over the interphone. We started falling out of formation and the plane exploded. I was in the tail and it blew the tail off. I bailed out a little later. The navigator, Lieutenant Don Johns, was blown out from the nose; fortunately, he had his parachute on. Just after I landed on the ground I was captured and taken to Wehrmacht HQ. I was questioned by a German officer. A little later I was taken and shown five of the bodies of the men I flew with. I recognized two of them. They were Lieutenant Veal and Sergeant Marion Hord. The rest were too badly burnt and mangled to recognize. Later that night I was told that they found the other two bodies but they did not show me these. They told me that one other man had bailed out but wouldn't tell me which one it was so I couldn't be sure who got out. Next day I was taken to Pinneberg, Germany, and put in the hospital for a severe back injury. On 4 April I was taken with twenty-nine other men to Stalag Luft I at Barth. Lieutenant Don Johns, the navigator on the crew, was in this group of men. That is when I learned who was the other survivor. He did not know if anyone else got out or not.
Sergeant Robert A. Herman, tail gunner, B-17 *Lil' Butch*, **486th Bomb Group, Hamburg, 30 March 1945**

On 30 November 1944 the ten-man crew of *The Sad Shack* in the 527th Bomb Squadron in the 379th Bomb Group at Kimbolton about 9 miles west of Huntingdon were destined to become 'guests of the Germans' when concentrated flak brought down their B-17 on a mission to synthetic oil targets at Zeitz, south-west of Leipzig. Typically, Eighth Air Force crews consisted of men from all points in the USA. Major Theodore George Ramsdell, the pilot, born in Great Barrington, Massachusetts, on 14 December 1915, had enlisted in Springfield, Massachusetts. Second Lieutenant Bernal Loraine 'Rusty' Lewis, the co-pilot, had been born in Canton, South Dakota, on 16 March 1923 and at the time of his enlistment was married to Helen of Stockton, California, and was working in the Stockton State Hospital at the time of his draft registration. He enlisted in San Francisco on 10 September 1942. Frederic Herbert Olander Jr, navigator, had been born in Kansas City, Missouri, on 4 October 1922 and had enlisted at Lawrence, Kansas, on 25 May 1942. First Lieutenant John William McDermott, also a navigator, was born at Williamsport, Pennsylvania, on 28 November 1924 and was living in Mayview, Pennsylvania, and working at the Williamsport Textile Corporation at the time of his draft registration in December 1942. He had enlisted in 1943. Forrest L. Kenyon, the bombardier, who was born in Richmond, Vermont, on 18 August 1921 had enlisted at Rutland, Vermont, on 26 August 1942. Robert E. Wogatske was born at Council Bluffs, Iowa, on 16 November 1923 and enlisted in Los Angeles on 18 June 1943. Tech Sergeant Peter Papas, radio operator, born Chicago, Illinois, on 11 August 1923, had enlisted on 2 July 1942. Staff Sergeant Robert Edward Reverdy, waist gunner, born on 6 July 1922 at Burbank, California, enlisted at Fort MacArthur, San Pedro, California, on 28 December 1943. Tech Sergeant Ivon Eugene McCarty, the tail gunner, born Clinton, Tennessee, on 3 August 1922, had enlisted at Camp Forrest, Tennessee, on 8 October 1942. First Lieutenant Morris Meyer Gropper, radar navigator, 'Mickey' operator, born Brooklyn, New York, on 31 October 1921 was living in Brooklyn in 1942 with his wife Cynthia when he enlisted on 17 July.

The mission began badly as 'Rusty' Lewis, who was flying his twenty-second mission, recalls: 'In order to maintain visual contact with the ground, our group leader dropped down through thick cloud, putting us in the low squadron at 23,000ft. Major Ramsdell and I attempted to relinquish the lead to the deputy lead, who was my ex-aircraft commander, on my right wing, but he ignored the green light. We were without radio communication so we pulled back and attempted to stall the aircraft so that we would slide ahead of us. Unfortunately, he stalled right with us. (I found out later that his co-pilot's control yoke was lying in his lap.)

BARTH – THE FINAL DAYS

'At last, the deputy lead crew realized that we wanted them to take over the lead. We made a turn to the right, making sure we had not passed the target. Maybe we had gone a little bit beyond it when we made a swing to the right and passed near Leipzig, where we encountered flak. During the 190° turn onto our secondary target at Merseburg, the deputy lead aircraft finally took over. We completed a 270° turn, taking us right back over the target area, where we were again showered by flak. The secondary target was obscured by cloud so we headed for the third target at Fulda.

'On the bomb run Morris Gropper, our "Mickey" radar operator, screamed over the interphone that the target was to the left. Then I heard, "No, we're on the bomb run itself." They were checking checkpoints but when we arrived over the target area the target was not there! We heard some explosions off to our left and realized that the Germans had camouflaged the checkpoints to fool our visual men in the nose. Most crewmen at the time always believed their eyes and instruments and not the "Mickey" sets, of which little was known except by the technicians who used them.'

In the resulting confusion the formation broke up and scattered in complete disarray. 'Rusty' Lewis continues: 'We got a fire in the number four engine and we had to shut it down. Aircraft from our squadron were going down all around us and we only had three aircraft left in the formation. [*Take Me Home, Dimples* and Lewis' ship; which were all lost together with *Landa*, *Lucy* and *Miss Lace*, which had already gone down.]

'Our intercom was dead. All electrical supply to the top turret was dead, we lost another engine and the propeller ran away. I looked out across the wing and saw that all the oil tanks appeared to have been riddled by rifle fire, although it was obviously flak. The oil ran low and the engines began overheating. Finally, a third engine went out and we had another runaway propeller. We were now flying around 4,000ft with lost power. It was time to leave the ship.

'I held the aircraft level, looking down between my knees through the escape hatch below me until the hills came up underneath. First Lieutenant John W. McDermott, the navigator, had been hit in the head and was unconscious. It was my intention to take him out with me in my arms with his "D" ring in my hands so that when we jumped out the airspeed would hit him and pull him away. Luckily, he regained consciousness just prior to our jump.

'We were over Heligolandstock, south of Hannover, when I went to bail out and I could see right over the town. I noticed it had a high pointed steeple. I had always rehearsed parachute jumping in my mind and had daydreamed about getting hung up on a steeple.

'I thought I might as well enjoy the parachute jump but all of a sudden, I realized I had left the aircraft at only 4,000ft! I quickly pulled the ripcord. I was wearing a 28ft back pack 'chute and its opening created a very big impact. The ring fell out of my hand and I thought, "Oh Hell, I won't be able to get into the Caterpillar Club without it." Then I noticed that those who had jumped before me were just opening their 'chutes! I thought how smart they were because they would not drift over the town like I was going to thanks to the prevailing wind. (It was only later that I found that three of the crew had to claw their 'chutes out of their chest packs with their fingernails after the rings had failed.)

'I landed right on the edge of Heligolandstock, where people were waiting with pistols. I gave my parachute to a pretty girl in the group. There was rapid firing. Did I make it back this close to the front lines? I asked a young German soldier, who was about sixteen years old and had a broken arm, if we were in Holland or Germany. A little nine-year-old German kid laughed and said, "No, Germany." The rapid firing was only the ammunition exploding in our burning Fortress.

'An old man took me to his house and put on a hat with a feather in it. I guess he was Volksstrum. I was led through the streets but people were becoming mean and angry and I got kicked in the crotch from behind. (This caused some bad urinary bleeding problems later.) I was taken to a police station and joined by a German enlisted man called Eddie Stang. He used 1930s slang, saying things like, "These fellers want to bump you off. They think you dived your aircraft on the village and I want to help you." (We had decided to crash our airplane rather than let the Germans get our "Mickey" set.) I said I understood all this, although I didn't believe a word of it. I told him I could not give him any information other than my name, rank and serial number. He tried to con me that he had visited the USA before the war and had lived in Chicago. I stuck to the "name, rank and serial number" routine.

'Later, a 6ft 5in German with a shaved head visited me. It turned out he was the burgermeister. He asked me through an interpreter what target we had bombed but I said I could tell him nothing. He mouthed and slapped me with his bare hand. I figured if he really wanted to hurt me, he would have used his fist. I looked him straight in the eyes and said to myself, "Don't look scared." In my mind I called him every dirty name I could think of. He gave up. Stang returned and said the crowd outside were calling for my blood because I had dived our plane into their village.

'About six hours later the Germans started bringing in the rest of my crew, including Major Ramsdell who had been flying with us. He was quite a soldier and the Germans recognized that they had a prize catch. The next day we were despatched to Frankfurt by train. We stood on the platform at the packed *bahnhof* and I had the urge to escape until I saw a guard with his eyes locked on me waiting for me to attempt an escape. Had I tried to get away I would have been shot.

'By tram we were taken to Oberursel, about 20 miles from Frankfurt. However, about halfway the tram broke down and we had to walk the rest of the way. At Oberursel we were herded into an overcrowded basement. Most were friends from my squadron, ten out of the twelve ships having been shot down. Next day we were put in solitary confinement. We had been shown a movie about Dulag Luft in England so we knew what to expect.

'It had said that there would be a Red Cross form and that we were to give only our name, rank and serial number. It also warned us that the Germans would try and peg us as extrovert or introvert. We were told, "Be as blasé as you can." Nevertheless, putting my ear to the wall I could hear men being sucked in by the Red Cross form, writing name, rank and serial number and then carrying on with information about where they had trained their squadron and group details and so on. Because it had "Red Cross" at the top of the form, people were filling it in and getting out of Dulag Luft in about a day. They inadvertently told the Germans all they wanted to know.

'During my interrogation I refused to give the Germans any information. I said I understood the Germans to be good soldiers and I was one too. I had been ordered to stick to "name, rank and serial number". My interrogator, a German captain, said, "We don't know if you are a spy. Your dog tags don't mean anything. We have to have more information about you and you will remain here until we get it."

'After four days in solitary confinement it became very tough going. Before the war I had been a psychiatric technician and having studied quite a bit about psychology I felt I could follow the dictates of my confinement and interrogations. I had been a "pumpster" all my life and I wanted to write a book about my religious beliefs. After about seven days' solitary confinement

STORIES FROM THE STALAGS

I think I would probably have become mentally ill had I not had the training in mental discipline. I could see where people had tried to scratch some messages on the wall with their fingernails and they had probably gone mad eventually. In the next cell to me was Count Daceagunsac. "Zac" was a Free French fighter and had been in solitary confinement for 56 days. Despite this he was still able to shout encouragement and taught me to sing "Alouette" and so on. Although I never met him face to face, I have always considered him a friend.

'After solitary I was taken before a "*hauptmann*"; another shaven-headed type. As I entered his office, I saw a complete mock of up a "Mickey" set. He asked me questions but I still stuck to the "name, rank and serial number" routine. On the wall was a board showing the squadrons in the 379th Bomb Group.

The *hauptmann* gave me a propaganda lecture and began by saying that my squadron CO was called the "Monster". (This was true; Major James E. Crosby Jr was a West Pointer and the men called him the "Monster" because of his size.)[1] This was just to impress upon me that he knew all about us. He added, "You will win the war but not as soon as you think. (Unknown to me the "Battle of the Bulge" had just started.) It won't be long after this war that you'll be fighting the Russians and we'll be on your side."

'Later, I found out that Major Ramsdell had been given the opposite treatment. The Germans discovered that it had been his birthday and gave him a big champagne party. One of the Germans got up and toasted him, saying, "Five or ten years ago I was in the United States enjoying myself." The Major returned the toast, saying, "One, two or three years from now I'll be in the United States enjoying myself." This showed the different type of treatment we were getting.

'On my 21st day at Dulag Luft I was told that if I did not give more information, I would be left to rot. I said, "OK, I'll give you my birthday, but that's it." The *hauptmann* laughed and said, "OK". A Lieutenant Colonel I later talked to told me that during his interrogation he was shown a clipping from his home town newspaper printed a month before, giving his promotion. My home town newspaper had stated that I had flown 21 missions. My

---

1. Major Crosby, who piloted *Pretty Olga* on the mission to Regensburg on 16 April 1945, put down at RAF Woodbridge on return. This B-17 survived the war and was scrapped at Walnut Ridge, Arkansas, in late 1945.

parents were able to pin down how many missions I flew because I had a little code system going with them. When we had gone overseas, we had painted a nude on our B-17 and called her the Sad Shack. I said I was going to kiss her fanny every time I got back from a mission. When I wrote that I had seen "fanny" that day they knew I had completed another mission. At one of the interim camps on the way to Stalag Luft I, I was allowed to write a message that would be sent over the Red Cross radio. All I wrote was, "All crew OK; am fine." A ham radio picked it up.

'After giving this information I joined a muster in a hall. My electric flying suit was returned to me and I found a piece of chewing gum in one of the pockets. Later, I tried to pass it through the door to "Zak" but a guard sneaked up from behind and got me by the scruff of my neck and the seat of my pants. He threw me across the room. Having been an accomplished boxer, my first reaction was to hit him but my crew shouted otherwise. I had taken a beating because the German thought I was a Jew.

'I was put on a long train journey across Germany. I was completely amazed at the German railway network. I saw there was no way we would ever knock out their railway system in the war. Every forest had camouflaged equipment, screw tracks and so on. At this time the Air Force effort was aimed at wiping them out and strafing trains was common. On Christmas Eve our train was strafed. Our guards jumped from the train and scrambled into ditches. They trained their guns on us while we stayed in the cars. They were especially angry that the Allies had strafed and bombed on Christmas Eve! Finally, we reached Stettin and East Prussia and went on to Stalag Luft I at Barth.'

'Rusty' Lewis arrived at Barth in Pomerania the day after Christmas 1944. The camp was sited near the town, which lay in the Zingsthof, a large inlet sheltered from the Baltic by the sandy, forested arm of the Zingst Peninsula. In strict contravention of the Geneva Convention, Luft I was built near a German anti-aircraft regimental school for army recruits. Barth's huge, ugly, square-shaped church with its spire dominated the area. The camp itself held between 9,000 and 10,000 Allied prisoners of war in four separate compounds. Lewis was put into North Compound 3. Many of Luft I's population were RAF prisoners, some of whom had been held captive since the first months of the war. Flight Lieutenant (later Air Vice Marshal) Harry Burton, a 149 Squadron Wellington pilot shot down on 6 September 1940, became the first Allied prisoner to escape from a German PoW camp when he got clean away from Luft I in May 1941. Despite this and other successful escapes the vast majority of RAF and American prisoners were destined to remain at Barth until the end of the war.

It seemed to bring together many colourful characters that would leave their indelible stamp on those around them. Lieutenant Colonel Charles Ross Greening, or 'CRG' as he was known, had been at Barth since January 1944. Greening was born on 12 November 1914, in Carroll, Iowa. He took his first plane ride in June 1921. After his father's bank failed, the family moved to Tacoma, Washington, in 1925. Greening received a bachelor's degree from Washington State College of Fine Arts in 1936, minoring in physical education and military science, and serving as the ROTC commandant. He entered the military on 23 June 1936 at Fort Lewis, Washington. On 9 June 1937, Greening graduated from the Air Corps Flying School at Randolph Field. He was then assigned to the 20th Pursuit Group at Barksdale Field, flying Curtiss P-6 Hawks and Boeing P-26 Peashooters. In 1938, he was assigned to Hamilton Army Airfield and the 7th Bombardment Group. Then in 1940, Greening volunteered to open McChord Field, where he flew the Douglas B-23 Dragon, and then the B-25 in the 17th Bombardment Group. In 1941, his unit was assigned to Pendleton Field, where they patrolled the Oregon coast for Japanese submarines. They then transferred back to McChord, and then onwards to Columbia, South Carolina, where Greening volunteered to help with the B-25 armament for Doolittle's upcoming secret and hazardous mission. Greening joined the Doolittle group at Eglin Field. Captain Greening eventually took over the role of piloting a B-25B Mitchell named *Hari-Kari-er* and on 18 April 1942 he and his crew took part in the raid on Japan mounted by B-25s from the USS *Hornet*. All the B-25s took off safely from the rolling deck of the carrier and none were lost over their targets but two crews crash-landed in China. Three men were executed by the Japanese and a third died in a PoW camp. *Hari-Kari-er* ran out of fuel and Greening and the crew were forced to bail out 200 miles inland from the China coast. They evaded capture for several weeks with Chinese assistance and finally reached safety with the help of Chinese guerrilla forces.

Following his leave, Greening reported for duty at McChord Field and training in the Martin B-26 Marauder bomber. He became a group commander and flew twenty-seven missions from a North Africa base before being shot down on 17 July 1943 on a mission to Naples when a German 88mm shell hit his right engine. 'CRG' parachuted out and landed on the

BARTH – THE FINAL DAYS

slopes of Mount Vesuvius! Luckily, a kind wind blew him away from the volcanic crater and deposited him in the midst of some enemy soldiers who made him prisoner. After spending two months in an Italian PoW camp, Greening and four English friends saw their chance to escape when the PoWs were moved northwards to Germany and away from the Allied advance in Italy. They got clean away during a bombing raid and Greening remained free for six months. His four friends were captured and shot for being in civilian clothing. Greening was finally cornered in a cave in Yugoslavia and sent to Stalag Luft I, where he passed much of the time painting and sketching other prisoners in the camp.

The large American contingent at Barth also boasted some very well-known fighter pilots who had been shot down towards the end of 1943 and throughout 1944. The first was Colonel Loren G. McCollom. Born in Ritzville, Washington, in 1914, he graduated from Ritzville High School in 1932, attended Washington State College in Pullman and graduated in 1937. In 1939 McCollom joined the USAAC and was commissioned as a reserve second lieutenant in 1940. His first assignment was aircraft commander in the 8th Pursuit Group at Langley Field, Virginia. McCollom was assigned command of the 61st Fighter Squadron, 56th Fighter Group, in 1942. In August 1943 he assumed command of the 353rd Fighter Group at Metfield, Suffolk, and was promoted to lieutenant colonel. On 25 November 1943 McCollom and fifteen other P-47D Thunderbolt dive-bombers each carrying a 500lb bomb, headed for the airfield at Ste-Omer-Ft Rouge in France. Heavy ground fire bracketed the formation as it approached the target and McCollom's P-47, *Cookie*, received a substantial hit underneath the fuselage, ripping away a large area and setting fire to a fuel tank. McCollom bailed out and was taken prisoner. He was sent to Barth and for a time became the Senior American Officer in the camp.

On 5 March 1944 Colonel Henry R. Spicer, commanding officer of the 357th Fighter Group at Leiston, Suffolk, was also brought down and sent to Barth. Spicer was born on 16 February 1909 in Colorado Springs, Colorado. He attended the University of Arizona and received a bachelor of science degree in economics in 1932. Spicer joined the Army Air Corps in 1933 and was commissioned a second lieutenant in 1935. Spicer was assigned as executive officer of the Eighth Air Force 66th Fighter Wing in October 1943. He took command of the 357th Fighter Group in February 1944. During a sweep over the Cherbourg Peninsula his P-51 Mustang, *Tony Boy* (named after his young son), was hit in the coolant by light flak and crashed into the Channel. Spicer was washed ashore after two days and nights in the water, unable to walk.

Later that month, on 18 March, the 20th Fighter Group at King's Cliffe, Northamptonshire, also lost its commanding officer. Lieutenant Colonel Mark E. Hubbard had scored four kills during command of the 59th Fighter Squadron, flying P-40Fs in North Africa and two and a half kills as CO of the 20th Fighter Group flying P-38Js for two weeks before he was shot down by flak and sent to Barth. For six months he was commanding officer of Group IV and was later attached to the Wing Staff after the camp was reorganised in November 1944. He was a capable, energetic and efficient officer and well-liked by the men at Stalag Luft I.

As if these losses were not bad enough, on 27 March 1944 Major Gerald W. Johnson of the 56th Fighter Group, an ace with eighteen confirmed kills, was shot down during a strafing attack on a road convoy. Light flak hit his Thunderbolt and he followed the path of other fighter pilots into the bag at Barth, where he became the security officer for North Compound III. He was joined shortly afterwards at Barth by 22-year-old Major Duane Willard Beeson of the 4th Fighter Group, who was also shot down by ground fire, during a strafing attack on 5 April. He was a leading ace with 22.08 victories, including 17.3 air-to-air kills, 12 of which were scored in the P-47C/D Thunderbolt, and 5.3 of which were scored in the P-51B Mustang.

On 20 July 1944 the Germans caught one of their biggest fish yet. Colonel Francis S. 'Gabby' Gabreski of the 56th Fighter Group at Boxted, Essex, was the leading ace in the European Theatre of Operations with twenty-eight victories, tying with his commanding officer, Colonel Hubert A. Zemke, who had given his name to 'Zemke's Wolf Pack'. During an attack on a German airfield 'Gabby' pressed down the nose of his Thunderbolt to fire at a Bf 109 just taking off. The American ace was too low and his propeller touched the ground. Gabreski scrambled out unhurt and managed to evade capture for five days. Two Hitler Jugend overpowered him and he was sent to Stalag Luft I, where he became commanding officer of North Compound 3.

Three months later, on 30 October 1944, his former Group Commander, Hubert 'Hub' Zemke, now commanding the 479th Fighter Group at Wattisham, Suffolk, was also brought down. This brilliant fighter leader, born 14 March 1914 to German immigrant parents and who had seventeen

BARTH – THE FINAL DAYS

and a half confirmed kills in the air, was once described by General Jimmy Doolittle as his 'greatest fighter group commander'. North of Hannover, Zemke's P-51 was thrown over on its back by violent winds and it entered a dive in which the wing parted from the fuselage. Zemke, who was probably on his last mission before being transferred to a desk job at wing headquarters, bailed out before the Mustang disintegrated and was captured. While being transported by train between interrogations before being sent to Barth, Allied fighters began strafing the passenger carriages. After realising that escaping in the confusion was impossible due to the surroundings, Zemke returned to the carriage to pull two young German girls from the line of fire as the fighters made another pass. For this action he was nearly awarded a Nazi medal for bravery.

He became senior Allied officer at Stalag Luft I on 16 December, commanding the 7,000 Allied prisoners of 'Provisional Wing X'. Conditions were deplorable. There was insufficient food, inadequate clothing and medical attention and a lack of military discipline among some prisoners. Zemke established his leadership of the PoWs, who numbered 9,000 by the end of the war, gradually developing working relations with the often indifferent or a hostile German camp commandant and staff and achieving some improvements in living conditions. Towards the end of the war, suspecting that the Germans might try to kill the PoWs rather than allow them to be liberated by the advancing Russian armies, Zemke prepared a force of commandos and stockpiled weapons (mostly home-made grenades), in order to resist any such attempt.

Of the bomber contingent at Barth, perhaps the best known was Lieutenant John Cary 'Red' Morgan, a 6ft, red-haired Texan, born in Vernon on 24 August 1914 the son of an attorney. Morgan graduated from a military school in 1931 then attended several colleges. While at the University of Texas at Austin he learned to fly aircraft and in 1934 dropped out of college. He worked in the Fiji Islands as a foreman on a pineapple plantation until 1938, when he returned to enlist as an aviation cadet in the USAAC. However, because of his poor education record he was refused enlistment. Working at an oil-drilling site for Texaco, Morgan suffered a broken neck in an industrial accident, and as a result was later classified 4-F by the Selective Service System. In August 1941 Morgan joined the RCAF, and after completion of flight training in Ontario and England, was posted as a sergeant pilot to RAF Bomber Command.

STORIES FROM THE STALAGS

On 23 March 1943 Morgan was transferred to the Eighth Air Force as a flight officer and assigned to the 92nd Bomb Group at RAF Alconbury. On his fifth mission, to Hannover, on 26 July, he was co-pilot on B-17F *Ruthie II*, which was attacked by enemy fighters when en route to the target and First Lieutenant Robert Lee Campbell, the pilot, was hit in the back of the head by a shell that had entered from the right side and crossed in front of Morgan. The pilot's upper body slumped over his control wheel, causing the bomber to start to become out of control. Morgan seized the controls on his side and by sheer strength pulled the plane back into formation. Campbell continued to try to wrest the controls away from Morgan and smashed at the co-pilot with his fists, knocking some teeth loose and blackening both his eyes. Meanwhile, the top turret gunner was also seriously injured when a 20mm shell tore off his left arm at the shoulder. He fell out of the turret position and was found by the navigator bleeding to death. The navigator bailed the gunner out of the aircraft in a successful effort to save his life. Unknown to Morgan, the waist, tail and radio gunners became unconscious from lack of oxygen. Unable to call for assistance because of the damaged interphone, Morgan decided to fly all the way to the target and back within the protection of the formation, holding position in the formation, flying with one hand and holding his mortally wounded pilot up off the controls with the other until the navigator entered the flight deck and he and the bombardier secured the dying pilot in the nose compartment of the B-17.

Morgan finally made a forced landing at RAF Foulsham in Norfolk. Campbell died an hour and a half later. On 18 December 1943 listeners to the BBC's evening news bulletin heard that Morgan had received the Medal of Honor, America's highest decoration, from Lieutenant General Ira C. Eaker in a special ceremony at Eighth Air Force headquarters.

On 6 March 1944 'Red' Morgan was flying with the 482nd Bomb Group, which was leading the Third Bombardment Division over Berlin, in B-17F 'Chopstick-G George' when the aircraft was shot down by heavy flak just prior to the target at Kleinmachnow. The B-17 exploded and Morgan was pitched out of the bomber still holding his parachute under his arm. He tried to get it on as he fell feet first but the pressure kept pushing it up too high. Then he fell head first and it pushed it past his chest. He finally got it on when he was on his back and a few seconds later he landed in a tree. He fell 30ft from its branches and was picked up by soldiers from a flak battery. Morgan was one of only four men who survived from the twelve-man crew.

BARTH – THE FINAL DAYS

Throughout 1943 and 1944 the full-scale American daylight raids from England and Italy produced many PoWs and a large number found their way to Barth. Richard Olsen, a 19-year-old radio operator in the 451st Bomb Group of the 15th Air Force in Italy, arrived at Barth in January 1945. He had been shot down on 11 December 1944 on his tenth mission, to the marshalling yards at Vienna. Although it was only their tenth mission, Olsen's crew was already a lead crew. It serves as an indication of the heavy losses that the 15th Air Force was suffering at that time.

His Liberator, *Round Trip*, was hit by flak over Vienna and the pilot, Captain William A. Harris, nursed the bomber as far as Goya, Hungary, where the thirteen-man crew bailed out. The crew's silent descent was quickly shattered by ground fire, which put fourteen holes through Olsen's 'chute and killed the rear gunner, Melvin G. Schwulst. Once down on the ground Olsen was surrounded by Hungarian soldiers, one of whom was riding a horse. Olsen raised his arms and the horseman rode forward and relieved him of his GI 'hack' watch and ID bracelet. However, he missed Olsen's escape kit, which included $50, hidden in his left trouser leg. The surviving members of the crew were taken to Komron and interrogated. The Hungarians realised they had captured an important bunch of fliers because only a lead crew would have thirteen men aboard. Next day they were stripped and the Hungarians would all stop and stare at Olsen in his electric suit with its wires protruding everywhere.

After moving to Gyor and Parpau in four-wheel boxcars riddled with bullet holes from constant air attacks, Olsen and six others in the crew were sent to Germany on Christmas Day. On the way they went through Vienna, their target only three weeks before. Vienna from the ground looked different from the view obtained through a bombsight and Olsen noticed that chaff dropped from their bombers was used as a substitute for tinsel on Christmas trees in the streets! While in Vienna, the bombing raids continued and the Viennese were very hostile towards them. They threw stones, hurled abuse and spat at them. One Austrian cursed Olsen for bombing his house three times!

At Oberursel Olsen's escape kit was discovered and it was confiscated along with his other apparel. During a short stay at Frankfurt the RAF made them feel at home with several bombing raids. However, the RAF always dropped a magnesium flare in the centre of the compound at Stalag IIIB nearby, to prevent the accidental bombing of PoWs. Olsen and his compatriots were not sorry to leave the havoc and destruction of Frankfurt and on 11 January they arrived at Barth, their officers having been sent to an officers' camp in Germany.

The following day William M. Sterrett, navigator on Fortress *Grumblin' Gremlin* in the 100th Bomb Group of the Eighth Air Force at Thorpe Abbotts in East Anglia, entered the forbidding barbed wire compound at Barth. On 31 December, *Grumblin' Gremlin* was one of twelve B-17s in the 'Bloody Hundredth' that were shot down on the mission to Hamburg. The *Gremlin* sustained a direct flak hit on No.2 engine shortly after 'bombs away' and as the B-17 began to lag it was attacked by two Focke Wulf Fw 190s, which came in on their tail. Moments later, an engine and the wings burst into flame, while one 20mm shell detonated in the cockpit. At the same time the engineer and waist gunner were killed. Second Lieutenant Billy B. Blackman, the pilot, who was momentarily knocked unconscious, on coming to, pushed the bail out button and strapped his parachute on. Hearing the bell, Sterrett slipped out of the front escape hatch and as he pulled the ripcord on his parachute, he looked back to see the *Gremlin* explode, throwing Blackman out of the nose. The next thing Blackman remembered was laying on the ground with several Germans standing over him. He was informed that the co-pilot was dead although his parachute had opened, as was the radio operator, who was found without a 'chute. The tail gunner and the ball turret gunner had bailed out safely, while the waist gunner was blown out of the waist. In all, four men died and five survived to be taken prisoner.[2]

'Two Germans who got to me first,' recalled Sterrett, 'had quite an argument over who should get the credit for capturing me. Finally, one of them told me to gather up my 'chute and put it on the back of their bicycle and push it down the road in front of him. A crowd built up and followed us. I thought they were going to lynch me but I was taken into the burgermeister's office and stayed there until 1800 hours when a major came in to find out my name, rank and serial number.

'An hour later the German guard returned and told me to pick up my 'chute and go with him. He and another guard put me in a buggy and sleigh combination pulled by a single horse and we started down the road. We rode

---

2. See, *Century Bombers: The Story of the Bloody Hundredth* by Richard Le Strange, 1989.

BARTH – THE FINAL DAYS

about a half mile and then turned off into some woods. I thought for a moment they were going to dispose of me. However, I was taken to a German airfield and reunited with two of my crew. On 2 January we were put on a train for Frankfurt.

'The trip took two and a half days on about six different trains. We really had a scare at noon on the second day. We were approaching Fulda when the train stopped. We heard the sound of sirens and aircraft engines but couldn't see any planes because of cloud. Everyone jumped from the train and lay in a ditch as bombs began to fall. It sounded like the earth was falling apart. When the raid was over the train could not move because the tracks had been destroyed directly in front of it. We had to walk all the way through town to get on another train. Bombs had dropped all over the place, killing lots of people and setting the whole place on fire. Some people wanted to lynch us but our guards would not allow that.

'At Frankfurt (Oberursel) we were put in solitary confinement, interrogated and accused of being spies unless we gave the information our interrogators needed. I said my dog tags were proof enough and refused to answer any questions. Finally, I was handed a piece of paper with answers to most of the questions and told to sign it. I refused and was taken back to my 8×13ft cell. The truth was they knew more about what was going on than I did. After a couple of days, I was put on a train for Wetzlar, where we had our first contact with the Red Cross. We were given a "Joy Kit" containing cigarettes, clothes and toilet articles. I was at Oberursel only two days before going to Stalag Luft I. We finally arrived on 12 January 1945, the day the Russians started their drive out of Warsaw. We felt we would not be at Barth long but the Russians only came so far and then stopped.'

'The old-time prisoners thought the war would never end,' 'Rusty' Lewis recalled. 'We had a radio in the camp and every night someone would come round and give us the BBC news. I remember how joyful we were when the Allies arrived at the Rhine and then for months and months when there was no movement, we got very pessimistic. Six months does not sound a long time but we didn't know if we would ever make it back. When we heard troops had crossed Remagen Bridge we were happy again.

'We were so hungry that we could not keep our minds off food and recipes. We all became expert cooks in our minds and our conversations often centred on food. Everyone got out their little blue Red Cross books and wrote down marvellous menus. Our diet consisted of four thin slices of very black bread, only about an eighth of an inch thick, and a bowl of soup a day. As a consequence, I lost about 45lb in weight.

'I saw a cat covered in sores and the thought passed my mind about catching and eating him. He disappeared so someone must have eaten him, sores and all. I also saw a black raven that someone later caught and ate. Even though I am half-Norwegian I gave away some stinking limburger cheese about half an inch thick because I could not stand it. I got a chocolate bar from a Red Cross parcel and chewed it one little square a day. One guy said, "Can't you just eat the whole bar or let us have it; it's driving us nuts?"

'I said I wouldn't sell it for less than $25. He said "sold" and wrote me out a cheque on a piece of toilet paper. Later, I had an operation to remove an ulcer and had most of my stomach cut out because of my PoW diet.'

'Two men were given one Red Cross parcel once a week plus some German food,' recalled William Sterrett. On 28 February we were given six parcels for 24 men and were not given any more until 1 April. This was the roughest period of the whole episode. The Germans gave us a 7th of a loaf of bread, a cup of Ersatz coffee and a cup and a half of stew a day. This is equivalent to about 1,000 or 1,200 calories a day; just enough to keep a person alive. Cigarettes were also scarce. Our morale was at rock bottom so someone would start a rumour just to build up morale. On Easter Sunday we were given some Red Cross parcels plus some potatoes and we really had a big feed. Some of the fellows ate too much and about 90 per cent of the camp went sick with dysentery.'

Tension increased when it became known in April 1945 that the Russians were nearing the camp. The presence of the British and American armies on the Elbe and the Russian encirclement of Berlin made everyone at Barth feel that liberation was not far off. When the Russians began a new, concerted drive, across the lower Oder towards the Baltic ports, tension reached fever pitch. In the Vorlager panic set in and the Germans were no longer interested in guarding the prisoners. On 29 April confidential reports were hurriedly put to the torch and the Germans even attempted to destroy the nearby airfield and flak school so that equipment would not fall into the hands of the Russians.

Finally, late in the afternoon, Canadian Group Captain Cecil Thomas ('Ginger') Weir DFC and Colonel Hubert Zemke, the Senior British and American officers respectively, were called to a conference with the camp Kommandant, Colonel Warnstedt. Weir was the station commander at

BARTH – THE FINAL DAYS

Fulbeck and was taken prisoner after bailing out of a 49 Squadron Lancaster after it was hit by a bomb from another aircraft during the raid on the Osnabrück Canal on 22–23 November 1944. He was the sole survivor of the crew. Warnstedt told the two senior officers that he had received orders to move the entire camp westward. Colonel Zemke stated that he had no intention of moving and asked in that case what the Germans' attitude would be. Warnstedt replied that he would not tolerate bloodshed in the camp and if the PoWs refused to move then he and his men would evacuate and leave the 'Kriegies' in sole possession.

At approximately 13.00 hours on 30 April Major Stienhauer informed Group Captain 'Ginger' Weir and 'Hub' Zemke that the Germans had evacuated the camp. When they awoke that morning, the prisoners discovered they were no longer under armed guard and comparatively free. However, the Russian forces were still not within sight so it was decided to send out scouting forces to make contact. An American major, a British officer who could speak German and an American officer who could speak Russian, set out with a German in a German staff car with an American flag and a white flag to investigate the real situation in Barth. They were then to proceed to the main Stralsund–Rostock-road about 15km south of the camp and wait there for any Russian spearheads in the proximity of the front line. However, the patrol returned in the early evening with no sign of news of the Russian army.

Meanwhile, the few Americans at a working party in Barth watched it become an open city and an open grave. The city had been in decay long before the Russian's imminent arrival. The streets were peopled only with children and old men. Most of the males were infirm; some lame, others blind. Shop windows were empty and in the baker's shop a sign said, 'Cake is not sold to Jews or Poles'. Now the shop would never again make 'brot' for Stalag Luft I. However, there were good things to be found in the larders in Barth. Many were requisitioned items like Nestlé milk from Denmark, wines looted from France and baking powder from Holland.

Once the first explosions reverberated through the streets of Barth, red flags and white sheets began to appear in the windows of the 'gingerbread' houses. The populace, or what remained, stood querulously in their doorways, wringing their hands and weeping, fearful of their fate. They could not take flight; there was nowhere to run to. All they could do was take down their pictures of Hitler and scatter the torn pieces to the wind.

STORIES FROM THE STALAGS

At about 08.00 on 1 May, Major Braithwaite and Sergeant Korson, two of the Stalag scouts, raced to a crossroads about 5 miles south of Barth. They searched southward for the Russians despite a rumoured curfew that meant that anyone seen moving would be shot on sight. Meanwhile, another patrol led by Wing Commander Blackburn had reached Stralsund. His telephone crew rang numbers in the city hoping a Russian would answer the call. It was suggested that they telephone the Burgermeister of Stralsund but a girl, who was still manning the Barth exchange, told them he had long since fled.

Major Braithwaite and Sergeant Korson had better luck. They pushed on another 3 miles from the crossroads and met up with the first Russian they had ever seen. He was a chunky, small, man who loomed up brandishing a variety of lethal weapons. '*Engliski*' shouted the scouts and without further ceremony they were taken to the nearest Russian officer, First Lieutenant Nick Karmyzoff, an infantryman from Tula. He had fought through to Barth from Stalingrad and three years of war across Russia, Poland and Germany.

Karmyzoff and the first vestiges of the Russian army entered Stalag Luft I through the main gate. Colonel Zemke and Group Captain Weir received him and Schnapps flowed freely. Toasts were exchanged and glasses were smashed against Hitler's picture. The 'Kriegies' had rigged up their radio to the camp loudspeaker system to hear the BBC Lucky Strike hit parade on Saturday night. The first song they heard was, appropriately, 'Don't Fence Me In'.

Now began the transition from German occupation to one of Russian occupation. The PoWs had not known how the Russians would treat them so just prior to their arrival they had dug slit trenches inside the compound. The Russians asked why no black armbands were being worn as a mark of respect for the late President Roosevelt. Contrary to regulations the Russians gave orders that the 'Kriegies' were to wear them while they inspected the prisoners. Although the Russians and prisoners drank toasts to the 'destruction of Germany' and the 'solid and enduring friendship' between America, Russia and Britain, the opposite appeared to be true.

'On 2 May the Russians began arriving in full force,' recalled 'Rusty' Lewis. 'The first one I saw was part of a bunch of Mongolian paratroops who were terrorizing the countryside. One shot a woman who was running away with her five-week-old baby. They fought, drunk, were completely undisciplined and lived off the land. The only equipment they had was American and British. They drafted 75 of our officers to work on a ship in a local port even though the war was not yet over and it did not come under any reparations clause. It was rumoured that they would not let Allied aircraft fly us out. It was also rumoured that they were going to march us a thousand miles to Odessa on the Black Sea. We could not have walked 50 miles without keeling over.

'But when the high echelon troops came through, they brought with them a dancing troupe and singers to entertain us. We rounded up cattle and potatoes and each man had a barbecue fixed up in the compound. The Russians brought in Red Cross parcels that they had been hoarding, saying that they had been delayed because of transportation problems. We ate and ate and almost gained our original weight.'

The Russians' apparent resolve to transport the PoWs to Odessa worried Colonel Zemke, despite American pledges to fly them out. Some men left the camp, trading with local people and picking up souvenirs en route. They finally got through to the Allied lines themselves, although rumours filtered through that some had been shot by the Russians. 'Rusty' Lewis recalls, 'It was said some Americans had their cigarette lighters stolen by the Russians and when they protested, they were shot. I heard that 26 people who left the camp never made it back.'

On 12 May the Russians finally permitted some Flying Fortresses to fly in over a 5-mile-wide corridor to airlift the PoWs to France and home. William Sterrett was among them. 'This really made us happy. B-17s in formation came in over the field and peeled off. We were waiting on the ground in groups of thirty ready to hop on the plane as soon as the wheels stopped rolling.'

John A. Holden, a pilot in the 452nd Bomb Group, flew in from Deopham Green. 'We put plywood floors in the bomb bays so we could carry twenty passengers at a time. During take-off and landing fourteen of these had to ride in the bomb bay and six in the nose because of the centre of gravity. We flew in and out of hastily constructed metal strip landing grounds several times a day until the task was completed.'

William Sterrett continues, 'We flew over Hamburg and the Ruhr at about 1,000ft and really got a good view of all the damage done by bombs. The first night we stayed at Reims. Next day we were put on C-47s, which took us to Le Havre and then we were taken to Camp "Lucky Strike" at Fécamp. "Lucky Strike" was in a bit of a mess because 90,000 men were brought in without any notice.'

STORIES FROM THE STALAGS

'We were detained at "Lucky Strike" for almost thirty days' recalled 'Rusty' Lewis. 'We were restarted on our PoW diet after eating properly for two weeks and we almost starved to death. General Eisenhower came through and walked up to one of the fellers and asked how they were treating him. He said, "Goddamit, "Ike", they're starving us to death." "Ike" took him over to the mess tent and told the cooks to fill up his mess tin with chicken!'

Sterrett, Lewis and many thousands of other PoWs sailed on troopships for the long journey home to the USA. It gave them time to readjust and recall their past experiences at the hands of their German captors and more recently, their Russian 'allies'. 'Rusty' Lewis recalls: 'I felt that we would be at war with Russia within five years and as bad as I wanted to get home, I felt that we should have gone right on through and cleaned them out. I came home from the war hating the Russians much more than the Germans.'

Chapter 11

'We'll be home for Christmas, if only in a dream'

PoW Len R. Clarke, shot down on 14 May 1940

'In April 1945 the bulk of RAF NCO prisoners of war were held in Stalag 357 at Fallingbostel, lying between Hamburg and Hanover in north-west Germany. The camp also lay under one of the main routes flown by the RAF at night and by day the bombers and fighters of the US 8th Air Force.

'During the intensive air operations in the closing months of the war, the prisoners saw many aircraft from both sides fall to the ground and sometimes a single or a cluster of parachutes hanging apparently motionless in the air.

'During night raids many relived their own experiences as they watched searchlights form into cones, encircling a single bomber now a target for the guns. Over the drone of the bomber stream muttered oaths were heard and cries of "For Christ's sake, weave!" as they saw stabbing points of light from bursting flak shells within the cones. All too often a huge conflagration followed the firework display, signifying the end of another bomber. One wondered – and hoped – for the crews.

'We had been at Fallingbostel since August 1944, having been evacuated from Heydekrug, East Prussia, in June and Torun in Poland two months later. The guns of the advancing Russian armies could be heard at both the latter camps and now Allied guns were moving close to Fallingbostel from the west.

'It had been a difficult winter for the prisoners. The Red Cross lifeline was broken and everyone existed on the bottom ration scale, designed to maintain little more than subsistence and reserved by the Germans for non-productives and criminals. Fuel was almost non-existent and the large huts packed with three-tiered bunks were constantly wet with condensation. Even sleeping, lying fully dressed in our bunks, was made uncomfortable. As a reprisal for German prisoners allegedly being forced to sleep on sand in the Middle East, our straw palliasses had been removed. To make matters worse, most of our bed boards had already been taken and burned for fuel. Many times, during the night startled oaths told where someone had fallen through gaps in their bed boards on to unlucky neighbours beneath.

'Although morale remained high, the main contributory factor to this being the BBC news received on hidden radios, there was a growing impatience for the war's end, particularly among the prisoners of four and five years' standing. It seemed as though the nearer the end came in sight, the more difficult it became to face the intervening period and its many uncertainties.

'As the sound of guns grew louder, rumours abounded about being marched off into the interior, possibly as hostages. Many of us had in mind the possibility of last-minute revenge by the Germans against airmen responsible for the destruction of German cities. On 6 April 1945 our camp leader, "Dixie" Deans, was informed by the German commandant that we were to march out of the camp. Sergeant James Alexander Graham "Dixie" Deans, a Whitley pilot on 77 Squadron, was shot down on 10 September 1940. He spoke perfect German and by displaying his natural quiet but persuasive leadership qualities, he commanded respect from his fellow PoWs and eventually the respect from the Germans, because of his numerous quiet, firm decisions which defused many nasty dangerous situations. Because of those personal qualities and acts of quiet courage, "Dixie" earned the life-long gratitude of thousands of fellow prisoners, was appointed Camp Leader, and throughout the rest of the war busied himself with prisoners' welfare and safety. Behind all those acts of courage, he was also hard at work masterminding an extremely efficient and powerful intelligence network, finding ways of getting important information he gleaned from the Germans through to Allied agents with whom he had somehow made contact.

'"Dixie", who had a splendid instinct for right decisions, advised compliance and go-slow tactics. The columns formed up very slowly and it was well into the afternoon before the group in which I was a member moved out, each man carrying his worldly possessions. We dawdled along the road; our guards, who appeared to have little enthusiasm for their task, were nevertheless treated with caution, as their attitude and temper seemed uncertain.

'WE'LL BE HOME FOR CHRISTMAS, IF ONLY IN A DREAM'

'It was dark when we reached our first night stop, a large barn only a mile or two from the camp. On this night there was a lot of air activity and soon a flare was dropped, lighting up the countryside as if in daylight. An aircraft was then heard diving down and it passed very low over our barn. A few seconds later there was a flash of light, followed by a loud explosion. The aircraft, believed to be a Mosquito, had hit some trees and crashed. Next morning a German brought along the identification tags of the two dead airmen.

'The next few days were a kaleidoscope of apparently meaningless wanderings around the German countryside with the noise of war a constant background; the distant rumbling of guns and Allied aircraft flying overhead. The latter were a particular worry to us, particularly the roving Spitfires looking for ground targets. We would see them wheeling in the distance, the sound of cannon reaching us after the aircraft had again attained level flight.

'We would wave frantically as the Spitfires banked over and circled above us. Much to our relief they always flew away, our ragged appearance probably satisfying the pilots that we were not a German column. Not so fortunate, though, for one group ahead of us. They were caught by Typhoons as they sat around eating some recently supplied rations. Thirty-seven died, including one a prisoner since April 1940. It was hard to affect the usual apparently indifferent shrug – so near the end and by our own Service as well.

'Most nights were spent in fields, the weather fortunately remaining mild and dry. One night, as the bomber stream flew towards us, a brilliant "Christmas tree" marker of red and green was dropped right above the field. The aircraft wheeled to the north and sometime later flashes of light and rumblings of sound showed where the target lay.

'During our wanderings we criss-crossed long columns of unescorted French prisoners and displaced persons pushing and pulling a weird assortment of prams, trolleys and carts. We envied them their apparent wealth of food and freedom, our meagre rations being supplemented by forages against potato clamps, beet stores and meal bags. Once I returned in triumph after foraging in a farm store, but alas the oats I brought back were heavily laced with fishmeal and inedible.

'One morning we found ourselves near a fast-flowing steam. We stripped off and got into the chilly water, the first real wash since we left the camp a week before. On one occasion we came across the remains of a German column which had been attacked from the air. Several dead horses lay alongside the road. We fell on these beasts with our knives and later that day enjoyed horse steaks grilled over fires which surprisingly enough the guards allowed us to light.

'As was customary in PoW camps, four of us pooled our resources into a combine and in discussing our situation had decided that we should watch out for the right moment to escape from the column. We bore in mind the German warning that those dropping out would be shot, as well as the possible dangers in meeting members of the German civilian population, many of whom had been evacuated from bombed cities. On the other hand, there was no guarantee that the Germans would release us safely at the end. One of the Combine began suffering the effects of privation and in spite of our pleas, could go on no longer. In answer to our warning about being shot, he merely said: "Sod it, I don't give a damn," and sat down by the roadside. The German guard spoke to him and much to our relief moved on, as did the next guard. He was lucky to be eventually picked up by some Germans, taken to Luneburg and lodged in the jail, where he spent the next four days before being released. That night, 14 April, was spent in a barn. The guards advised us to get a good rest as it was their intention next day to cross the Elbe, some 30km distant.

'The Combine agreed that this was the moment to get away. We felt that once across the Elbe it would not be possible to get back again across the river. That night we burrowed deep into the straw and next morning waited until everyone had gone before emerging. We were sitting just inside the barn, brushing ourselves down and gathering our things together, when a German soldier armed with a rifle walked through the doorway. This was the sort of encounter we feared most, but fortunately he merely asked what we were doing there. We said that we were sick and had to rest. He appeared to be satisfied with our answer and after a few further exchanges went on his way, much to our relief.

'We started off, keeping to paths and by-roads. Except for aircraft wheeling overhead, the countryside seemed strangely empty. We reckoned the Allied forces were only a few miles away and hoped to avoid any retreating German troops. After some time, we came across a horse-drawn cart containing some sick British prisoners and others walking alongside. They were making their way toward a central point for sick prisoners at Melbeck, 10km away. Melbeck, a small village 12km south of Lüneberg, lay in the general direction we were taking. We joined the party and eventually arrived later that day. In

'WE'LL BE HOME FOR CHRISTMAS, IF ONLY IN A DREAM'

a farmyard at the end of the village a busy Army doctor was looking after a number of men lying on the floor of a barn. Occasionally a nervous-looking farmer's wife brought over milk, her three children peeping around the door. We were glad of the opportunity to rest and planned to stay a couple of days before pushing on.

'In the farmyard under a tree was a group of young German soldiers, the crew of a mobile flak gun. They were friendly enough and showed us the damage to their vehicle after an air attack. The driver was particularly pleased that he had escaped injury in spite of severe damage to his compartment. The crew were now sitting the war out and waiting for the end. That night they drove off with a cheery "*auf Wiedersehen!*" In a stable a horse with a blown stomach through eating grain was dying. Someone borrowed a gun and put the beast out of its misery. From then on there was plenty of meat stew available at all times.

'Nothing moved on the road outside, except on one occasion a fire engine went past at high speed towards Lüneberg. It had travelled only a short distance when it was caught by three Spitfires firing their cannon when over the farm. The cannon roar reverberated among the farm buildings. There was a flash of fire and smoke as the fire engine crashed into the side of the road.

'Nothing else moved. It was obvious that the end was now near. The sky that night of 17 April glowed from fires quite near. It was wise to stay where we were.

'Early in the morning of Sunday, 18 April the sound of approaching tanks was heard. White flags were already hanging from windows in the village. We rushed to the road and saw a mass of tanks and trucks piled with troops. Soon we were part of a milling mob with men of the King's Shropshire Light Infantry. We climbed on to the tanks in a delirium of excitement, our pockets being filled with cigarettes, chocolate and rations.

'A member of the KSLI [King's Shropshire Light Infantry] invited me to go with him checking houses for hiding Germans. We marched into a house but I did not like the sight of these cowering, frightened people, who were now completely at the mercy of their conquerors, even though I speculated that these same people had probably no such qualms when their own troops were marching in triumph across occupied countries.

'The next few days are a misty memory of shattered buildings where stands had been made, empty shell cases where tanks had stood and fired, crashed aircraft and the litter and waste of war everywhere. And everywhere, white flags. We cadged lifts in returning supply trucks, spent a day or two at Nienburg and then on to Rheine, the airfield a scene of utter destruction following Allied air raids. But craters had been filled in and RAF Dakota aircraft were busy flying in and out. Prisoners were now arriving in large numbers and waiting for flights to take them home. I just missed the last aircraft leaving that day for England and was standing around looking at wrecked German aircraft in the shattered hangars and at a Dakota which had run into a crater and tipped over, when a Canadian pilot asked me how long I had been a prisoner. On learning five years, he said: "Heck, I guess you'd like to get back then. If you don't mind riding on crates, I'm just leaving for Wing, one of the PoW reception centres." Those of us in the vicinity accepted the offer with alacrity.

'I wondered how I would feel about flying again. It was three weeks short of five years since I was last in an aircraft and from that occasion, I still had the feel of cordite, spilling oil and glycol, smoke and fire in my nostrils. We lifted into the air and the intervening years disappeared. The drill came back, wheels up, flaps up, change from fine pitch. I envisaged the wireless operator sending his messages and wondered whether the procedures had changed very much. I lay back on my crate and looked at the roof and wondered whether the last five years had happened. My dirty khaki battledress was enough to remind me it had. I looked down on the fields of England and soon we were landing at Wing. I called to the pilot: "Thanks for the ride." He laughed. "Well don't stay away so long next time." I jumped from the aircraft. I was on English soil again. It was 23 April 1945, just five years and two months, a fifth of my life, since I last left England to return from leave to my squadron in France. I would be home for Christmas this year, the first for seven years.'

Index

'Tom', 'Dick' and 'Harry' (escape tunnels at Sagan), 76-7

Agur, Flying Officer Patrick Graham RCAF, 92
Alkemade, Sergeant Nicholas S., 65-7

Barth (Stalag Luft 1), 105-109, 145-64
Beeson, Major Duane Willard, 154
Bergsland, Per RNZAF, 78
Bernadotte, Count, 121
Blackburn, Wing Commander, 162
Blackman, 2nd Lieutenant Billy B., 158
Braune, Oberst Werner, 79
Bridgeman, Phil, 8-13
Brooks, Wing Commander, Hubert, 18
Buckley, Jimmy RN, 75-76
Bury St Edmunds (Rougham), 84-85
Bushell, Squadron Leader Roger, 74-75, 79

Cady, Doug, 122-144
Carfoot, Flight Lieutenant Norman Henry, 22

Cawthorne, Pilot Officer C. A. DFM, 102
Chivenor, 6
Church, Sergeant Harold 'Harry' Church, 22-45
Churchill, Geoff, 14
Churchill, Mr. Winston, 14-15
Collins, Staff Sergeant Levi, 85-86
Cooper, Flight Sergeant James RCAF, 9
Cordes, Oberstleutnant Erich, 79
Cotner, Second Lieutenant Franklynn V. (Frank), 82-84
Cranwell, RAF, 15
Craske, Warrant Officer Basil, 65-72, 91

Day, Wing Commander 'Wings' SBO, 75
Dieppe raid, 19
Dulag Luft, 8, 27, 57-58, 68, 75, 87
Duncan, Sergeant John, 18

Elliott, Denholm, 11
Escape, The Great, 78
Eugen, Prinz, 1-3

Fallingbostel (Stalag 357), 149, 165
Fier, Second Lieutenant Rueben 'Ruby', 84-87
Fischer, Unteroffizier Hans, 46
Frankfurt (Oberursel), 7, 8 (FN), 57, 65, 84, 87-88, 95, 104, 115, 117, 157, 159
Fresnes Prison, 87

Gabreski, Colonel Francis S. 'Gabby', 154
Göring, Reichsmarschall Hermann, 78
Great Escape, The, 1, 2, 12, 67, 72, 77, 79-80, 82

Halesworth, 122
Hamburg, 145
Harris, Sir Arthur T., 15-16
Herman Sergeant Robert A., 8th US Air Force, 145
Heydrich, Reinhard, 75
Himmler, Reichsführer Heinrich, 79
Holden, John A., 163
Horsley, Squadron Leader Hugh Wilkinson AFC, 102
Hoskisson, Sergeant R.T., 102
Hubbard, Lieutenant Colonel Mark E., 154
Humes, Sergeant Edward Leo, 46-64
Humphrey, Flight Sergeant Denis Innell, 111-121
Hurrell, Allan, 2-13

Île de France, SS, 21

Johnson, Major Gerald W., 154
Joslin, Pilot Officer Peter Clement Vellacott, 9
Junge, Major Heinz, 89-90

Keitel, Field Marshal Wilhelm, 78-79
Kimbolton, 145
King's Cliffe, 154
Kramer, Major Ronald V. US 8th AF, 87-88
Kubisch, Leutnant Walter, 9

Lambertson, Captain Richard T. Lambertson US 8th AF, 87
Lamsdorf, Stalag VIII-B, 8, 18, 61-64
Leiston, 153
Lent, Oberleutnant Helmut, 9
List, Flight Sergeant Dave McCarthy, 23-24

Massey, Group Captain Herbert, 68, 69, 72
McCardie, Lt Colonel, the South Staffordshire Regiment, SBO, 104
McCollom Colonel Loren G., 153
Metfield, 153
Mildenhall, RAF, 14
Miller, Colonel Joseph A. US 8th AF, 89-90
Mitchell, Captain the Reverend H.A.M., 108-109
Modrow, Hauptmann Ernst-Wilhelm, 102
Moreton Bay, SS, 18

INDEX

Morgan, Lieutenant John Cary 'Red', 155
Mühlberg, Stamalager 4B, 29
Müller, Jens Müller RNAF, 78

Nebe, SS Gruppenführer Arthur, 79
Newman, Flight Sergeant Jim, 66
Nuremburg, 122

O'Brien, Major Jim USAAF, 69-70, 76
O'Shea, First Lieutenant USAAF, 70-71
Oberursel, 8 (FN), 27, 87, 89, 95, 98, 104, 149, 157, 159
Oflag XC, Lübeck, 75
Oflag IVC, Colditz, 75
Oflag VIB, Warburg, 75
Old Buckenham, 89
Oslo, 7

Parker, Reginald, 15-21
Parker, Sergeant Winston Churchill RCAF, 14-21
Pitkin, Roy, 2
Play Boy crew, the, 82-84
Pleasence, Donald, 12 (FN)

Quisling, Vidkun, 5 (FN)

Rodney, George, 12

Scheidhauer, Souse Lieutenant Bernard W.M., 79
Schneider, Feldwebel, 102
Schulz, Emil, 79
Seething, 87

Skellingthorpe, 102
Spann, Dr. Leopold, 79
Spicer, Colonel Henry R., 153-154
Spivey, Colonel Delmar T., 68-69
Stalag Luft IXC Kraysburg, 58
Stalag Luft III, Sagan (Żagań), 8, 39, 65-66, 71, 74, 90-01
Stalag Luft IV, 44
Stalag IIIE Kirchhain escape, 65
Stalag VIII-B, Lamsdorf, 8, 18, 61-64
Steainstreet, Pilot Officer Arthur, 123-144
Sterrett, William M., 158-160, 163-164
Stienhauer, Major, 161
Stirling Castle, RMMV, 14

T.T. Schmidt, 89-90
Taylor, Geoffrey ('Sqizzy') RAAF, 101
Thompson, Cliff, 1-2
Thompson, Walter H., 15
Thorpe Abbotts, 158
Trent, Squadron Leader Leonard Henry VC RNZAF, 78
Tucker, Flying Officer Clifford, 85

van der Stok, Bram, 78
von Graevenitz, Major General, 78
von Lindeiner, 78-79

Warnstedt, Colonel, 160
Warrington, Sergeant Jack, 429 'Bison' Squadron RCAF, 92-100
Waterbeach, RAF, 46
Wattisham, 154

Webber Flying Officer J.C., 102
Weir, Canadian Group Captain Cecil Thomas ('Ginger') DFC, 160, 162
Westhoff, Major General, 78
Wheeler Flying Officer Johnny, 102-109
Wick, 6
Wiley, Lieutenant Eugene M. USAAF, 68
Williams, Eric, 71
Williams, Wing Commander Mervyn DSO, 2
Witchford, RAF, 66
Wooden Horse escape, The, 71-72

Zafouk, Pilot Officer Jaroslav, 75
Zemke, Colonel Hubert 'Hub' A., 154-155, 160-163